Praise for Not-Two

At this critical moment in the hi[story]
when the very foundations of [life are chal]lenged, there is a message of compassion being spoken by one grounded in enduring wisdom and true discernment. In *Not-Two Is Peace*, Adi Da writes of the urgent need for a new form of global discourse, based on the recognition of the underlying unity of humankind. Such discourse would renew the ideals that originally underlay the foundation of the United Nations. And it would require humankind as a whole to listen to the ordinary people all over the world who are in dire need of greater human security.

BRYAN DESCHAMP
Former Senior Adviser, United Nations High Commission for Refugees

In this book, Adi Da powerfully and elegantly cuts through the collective delusion of separateness upon which modern society is founded. He calls for the establishment of a Global Cooperative Forum based on the presumption of our prior, underlying, and inherent unity. He writes his wisdom into a time on this planet when, if we do not all start acting, all at once, for the common good, life on this planet will become unlivable for all of us. This book establishes the essential foundation for a new cooperative world order arising from the unity which is prior to our diversity.

BOB ANDERSON
Founder and Chairman, The Leadership Circle

At the Dawn of this New Divine Springtime, Beloved World-Friend Adi Da clearly enunciates the Sacred State of Consciousness—Prior Unity and Oneness—needed to actualize a Global Cooperative Forum, a dynamic and vital step toward Universal Peace, long prophesied by the Ancient Ones. Without a doubt, through the Everywhere Spirit that is manifesting in digital technology, we will unify "everybody-all-at-once" and take this historic step together, with One Heart and One Mind in many bodies.

HEREDITARY CHIEF PHIL LANE JR.
Chairman, Four Worlds International Institute
Global Trustee, United Religion Initiative

A di Da demonstrates the illusion we are living in and the separateness and greed that run both nations and large institutions, thereby affecting our lives. He presents a blueprint for a world that works but also points out the steps each individual can and must take to transcend the ego. His book is both visionary and practical, showing that cooperation is the only road available to us to avoid total destruction.

GÖRAN WIKLUND
Partner, U&We (a leading Swedish sustainability consultancy)
Board Director, ZeroMission (climate calculation and offsetting)
Founder, Stockholm Loves Pollinators

N ot-Two *Is* Peace is Adi Da's urgent wake-up call to all men and women of conscience. Now is the time to bring together all our diverse gifts and talents into one shared project to make our world fit for all human beings to inhabit. We are united by the same need to live free of want, free of fear, and free to live a life of dignity. At the heart of the human condition lies the recognition that freedom for one must mean freedom for all. Peace is the prime directive. Peace is prior unity. The Global Cooperative Forum is the way.

HILDE RAPP
Co-Director, Centre for International Peacebuilding, London

N ot-Two *Is* Peace contains wisdom that can transform the current and ongoing world crises that so desperately need effective conflict resolution. If truly acted upon, what Adi Da advocates has the power to bring an end to the horrors and suffering that are the result of our mad need to differentiate between "us" and "them".

HUGH O'DOHERTY
John F. Kennedy School of Government, Harvard University

This extraordinary collection of illuminating essays offers a deep diagnosis of humanity's predicament. The cure Adi Da prescribes, based on higher laws, is simultaneously radical, urgent, and straightforward. Adi Da's is a uniquely authentic and compelling voice in this global age.

ROLF C. CARRIERE
Former UNICEF Country Representative in Asia
Board Member, Nonviolent Peaceforce and the Free Yezidi Foundation
Founder, Global Initiative of Stress and Trauma Treatment (GIST-T)

Adi Da offers not just one peace-making strategy among others. He goes deeper, reminding us that the very concept of "other" is a false basis from which to begin. He is right to insist that we must go beyond seeming divisions to the deeper reality that there is one singular whole of which all existence is, and always was, a part. His recognition and articulation of this "prior unity" offers a guiding light on the path forward.

SISTER MAKRINA FINLAY, OSB

Adi Da quietly arrives on the doorstep of the evolution of consciousness, revealing, step by step, what is required to sustain humanity and this beautiful planet. We should all be very interested in the mysterious state of "prior unity". Let us invest in this work of genius immediately. Let us never put this book on the shelf. It is a living document, forever active.

PATRICIA KAREN GAGIC
Award-winning Artist and Author
WXN Top 100 Most Powerful Women in Canada
Former International Director, Colours of Freedom Foundation

Adi Da's poignant and profound *Not-Two Is Peace* reminds us to rise above prejudice to seek commonality over differences. We are living on a planet of increasingly finite resources. Adi Da reminds us of the interconnectivity of all things that ultimately binds us to each other and our planet.

LAURENCE BRAHM
Founding Director, Himalayan Consensus
Senior International Fellow, Centre for China and Globalization

As we cross into the twenty-first century, it is clear humanity has entered an unprecedented global age. This global age, of course, has been emerging over millennia, but we now face a range of global crises that call for new ways of thinking and a new kind of consciousness to get to the source of the challenges. A number of initiatives have emerged which center on the collective wisdom of the ages—an emergent global wisdom that resonates across our diverse worldviews and traditions.

In this context, Adi Da's book *Not-Two Is Peace* taps this global wisdom. And the title of the book is right on the mark. He has said that the real (even genetic) situation of the human species is prior unity, and peace requires that prior unity be the "working-presumption" of humankind. This simple and powerful principle reflects a consensus truth of global wisdom that there is That Which is First—an ultimate, unifying, infinite Force (whether we call it Tao, Aum, Brahman, Yahweh, Allah, Energy, Buddha Nature, Sunyata...) that is the ground and source of all life, all existence, all worldviews, religions, cultures, forms of life. This is "Prior Unity", and the collective wisdom of humanity has urged that unless and until humans center our lives in this Unifying Principle and Holistic Unified Field, we are not sustainable and we cannot flourish, individually and collectively. And we will not realize true peace.

The narrative of Adi Da's book is simple, powerful, accessible, and compassionate. And his message, grounded in global wisdom, is urgent and timely—he suggests that former ways of seeking peace have not worked and cannot work. Instead, we must mature and advance to a new form of consciousness that is grounded in "Prior Unity", wherein we find our common ground, mature as humans, and touch the sacred space of true peace—hence "Not-Two Is Peace". Adi Da recognizes that the wisdom of the ages—the awakening of this integral consciousness—calls for a radical networking from the heart and mind and urges that we form a Global Cooperative Forum to facilitate our transition to a true global culture of peace. So there is a powerful diagnosis and prescription for our human sustainability. This important book should be read carefully and put into practice by all global citizens.

ASHOK GANGADEAN
Margaret Gest Professor of Global Philosophy, Haverford College
Founder-Director of the Global Dialogue Institute

The work of Adi Da invites humanity to step through a portal into the nature of Reality Itself. With the power and poise of a true spiritual master, Adi Da uses this book to plant the seeds for a morally enlightened civilization based in the principle of prior unity, rather than in separation, domination, and control. At times fierce, at times gentle, Adi Da's teachings shine like a bright star of hope that humanity can use to navigate its way forward. In humanity's curriculum, this book is required reading.

DUSTIN DIPERNA
Author, *Streams of Wisdom*

Through the ages, people have struggled with the idea that consciousness and being are *a priori* to physical manifestation. Today, our awareness of timeless union and inner value finds fragmented expression in a myriad of linear phenomena that we take for reality, including sovereign boundaries, property rights, market prices, interest rates, cyclical bubbles, and externalities such as pollution, poverty, social conflict, terrorism, and war. In this visionary and epochal book, Adi Da reminds us that humanity is already always a mass subjective unity and beckons us to fully externalize this conscious interconnectivity and ontological interdependence through our economic, social, and political institutions and collective decision-making.

JAMES B. QUILLIGAN
Managing Director, Economic Democracy Advocates

In Adi Da's wonderful book, this great friend of the whole world reaches out, with impeccably loving truth, profound compassion, and enlightened insight, to offer humanity a way forward to heal and re-solve our dis-membered psyche and thus our dysfunctional behaviors that continue to arise from its schism. Adi Da identifies its cause as our ego-based illusion of the apparent separation of the world and our collective forgetting of its and our "prior unity". Not only is his understanding of unity-expressed-in-diversity vital at this pivotal moment in human history, but it is gaining compelling and transformational validation from the latest scientific evidence.

DR. JUDE CURRIVAN
Cosmologist, Planetary Healer, Futurist
Author, *The Cosmic Hologram:*
In-formation at the Center of Creation

Not-Two Is Peace

The World-Friend Adi Da speaks out of his concern for the current plight of humanity. Adi Da invites you to consider his urgent calling for the founding of a Global Cooperative Forum—to address the profound ills of today's world, and to re-establish human civilization based on principles of mutual trust, cooperation, tolerance, prior unity, and the limitless participation of all of humankind in transforming its own destiny.

The old moral, social, and political "order" of humankind is now dead.

A new and true and right order of humankind is, now, and forever hereafter, necessary.

This Free Declaration is the Seed-Utterance of that new and necessary true and right (and truly globally, totally, and universally cooperative) order.

World-Friend Adi Da

Not-Two Is Peace

The Ordinary People's Way
of Global Cooperative Order

BY THE WORLD-FRIEND

Adi Da

IS PEACE 723
CHICAGO

ABOUT THE COVER

The image on the cover is a flag design created by Adi Da specifically for the Global Cooperative Forum. He explains the significance of the flag as follows:

National flags represent the already presumed separateness of national identities. In contrast, the Global Cooperative Forum is represented by a single flag, consisting of the simple spectrum of colors on a white field.

The white field is a "tabula rasa" (or blank slate), symbolizing the absence of all the kinds of "self"-imagery by which human beings create differences between themselves and others. In addition, the plain white flag is a traditional sign of truce or surrender. The party waving the white flag is signalling that it does not want confrontation, and that it is not posing a threat.

The Global Cooperative Forum is not there to confront anyone. It relinquishes all confrontation and all war, and it upholds no self-imagery beyond the simple reality of being part of the totality of humankind.

The presence of the rainbow straight across the flag indicates that the Global Cooperative Forum is actually functioning as a global institution. The spectrum of color on the white field symbolizes inclusiveness in every sense—all flags, all races, and all nations.

The "723" in the lower left corner stands for the date July 23, 2006. In his essay entitled "723" (Essay XXIV of Part Two in this book), Adi Da comments on the unique and decisive significance of this date in global human history. ■

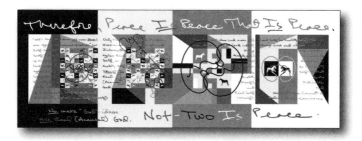

ABOUT THE *NOT-TWO IS PEACE* IMAGE

Throughout his life, Adi Da worked to develop literary and artistic means of conveying his communication to the world.

Included in this book, between pages 276 and 277, is a work of art by Adi Da (made in 2006) which bears the same title as this book—*Not-Two Is Peace*. In this image, Adi Da makes a visually joyous communication about the prior unity of the entire "spectrum" of the human race. The text in the image (a slightly varying version of a passage from this book, page 278) was hand-calligraphed by Adi Da.

This *Not-Two Is Peace* image was hung as a monumental banner at the "Religion after September 11" World Congress in Montreal (September 2006).

In the following year, ten works of image-art by Adi Da were shown at the 52nd Biennale di Venezia (2007), in the Collateral Exhibition *Transcendental Realism: The Art of Adi Da Samraj*.

Examples of the artwork of Adi Da, together with discussions of his artwork and his own statements about it, may be seen online at:

www.daplastique.com

The *Not-Two Is Peace* image is published (together with many other works of Adi Da's image-art) in *The Spectra Suites* (New York: Welcome Books, 2007). ∎

C O N T E N T S

Not-Two Is Peace

INTRODUCTION

by Ervin Laszlo

Every once in a while a prophetic voice is raised in the midst of crisis and chaos. It cuts through the walls of indifference, neglect, and just plain ignorance, and exposes the heart of the issue. The book in the hands of the reader is such a voice. Not surprisingly, it comes from one who is not part of the hustle and bustle we charitably call the business of living, and less charitably the daily rat-race. It comes from one who decided early in life to keep the distance needed for clear vision, and enter the silence needed for true audition. We see things best when we have them in perspective: then we see the forest and not only the trees. And we hear best when we silence the cacophony of competing voices clamoring for attention. The source of deep insight is the emptiness that is also a fullness and the profound silence that allows the voice of true reason to be heard.

The voice of the World-Friend, Adi Da, which speaks to us through these pages, addresses none other than the issue of our collective survival—the survival of the species that calls itself homo sapiens: homo the knower, homo the wise. We have reached the very edge of our species' viability on this planet. The problems are becoming every day more evident; I have enumerated them myself in recent writings. Adi Da states them succinctly: ". . . environmental pollution, global warming, climate change, the abuse of power by corporations and governments, the necessity for new technologies and new methods in every area of human life, the scarcity of fuel resources and of natural and human resources altogether, disease, famine, poverty, overpopulation, urbanization, globalization, human migration, territorial disputes, violent crime, the pervasive accumulation (and the sometimes actual use) of excessively (and even catastrophically) destructive weapons, the tendency of nation-states to avoid cooperation and mutual accommodation, the tendency of nation-states (or factions within nation-states) to use war (and, otherwise, unspeakably dark-minded violence) as a method for achieving the goals of national and otherwise culturally idealized policies...." The list could be continued; it is long and somber. Every scenario of BAU (business-as-usual) leads to a dead end.

Yet our fate is not sealed. Unlike other species that reached a critical point of existence and succumbed, homo sapiens has a chance: it is a unique chance, for his is a unique situation. Other species went toward and into extinction through little or no fault of their own: the environment around them changed, or other species invaded their niche. Homo does not have more powerful species to contend with, but his environment is changing, and may do so irreversibly. The planetary environment is changing because homo is changing it. Homo the wise, the knower, is too smart for his own good. He is creating untenable conditions in the biosphere, and stressful and potentially catastrophic conditions in the sociosphere.

What makes homo create such conditions? Not his instincts: those are oriented toward individual and collective survival. But human instincts are no longer dominant: they have been overlaid by human reason that has the awesome freedom to ignore the basic instincts. It is the egoic, shortsighted rationality of modern man that guides his steps, it is what creates his values, governs his perceptions, and creates the complex superstructure proudly called modern civilization. This rationality is now testing the limits of the viability of our species.

The unique freedom of homo is also his unique salvation. For what has been repressed has not been lost; what is now ignored is not beyond recovery. It is not raw instinct that we need to recover, for it alone is not sufficient to turn around the current rush toward unviability and extinction. Deep insight welling from the most basic instincts of our species for individual and collective survival is what we need, for that alone can lead us to a civilization that is peaceful and sustainable—to a condition that is truly viable.

Deep insight is our most reliable remedy, for it is the purest contact we can have with reality—contact uncorrupted by pretension and unadorned by sophistry. Were it not for the emergence of such insight at crucial epochs in our history, we would not be here today. But in our history such insight has emerged again and again, and so we are here today. And because it is emerging again today, we have a chance of being here tomorrow.

The insight the voice expresses in this book is that we are not only threatened; we can also be saved. The threats come from our egoic separateness, and the salvation from the rediscovery of our unity: the unity that is prior to all other facts and considerations. It is there: it is a fact. Unfortunately for us, it is a nearly forgotten fact. But, fortunately, it is a fact that can be, and is now being, recalled and rediscovered. It is recalled by spiritual masters such as Adi Da, and rediscovered by front-line thinkers and scientists among whom I aspire to be included.

Particles are entangled—nonlocally connected—with each other throughout space: theirs is a prior unity that is never repressed. Living things of all kinds are nonlocally connected throughout the biosphere; theirs is a subtle connection that is real although it is has been only recently discovered. So-called primitive people, too, are nonlocally—telepathically—connected with one another, with their homeland, and with their environment, as anthropologists have found. They did not repress their prior unity. But modern man, homo the knower, homo the wise, did repress the recognition of his prior unity and then, emboldened by his misguided rationality, denied its very existence. We are now witnessing the consequences: allegiances fragmented into "my country" and "my company" and "others"; nature over-exploited and despoiled, and thousands of millions pressed into deep and seemingly hopeless poverty.

Return to unity—to seamless wholeness, as in the legendary paradisiacal state. Utopia? No: the uncompromising requirement of homo's physical, biological, and socio-psychological survival. Will this requirement be met? Time will tell, and it will not be long before it tells.

I strongly believe that the answer will be yes. We are not alone. Not only are we not alone in the universe—for there is an overwhelming probability that many civilizations exist on some of the innumerable planets of this and billions of other galaxies—we are not alone because there are unseen yet now increasingly manifest forces guiding our destiny. The evidence speaks loud and clear. Voices of true reason rise, a new spirituality evolves, a higher frequency of radiation emerges on the planet. The insight to which Adi Da gives voice is the same insight that is dawning on increasing numbers of people: a decade or two ago thousands, now millions.

The transformation of the human species has begun. A new epidemic is spreading among us: more and more people are infected by the recognition of our unity. The fragmentation of human communities, the separation of man and nature, were but an interlude in human history; and that interlude is now coming to a close. We are recovering our unity not by returning to a prior culture and consciousness, but by moving beyond the fragmented, egoic civilization that dominated humankind for the past two centuries—moving toward a cooperative world that could be, and should be, initiated by the worldwide consultation of people representing no interest other than that of the species itself. The establishment of a Global Cooperative Forum for this purpose is at the heart of Adi Da's calling in this book. As he writes, "rather than playing the global competition-game to its terrible end, . . . there must be the establishment of a true Global Cooperative Forum, based on the working-presumption and enactment of prior unity—and, thus and thereby, the globally-extended establishment of a no-nonsense, getting-down-to-business disposition and practice in humankind at large. And, in this Global Cooperative Forum . . . , everyone will—and, indeed, must—focus on the genuine necessary issues that everyone has in common."

It is high time to move on: the hour of decision approaches. If a critical mass among us recovers the lived experience and attains the felt realization of our prior unity, we shall take action, and can await the hour of decision with confidence. The spread of messages coming from the deepest intuitions of which our species is capable is both the means of achieving this paramount condition, and an indication that achieving it is not a question of serendipity, but the fulfillment of the destiny of humankind: the destiny of accomplishing the further evolution of the spirit, mind, and consciousness that is both the blessing and privilege of our species, and its ineluctable responsibility to safeguard and evolve for the benefit of all things that inhabit the Earth, our precious home in the universe. ■

March 2007

Note on the Fourth Edition of *Not-Two Is Peace*

The expanded fourth edition of *Not-Two Is Peace*, published ten years after the third edition, retains the three-section structure established in the third edition. Part One comprises seven sets of "Principles", or summary points, formulated by Adi Da. These Principles are Adi Da's summary of many crucial points regarding the current state of the world and the characteristics of the Global Cooperative Forum he describes. In these Principles, which are a microcosm of *Not-Two Is Peace*, Adi Da speaks in direct, uncompromising language about the perilous predicament of humankind and what must now change.

Part Two consists of essays in which Adi Da elaborates on and further contextualizes many of the points made in the Principles. Three new essays that Adi Da designated for inclusion in *Not-Two Is Peace* have been added to Part Two in this edition:

● "All Modes of True Religion Point To Reality Itself" (pp. 117–22)

● "Humankind-As-A-Whole Must Collectively Address Its Real Issues" (pp. 201–4)

● "No Enemies" (pp. 243–51)

Part Three is devoted to essays on the root-nature of Reality, and, thus, on the ultimate meaning and significance of "prior unity" and "Not-Two".

The Epilogue, "I Am Here To Awaken A Bright New Age of Global Humankind", is Adi Da's extraordinary vision of a new civilization on Earth, founded in prior unity.

The last piece, "Final Word", was spoken by Adi Da hours before he suddenly departed from the body, on November 27, 2008. ■

Not-Two Is Peace

The Ordinary People's Way of Global Cooperative Order

BY THE WORLD-FRIEND

Adi Da

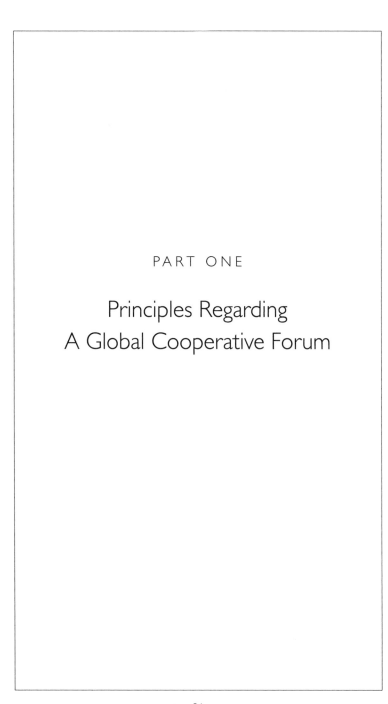

PART ONE

Principles Regarding
A Global Cooperative Forum

Adi Da's Vision of a Global Cooperative Forum

It is now common knowledge that the Earth-system is fast deteriorating into a degraded and unsustainable condition from which there may soon be no going back. The human world is threatened by an ever-widening gap between the rich and the poor, unbridled exploitation of resources, an energy crisis, food shortages, overpopulation, and increasing areas of social breakdown, political oppression, and armed struggle.

In the face of all this, the global human system is becoming dysfunctional—incapable of managing itself to establish and maintain integrity. Human society is a chaos of separate institutions, both public and private (nation-states, ethnic and religious groupings, intergovernmental organizations, civil society organizations, multi-national corporations), all doing their own managing in their own jurisdictions, with only partial reference (if any reference at all) to the interdependence of the whole. The result is the growing imbalance and conflict that threatens to become terminal for humankind and the Earth.

In this book, the World-Friend, Adi Da, speaks to this situation with a passionate calling for global change in the form of the "Global Cooperative Forum", a unique global institution founded in the inherent truth of prior unity.

The Origin of Adi Da's Call for the Global Cooperative Forum

In the course of the Kosovo war in 1999, an individual who was working on the refugee commission of the United Nations asked Adi Da if he would write an open letter to the human family about the urgent issues facing humankind.

Adi Da immediately did so, and his passionate statement was published, and also privately conveyed to individuals in positions of influence. That "open letter" was an early version of what would later be elaborated in *Not-Two Is Peace*. Adi Da was calling for humanity to abandon its "tribal" conflicts and "lose face"—in other words, to stop defending one's self-image (both individual and "tribal") and relate to others in the disposition of vulnerability and openness. Only by "losing face", Adi Da was saying, could humanity move forward together on the basis of genuine moral authority. He was calling for human beings to deal with all global issues on the basis of recognizing the prior unity in which everything is inherently connected, rather than separatively destroying the possibility of civilized life on the planet. And to establish and maintain this transformation, Adi Da emphasized the necessity for a new structure of human cooperative order, in the form of a Global Cooperative Forum—"based upon the working-principle of the prior unity of all of humankind".

Human beings must accept, with humility, that their rightful position (and that of every one) in the naturally indivisible world-family of Earthkind (including humankind) is not the "ego-place" of prior dis-unity (and, thus, of separateness, separativeness, domination, and control), but the "heart-place" of prior unity (and, thus, of ego-transcending cooperation and tolerance). . . .

Indeed, this Call to Right Life and Peace is a great and absolute moral Law, which I have Epitomized in the Formula C + T = P, or "Cooperation + Tolerance = Peace".

It is absolutely essential that the universal collective of humankind formally embrace and really enact this universal moral disposition.

—Adi Da, *Not-Two Is Peace* (p.100)

Key Term: "Prior Unity"
(as used in *Not-Two Is Peace*)

To rightly appreciate the book *Not-Two Is Peace*, and Adi Da's vision of a Global Cooperative Forum, it is important to understand what he means by the term "prior unity". By "prior", he does not mean "previous". He is not pointing to some past "golden age" of unity on Earth. Rather, Adi Da is speaking of the inherent, or "a priori", unity of existence—the primal, irreducible state of being in which the world and all things continually arise and pass away. This original state of being is, by its very nature, one and indivisible, regardless of the apparently separate happenings that arise within it. We can understand this by looking at the ocean, which is a single body of water supporting an ever-changing pattern of individual waves.

Prior unity, in this sense, is reflected in every dimension of the world and of the human being. For over one hundred years, physicists have been demonstrating, in ever more sophisticated ways, that so-called "matter" is a unified continuum of energy, not merely an assembly of separate particles. At the same time, biologists have shown that the genetic structure of the human being is almost exactly identical throughout the entire human species, and that the apparent differences between the world's races are very superficial.

Adi Da is saying that a clear awareness of the truth of prior unity enables intelligent collective action—action that starts from the working principle that prior unity is already so, rather than action that simply "works toward", or struggles to establish, unity. In other words, he is saying that the "real" or "realistic" politics of our time must come from understanding, and acting in accordance with, how things really are.

But, as Adi Da points out, there is an immediate obstacle to such intelligent action, and that obstacle is "ego", or "egoity". What does he mean by ego? He means the false assumption that separateness is the case, and acting on that basis. Ego makes, or is, "two-ness"—the sense of "self" versus "other". Adi Da places "self" in quotation marks throughout *Not-Two Is Peace*, indicating that the separate "self", while constantly presumed, has no real existence. Human society is based on ego, or "two"—the subject and the object. Prior unity is "Not-Two". And "Not-Two" is peace. ■

What the Global Cooperative Forum Would Do

How is the Global Cooperative Forum to be actualized? How do we get there? What would prior unity look like in actual practice, as the basis not merely of one's personal life but of collective human living? In Part One, "Principles Regarding A Global Cooperative Forum", Adi Da elaborates on this vision.

A Global Cooperative Forum, founded on the principle of prior unity, would address, on behalf of all the people of the world, all the crucial issues that humankind has in common. Adi Da introduces the term "everybody-all-at-once" to express the simultaneity and unique force potential in humankind when it wakes up and becomes aware of itself as one family, one collective, even one "system", existing in unity with, and responsible for, the entire Earth-system.

Such a Global Cooperative Forum would provide an institutional structure capable of bringing to life the principle of prior unity, and, thus, restoring to the Earth-system (both human and non-human) its inherent capability to self-correct and self-organize. In summary, the Global Cooperative Forum would regenerate and maintain the integrity of the Earth-system at all levels through a global cooperative process of self-governance on the part of the people of the world.

How the Global Cooperative Forum would function is, to some degree, suggested in the Principles given by Adi Da in Part One (and in *Not-Two Is Peace* as a whole), but *Not-Two Is Peace* is fundamentally a blueprint that must be fleshed out by a "morally-enlightened" leadership composed of individuals who carry no baggage of self-imagery or "tribal" agenda and are thus capable of representing "everybody-all-at-once".

Key Term: "Tribalism"
(as used in *Not-Two Is Peace*)

When Adi Da uses the terms "tribal" and "tribalism", he is referring to ego in its collective form. He notes that human societies do not operate on the assumption that human beings are all basically the same. Rather, human societies operate based on what he calls "the presumption of 'difference'", or the notion of "us" and "them". Identifying with one's local grouping, or groupings—be it village, clan, town, religion, political party, nation-state, and so on—has an enormous amount to do with how human beings think and act. There is an instinctive assumption that those who are not part of "our group" are "foreign" or "alien". These are key words in the common psyche and run through our social and political language.

Adi Da refers to the psychology of identifying with one's own group first, over against other groups, as "tribalism". He is not thereby criticizing the positive bonding between individuals in any human grouping, but pointing to the reflex of separativeness. It is said in the ancient Upanishads of India that wherever there is an "other", fear arises. What is true in the individual case is true also with collectives. The fear of the "other" is the age-old root of human conflict, and, when extended collectively, is the root of war.

It is obvious to all who face the facts, that, at this critical point in human history, "tribalism" has been pushed to terrible, and potentially terminal, lengths. Earth-systems are breaking down, and the social, economic, and political order is under severe stress in many parts of the world. The nation-states—and the various associations of nation-states—are inadequate to deal with the urgent global realities, which cross all borders. A new human process that gives form and life to the fact of prior unity is urgently required. ∎

Adi Da points out that no global organization presently is equipped to deal with the complexity of the world situation, in a way that accounts for the whole, because of the prevailing paradigm—which is that of separate interests negotiating toward settlements that are most advantageous for themselves. The global good (both human and non-human) is thereby subordinated to the aims of the separate interests.

In the current world, human beings are simply suffering this situation, or exploiting it, or both. Therefore, a shift of consciousness is essential, from the mind of "tribalism" to taking responsibility for the whole. A new global institution needs to emerge—one which genuinely represents humankind altogether, or "everybody-all-at-once", and, thus, empowers the human population as a totality.

Such a forum would allow humankind to become conscious of itself as one great coherent force—the only force capable of requiring and implementing systemic change that takes all factors into account. The purpose of the Global Cooperative Forum is to create the context for a new cooperatively-based global civilization to emerge, rather than the current "non-civilization" that is being imposed worldwide by exploitative, consumer-driven economics and related military agendas.

The Modus Operandi of the Global Cooperative Forum

The Global Cooperative Forum would be a form of global representative governance, in which each and every representative would be representing humankind-as-a-whole, rather than only a part of the whole, or an aspect of the whole. Thus, there would be no "flags" or "labels" or self-imagery or separative agendas introduced by the representatives. Every participating representative in the Global Cooperative Forum would set aside his or her personal national, religious, ethnic, or other forms of identity, and merely be there as a human being representing all of humankind. (This is not to deny the validity and natural expression of these forms of identity, but only to indicate that the <u>advocacy</u> of personal or tribal identity has no place in the workings of the Global Cooperative Forum.) Likewise, the equality of all representatives would be presumed, rather than any hierarchy of status.

The basis for discussions would be the "working-presumption of prior unity", meaning that the orientation would not be a <u>seeking</u> for solutions, but, rather, a disposition of <u>enabling</u> solutions that work in the context of the whole. In other words, it would be a matter of allowing the reality of prior unity to emerge, rather than continuing to obstruct that reality.

However, it is not going to work to merely "inject" the working-presumption of prior unity into this or that circumstance. The chronically leaky global boat will not be made seaworthy by patching it up here and there. For the working-presumption of prior unity to be truly effective, it would have to become the governing principle of global affairs as a whole. This is the task of the Global Cooperative Forum. ∎

Principles Regarding
A Global Cooperative Forum

I.

On The Dangers of The Old "Tribalisms", and The Necessity For A Global Cooperative Forum Based On The Prior Unity of Humankind

1.1 The old moral, social, and political order of humankind is now dead.

1.2 This is the moment when it will be decided what the future is going to be.

1.3 The future is either going to be catastrophic disaster, or it is going to be the turnabout moment in human history, in which humankind will step out of its dark ages of "tribalism" into a new mode of human cooperative order.

1.4 This next handful of years is the period in which this choice has to be animated, one way or the other.

1.5 All generations now alive will have to make things right, or everything is lost.

1.6 The old civilization is about "tribalism". The new politics is about the civilization of "humankind-as-a-whole", and only this has the potential for a viable human future. Humankind cannot survive a "tribal" world.

1.7 Starting in the nineteenth century and through the twentieth century, all the "tribes" found themselves face to face—and terrible wars, using the means of industrial civilization, have been the consequence.

1.8 At the same time, there are all the other effects of humankind's impact on the Earth—from climate change to migrations, urban chaos, shortage of crucial resources, disease, and poverty.

1.9 At present, most of the energy of humankind is going into industrial-age warrior conflicts rather than addressing urgent global realities.

1.10 Wise leadership is essential for humanity now. The necessity is for those who have the clarity to see what is going on, and who know what to do about it, to get the support of the human populations.

1.11 The kind of leadership needed begins with disciplined individuals who are responsibly managing their own lives, rather than merely going along with the consumerism of conventional society.

1.12 The modern "everyman" of consumer society is a propagandized individual, participating in illusions and, effectively, self-destructing.

1.13 The modern "everyman" is being created by the power system of the world, because it is in the interests of that power system for there to be consumer-egos who are "self"-involved, "self"-seeking, and stupefied.

1.14 Generally speaking, politicians have to stay identified
with the common mind and common illusions. But
it is too late for that. The world cannot afford leaders
who are deluded by the old patterns of culture and
of mind.

1.15 If the global chaos that is now happening is not
re-organized by the force of truth, it is going to be
done by other means—including totalitarian and dark
materialistic means.

1.16 Humankind now needs to choose its collective
survival and well-being in the real world, rather than
determining its politics based on old mythologies.

1.17 There has to be a global understanding that world
peace requires stepping beyond both religious
mythologies and secular ideologies.

1.18 The old "tribal" mythologies may touch upon Reality
and the Absolute, but they are also human inventions—
and their exclusivist and absolutist claims must now
be relinquished.

1.19 If there is not this relinquishment, there is going to be
nothing but disaster, created by the psychotic struggle
for one or the other to be the winner.

1.20 History is filled with the destruction of past cultural
monuments and temples, and the conquering of
homelands. But industrial-age "tribal" wars cannot
reclaim what has been lost. Rather, they threaten to
bring an end to everything.

1.21 The idea behind nuclear weapons is the idea of total war. Total war is not about conflicts based on confrontations between the armies of the warring states. Total war is about a practice of war in which the people are the target.

1.22 Total war is an obscenity. It is evil. Total war would destroy the people, and it would destroy everything— for a political advantage.

1.23 The seed, or root, of the idea of total war is the commitment to global dominance. Total war has no function except for a nation-state, or an alliance of nation-states, that is interested in global dominance.

1.24 This kind of warfare has become global policy in the course of the twentieth century, and now into the twenty-first century.

1.25 Total war is absolutely unacceptable, and so the current warlike posturing must stop. It is on the verge of producing its ultimate catastrophe.

1.26 It is not that this or that nation-state should not have nuclear weapons. Absolutely no state and nobody should have nuclear weapons.

1.27 There needs to be an immediate intervention on behalf of humankind to eliminate all nuclear weapons and to establish a working process for settling issues.

1.28 At present, a culture of total war, a culture of death, is ruling, while the people are engrossed in consumerism.

1.29 The only power on Earth that can stop the trend toward total war is the power of the human population declaring it will not cooperate with this nihilistic culture of total war and the ideologies of total dominance.

1.30 In the present day, declarations of independent nation-states based on ethnic and religious traditions are creating huge problems. Previous larger confederacies are breaking down.

1.31 This trend is all about "tribalization", setting up absolute pockets of power—based on the mythologies of the past, the traditions of the past, the separateness of geographical zones, the separateness of particular classes or races of people.

1.32 This disastrous fragmentation of humanity has to stop. What is needed is exactly the opposite of that.

1.33 The absolutization of "tribal" minds is the happening of the human race in this moment, and this is exactly what must be transcended. That requires a new kind of political orientation.

1.34 Right leadership, disposed toward global cooperation—based on a comprehension of the inherent and always prior unity of humankind and the total Earth-system—is now needed.

1.35 What needs to be supported everywhere is cooperative, participatory existence for the entire human population globally—and the establishment of a Global Cooperative Forum to express and implement that reality.

1.36 A Global Cooperative Forum representing humankind-as-a-whole would operate based on the principle of "prior unity"—meaning an acknowledgement of the fundamental unity of humanity and of all existence.

1.37 The human family would be represented at a Global Cooperative Forum by morally-enlightened leaders capable of moving the world population into a separatism-transcending view, and, thus, into modes of cooperation.

1.38 On the basis of the working-presumption of prior unity, such a Global Cooperative Forum would deal with all the urgent issues that humankind has in common.

1.39 There are, at the present time, nation-states, but nation-states would need to allow and cooperate with the Global Cooperative Forum that represents humankind-as-a-whole. That is the only politics that is viable for humankind now.

1.40 The nation-state configuration of the world is a leftover of the "tribal" past, in which larger regions of humanity were separated from the others and, generally, just kept their distance from one another.

1.41 Representatives of the nation-states getting together as the means of creating global order is not working. The "multiple-flags" model for global discourse represents the old "tribal" orientation, which now needs to be abandoned and replaced by a global cooperative.

1.42 Within a global cooperative there would be certain multiplicities of difference. Those differences should be largely cultural—simply part of the texture of humankind—and there should no longer be any effort to establish certain human groups as separate absolutes.

1.43 The principle of the Global Cooperative Forum is that the prior unity of everybody-all-at-once must become the basis of global politics.

1.44 The purpose of the Global Cooperative Forum is to ensure that the totality of humankind, or everybody-all-at-once, is participating in a global political reality, and demonstrating the self-organizing means for making it right and keeping it right.

1.45 Presently, the powers of the separate nation-state are being used to control populations all over the world.

1.46 The power of industry and money has actually become senior to the power of governments, and is now controlling the entire world.

1.47 The only power that can deal with these powers that are on the verge of destroying the Earth-world is everybody-all-at-once—meaning not merely mob power, but a new cooperative system for dealing with issues.

1.48 The efforts of separate nation-states and vested interests to control the people are not going to work forever. Sooner or later, the global population is going to demand a cooperative, benign situation.

1.49 That is why there needs to be a Global Cooperative Forum, in which all of humankind participates through right representation.

1.50 Such a Global Cooperative Forum would not be subordinate to a "tribalization" program imposed by nation-states, but would inform all of the existing political entities benignly and cooperatively.

1.51 Humankind has got to get down to its own business and choose itself—and the Global Cooperative Forum is the means to do that.

1.52 Humankind needs to be relieved of the burden of its past, and step beyond its past, like a butterfly out of a cocoon, or like a snake shedding its skin.

1.53 The self-ordering system of humankind must be free to put itself in order. Humankind will self-organize itself if it is free to do so, and it must no longer be prohibited from doing so by the separatist factionalisms of the "tribal" mind.

1.54 "Not-two" is peace. "Not-two" is prior unity. Conversely, "two" is separateness, prior dis-unity, "difference", otherness, competitiveness, opposition, confrontation, chaos, and war.

1.55 In the "room" of humankind-as-a-whole, the "room" of everybody-all-at-once, there is no "two"—there are no "flags", there are no religions, and there is no "self"-imagery that may be exclusively asserted. Rather, humankind must simply represent itself, and get together to create a new global domain for human existence. This is the great project.

II.

On The Necessity To Give Institutional Form
To The Principle of Prior Unity

2.1 Virtually every kind of human collective—a household, a family, a village, a county, and so on—is made subject to agreements, limits, laws, rules, and means of keeping it straight, productive, and positive.

2.2 The totality of the human world is an exception to this. Humankind-as-a-whole is not managing itself. Instead, it is managing all of its separate, "tribalized" elements. There is no instrument of order applied to the whole.

2.3 This is because another principle has been traditionally presumed about how the human totality is supposed to work—the principle of competition, involving warfare, mutual struggle, and dominance of one over another.

2.4 The notion that everything outside of one's own territory is a kind of wilderness is the traditional idea at the root of this situation.

2.5 This presumption about "out there" being a wilderness, and a place where you cannot and should not go, is the mythology that is now being applied by human beings relative to the totality of the Earth-world.

2.6 Because the Earth-world (as a whole) is presumed to be a wilderness, it is also presumed that human beings are not required to be responsible for the Earth-world, but are simply to avoid that wilderness.

2.7 The Earth-world can no longer properly be thought of as a wilderness. It is more like your local village or town or county or nation-state. It is a domain of necessary human responsibility.

2.8 The totality of humankind is intrinsically a unity. And that prior unity must be institutionalized as a cooperative of self-managing human responsibility, like any other area of human concern or enterprise.

2.9 At present, the voice for changing the world is a fractioned voice, coming from multiple individuals and civil-society organizations—all speaking of the necessary changes as something that will occur in the future.

2.10 It is in the interest of the institutionalized forces that are in power to keep the voices that want a world of peace and unity separate, weak, and vulnerable.

2.11 NGOs* are tending to function within the institutionalized power-structure of global "tribalism". They must, instead, become part of the global strength of everybody-all-at-once.

2.12 The Global Cooperative Forum would institutionalize a non-"tribal" world of prior unity that is in the interest of everybody-all-at-once.

---

* "Non-governmental organizations"—organizations created by private individuals or groups who do not represent any particular government.

2.13 The Global Cooperative Forum must be a functioning, systematic, institutional presence. It must not be reduced to a mere idea, which all kinds of separate parties can vouch for, saying they stand for that, too.

2.14 Mere ideas are not going to create an institution based on prior unity. The Global Cooperative Forum must be created by everybody—not everybody-one-at-a-time, but everybody-all-at-once.

2.15 There is terrific political resistance to the notion of a true global cooperative. However, what must be understood is that a true global cooperative order is not a globally-extended super-state (which would be a kind of totalitarian power), but a global cooperative order in which all freely participate.

2.16 The globally-extended super-state is what the big warrior-states are moving toward. They are looking for there to be a winner that can control the world in a totalitarian manner.

2.17 This absolutely must not be allowed.

2.18 The means to bring about the Global Cooperative Forum is not some council of highly-placed morally-enlightened individuals merely making a proposition to everybody that this is necessary.

2.19 The role of the initial council must be to accomplish the connecting with the human totality.

2.20 Without that participation of the world population, the Global Cooperative Forum would be just another group of highly-placed people communicating high-minded notions and struggling to achieve them. It would be back to the same old process.

2.21 The initial leadership of the Global Cooperative Forum will come from individuals who are disillusioned with power, and who see that the current efforts to improve the situation of humanity are not sufficient to transform the whole.

2.22 If the initial council knows how to make the connections, and does so, and establishes right representation for the global population, then the Global Cooperative Forum will emerge virtually out of the woodwork.

2.23 It is essential to fully connect the nearly eight billion* people to a process. That means that the total human collective, or everybody-all-at-once, must become conscious of itself.

2.24 Everybody-all-at-once must be communicated with by the initial council, and enabled to make itself known.

2.25 Everybody-all-at-once must be able to require that it be heard and that its requirements be acted upon in every positive sense.

2.26 This is the happening that is not in the works. Making the connection to the nearly eight billion people has never been done.

2.27 The Global Cooperative Forum is the institutionalized face for the nearly-eight-billion to manage itself.

2.28 The initial council is needed first. That council defines the issues and also organizes all the means of connectedness to the human totality. Then an effective, participatory process of global dialogue can begin.

* All such number references in this text have been updated per world population estimates at the time of publication.

2.29 The Internet would be the necessary means of this connectedness.

2.30 The human population would need to be able to be tuned into the Global Cooperative Forum websites every day, and then—having an organized, manageable circumstance for communication—to be getting down to business.

2.31 It would have to be determined how the Global Cooperative Forum needs to be fashioned in order to manage each of the large issues that humankind-as-a-whole must address.

2.32 Each of the primary issues that need to be dealt with would have to be outlined, including the agreements that need to be made.

2.33 This mobilizing of the human population is not some strange revolutionary happening. It is an orderly process of getting down to business. And there is no instrument for it now, nor even the consciousness that there should be an instrument for it.

2.34 That is what the Global Cooperative Forum is about—a completely different, unique, awakened orientation, the orientation of prior unity rather than everything else.

2.35 To establish the Global Cooperative Forum, "pure warriors" are what is needed—those who will bring the truth of prior unity into the domain of humankind, where truth has never really taken hold.

2.36 It is not possible to "get to" the point of unity in the human world. You have to begin with it, and then the process covers everything.

2.37 In the domain of the human collective as a totality, it is about a Global Cooperative Forum operating on the basis of the working-presumption of prior unity—which is an entirely different way for humankind to self-govern itself, never done before because humankind has been divided into countless individuals and nation-states, or "tribes".

2.38 The "tribes" still exist. The mode of the "tribal" mind still exists. But the "tribes" are also all defeating one another. The "tribalized" world now exists only in a kind of ashen state and has shown itself to be completely and obviously unworkable.

2.39 Something can and must replace the "tribalized" world—something that is authentic at the root, and something that can take responsibility for the governing of human affairs, take responsibility for the context of human life and engineer the new, rather than struggle with the old.

2.40 Prior unity is always already the case, and the old now is finished. If it is understood that what was is finished, great clarity can awaken.

2.41 This is the "ground zero" moment of human history, but not merely referring to an empty pit in New York. The whole world is at ground zero now. The entire basis for positive human civilization has been totally destroyed.

2.42 Prior unity then can be the basis for the establishing
of an entirely new mode of human civilization, the
human civilization not of "tribes", but of the human
totality.

2.43 Great energy for what needs to be accomplished resides
in the generation now coming to adult maturity, whose
vitality and mutual connectedness and impulse toward
rightness need to be brought to bear in the big picture
happening all over the world.

III.

On Competition, Prior Unity, and Self-Management

3.1 The current situation is one of global competition relative to the acquisition of goods and power.

3.2 There is no control over the excesses of competition, no force that speaks for the whole and subordinates all to the good of the whole.

3.3 This lack of control over competition is affecting not only the environment but every level of human life.

3.4 There is no over-arching principle that would act as a discipline so that the will to consumption and the activities of consumers are prevented from destroying the very system on which everybody is depending for life.

3.5 The supposed purpose of competitiveness—to get to the point where things will eventually be made lawful and sustainable—is being idealized. Excesses are permitted in the meantime everywhere.

3.6 In certain contexts, competition has a lawful place, and is virtually harmless relative to the great systems on which life depends—for example in sporting events, which are a way of people exceeding themselves and developing creative intentions.

3.7 The only right competition is one that occurs in a context of prior unity. Now all competition is happening in a circumstance of presumed dis-unity.

3.8 Consumerism is the society of systems-in-competition. The consumers in one "tribe" or other are looking to be big consumers exploiting the others.

3.9 The rulers get to consume. The defeated, or the subordinates, get to live in poverty, or with little.

3.10 The current situation in the world is that everyone wants to live the "good life" and be super-consumers. That is simply not possible. The Earth-world cannot sustain it.

3.11 Governments are afraid to limit the economic process to control pollution and environmental damage. They have no accountability relative to these things.

3.12 During the American Revolution, there was the cry that taxation without representation was tyranny. This should now be a global outcry. Governments everywhere are taxing people, and they are not rightly representing the interests of the people.

3.13 The exploitation of resources and means by corporations that are essentially independent of accountability is part of what is wrong.

3.14 Governments have the responsibility to maintain a viable global circumstance for human life, including business. But all things have to be happening in a system in which the integrity is protected, so that excesses will not destroy the system.

3.15 There needs to be a global cooperative means whereby transitions are made in all kinds of areas of industry, government, and so on. Resources from each mode of happening would be put into a process for research and development, creating new methods and means of approach.

3.16 All of it requires one thing: the principle of prior unity institutionalized through a Global Cooperative Forum. That would be the means for addressing all issues in a systems-based manner. Until that exists, no issues are going to be systematically addressed.

3.17 Every kind of system within the total global system has the same requirement—to be functioning on the basis of prior unity and enacting that through the discipline of self-management.

3.18 Every kind of problem in the human domain can be analyzed exactly in these terms: prior unity and self-management.

3.19 For corporations and governments, this means systematizing their own process in association with all other processes and the global whole, based on the principle of prior unity.

3.20 A right understanding of how to live in accordance with this principle, enacted as self-management, is the essence and the life-application of wisdom.

3.21 This is what is absent in the world—people are being propagandized to presume competitiveness, mutual opposition, and difference.

3.22 Prior unity and self-management must coincide with one another—one cannot merely communicate the idea of prior unity and have it change anything, any more than one can give speeches about stopping global warming and get a result.

3.23 So the principle of prior unity must have governing force. It must be a literal control over the system. It must take the "stave" out of the "wheels" of the system to generate the results that are intended or desired from the big-picture perspective.

3.24 When you eliminate the input, or "stave", that is creating chaos, then the system re-unifies the Earth-world, doing what it needs to restore its balance. This means that various kinds of input that are creating chaos or dis-unity in the Earth-domain have to be eliminated by responsible choices on the part of the human collective.

3.25 Everything that human beings do should have a focus in this Global Cooperative Forum, including every kind of industry and government. Everything will then be interconnected, and there will be a systems method for dealing with the global system altogether.

3.26 It would be a principled process—not merely a power-game played between competing factions. Competition and mutual opposition would be brought into order by this larger-systems means, which must be institutionalized, and, thus, be in a position to control the excesses.

3.27 There is a Universal Conscious Force That Is Indivisible, egoless, Acausal, and Absolute. And everything is arising as an apparent modification of That.

3.28 Reality Itself Is a Prior Unity. Therefore, everything that is arising is part of a prior unity. It is not just that things are connected to one another in a unified sense. Everything is arising <u>in</u> That Which Is Indivisible and Self-Evidently Divine.

3.29 This is a Spiritual matter, not a religious matter. It is a profoundly human matter, not a subject for disputes or "tribal" differences. That Which Is One and Self-Evidently Divine Transcends all religions, all differences. And "It" is not Itself "different" from anything.

3.30 At present, people do not understand the principle of prior unity as being the principle of Reality Itself, and, therefore, All-Pervading. And, so, it is essential to educate people about prior unity as being intrinsic to Reality Itself, and, therefore, the real picture everywhere.

3.31 On that basis, self-management can be introduced— individually, and in all modes of complex association, or collectivity.

IV.

On Globalizing Humankind
On A Cooperative Basis

4.1 The globalization of industrial society has worked to a certain degree up until now, but serious global imbalances have been the result. Further globalization of industrial society will only increase the toxification of the environment and make further chaos out of human existence.

4.2 Industrialized productivity throws waste products into the air and the entire environment, contributing to global warming and disastrous effects of all kinds.

4.3 And, so, humankind must be globalized by making all aspects of human life into something associated with a cooperative.

4.4 For example, cooperative food production would replace the effort to give the world population access to the global industrial society's food production means.

4.5 At present, relative to food production, there is the grossest exploitation of non-humans by the methods of industrialization. It is the same with land, which is being destroyed by the mono-culture of industrialized farming.

4.6 One purpose of the Global Cooperative Forum would be to unlink people from exclusive dependency on the methods of industrialization. A Global Cooperative Forum would see to it that natural resources are cooperatively managed at the local level and at every level.

4.7 All resources ultimately belong to Earth itself. They are the province of everybody-all-at-once, and not for any separate entity within the whole to exploit and own.

4.8 A global cooperative endeavor that produces the means of survival by making responsible and cooperative use of the Earth's resources needs to supersede the power politics of oil dependency.

4.9 Altogether, there are two now-global forms of dependency which must be gone beyond: dependency on fossil fuels and dependency on animal protein as food.

4.10 Both of these dependencies have broad political, social, and economic implications, and both are associated with conglomerates of corporate power which wield a great deal of influence.

4.11 Fossil fuels are already causing global warming and extreme weather, as well as negative effects on global economics and politics.

4.12 The "farming" of animals as food is also a major contributor to global warming—from the transmission of methane gas into the atmosphere (a natural by-product of the "farmed" animals themselves) and otherwise through use of fossil fuels in the industrialized production of animals as food.

4.13 Dependency on animal protein as food is also now beginning to be acknowledged as having a seriously negative effect on health.

4.14 Thus, the human world is being overwhelmed by its own waste and by the toxicity of what it is ingesting at every level, industrial to personal. That toxicity is at the root of the current world-situation—toxic energy-sources and toxic food-sources.

4.15 But it is not that industrialization, which is presently creating such destructive effects, should merely be treated as an enemy. There would always obviously be technological and science-based means required by the human collective.

4.16 Rather, existing patterns of industry should be converted and new industries made by re-tooling what is already there.

4.17 It is a matter of reorganizing what now exists in the form of the current corporations and adapting them to processes of manufacture that are life-positive and Earth-positive. This will necessarily involve addressing imbalances in the accumulation of wealth.

4.18 As soon as there is a class of wealth established in a culture, or a nation-state, or group of nation-states functioning together, the motives of greed, exclusivism, and "self"-protection begin to appear.

4.19 The power of wealth—extended through corporations, as well as through individuals—is used to acquire goods, power, and territory outside of the domain of the culture, or the nation-state, or the alliance of nation-states.

4.20 The situation has arisen that wealthy people, wealthy nation-states, and wealthy corporations everywhere are acquiring property and goods all over the world.

4.21 The power of wealth is upsetting the balance of how things were, and is having a dramatic effect on the global system.

4.22 And, so, there are not only military extensions of "tribalism", there is also the "greed effect" (which may call on military means).

4.23 As long as there is global fragmentation, the power motives of wealth can exploit that fragmentation. On the other hand, a cooperative global system would prevent the exaggerated use of national, corporate, and personal wealth-power from creating an imbalance in the world.

4.24 The inclination to acquire wealth, and even the tendency toward greed, is not something itself that is going to disappear as a human characteristic. But a global cooperative system would manage itself to maintain integrity and avoid the dramatic conflicts that result from gross imbalances.

4.25 It is not about waiting for greedy powers to agree. Rather, they must be obliged by a system that enforces the prior unity of the whole.

4.26 The role of the Global Cooperative Forum is to replace the absence of systematic responsibility with the presence of systematic order and integrity—a system that is self-governing, self-organizing, self-correcting, and self-rightening.

4.27 The Global Cooperative Forum is "global-systems management", to use a technical term. But it is also a very human mechanism, a cooperative mechanism. It gives the totality of humankind a means, not just a voice.

4.28 The Global Cooperative Forum is also the voice of the Earth-system as a whole.

4.29 The real purpose of the spreading of knowledge is to give the basis for cooperation and not merely the basis for power and exploitation.

4.30 The human world managed by a Global Cooperative Forum would be a fully participatory world—not a kind of totalitarian state, simply enforcing ideals and controls over people.

4.31 The Global Cooperative Forum should be a vehicle for the promotion and enactment of the universal re-bonding of humankind, through modes of mutual dependence and cooperation. That re-bonding will counteract the general tendency of ego-based civilization to establish a relationship of competition between individuals and between nation-states.

4.32 It is a matter of the human totality enacting the rulership of cooperation—not order for its own sake (because mere order can suppress cooperation), but a cooperative order, benignly maintained as an extension of everybody-all-at-once.

4.33 The Global Cooperative Forum is about everyone participating in a cooperative in which all are part of a process through their action that generates survivability and well-being for everybody from local to totality, and from totality to local.

4.34 When the old "tribal" mechanisms are superseded by the global cooperative whole, that transformation will change everything, including the whole complex of industry and productivity.

4.35 The "tribal" model is associated historically with persons in high places governing that "tribal" sphere. But, in the sphere of human activities that belong to the collective of the human totality, there are no "high persons", because that is a "tribal" sign.

4.36 Thus, it is a false hope to expect that a council of "high persons" is going to result in a right managing of humankind or of the interests of humankind.

4.37 In the Global Cooperative Forum, the gathering of representatives would not be "high persons". They would have no status, no separate position. They could even put on same-colored clothing when they sit down in the same council together, to indicate that there are no distinctions.

4.38 There must be an entirely new structuring of the human domain, and also a process wherein that entirely new structure can actually be given birth.

4.39 The old order will insist on its own persistence. And, so, it is a matter of the old order getting up one morning and finding out that there is a Global Cooperative Forum instead.

V.

On Non-Cooperation With What Is Wrong and On Mobilizing The Human Totality Based On The Self-Evident Truth of Prior Unity

5.1   The Global Cooperative Forum would not be some kind of a global parliament coming up with ideas, and saying, "Would all you governments out there please respond?" and, "Would all you corporations please change your act?"

5.2   There is a global collapse happening, and it is not going to be stopped merely by education, or by appeals to people's good nature, based on information only.

5.3   The Global Cooperative Forum has to have the means of the nearly eight billion people saying they insist on change.

5.4   The nearly-eight-billion can, on the one hand, cooperate with one another and engage in a global cooperative, and, on the other hand, they can practice non-cooperation with patterns and systems that are not serving human life and well-being. That capability to refuse to cooperate with the status quo is what gives the global collective its force.

5.5   If the human totality understood what the issues were, and organized itself to refuse to cooperate, refuse to buy, refuse to consume, relative to what is intrinsically and clearly wrong, then that is a means for change.

5.6   It is simply taking the power of the human totality and systematically applying it to its own business— it is not revolutionary and not intended in any kind of negative sense.

5.7   As fragmented cells or "tribes", human beings do not have the power to change the human domain, but humankind as a totality has the power, and so humankind must assume the power that is intrinsic to itself.

5.8   It is not a matter of separate little movements attempting to change things, but one force of humankind functioning intercommunicatively and cooperatively, and taking action relative to what needs to be changed.

5.9   The method of collective non-cooperation is most effective if applied by total populations, and best applied by the totality of humankind.

5.10 In fact, the only way for non-violent non-cooperation not to end up being divisive is to begin with everybody-all-at-once.

5.11 If non-violent non-cooperation is only applied in certain zones of action, there are people on the "yes" side, and people on the "no" side, resulting in divisiveness that can be surrounded by a lot of violence, no matter how non-violent the original intention.

5.12 Non-violent initiatives in violent zones have to be truly protected by the larger environment of everybody-all-at-once. That is the force that undermines misuse of power everywhere, including violent power.

5.13 If the method of non-violent non-cooperation is
applied at the scale of the totality of humankind,
there is effectively no "other side".

5.14 When the whole system is applying the principle of
prior unity to itself, the outcome should be entirely
positive, because the Earth-system, which is intrinsically
a unity, is being restored to its integrity.

5.15 The Global Cooperative Forum is a new basis for
politics, society, culture, economics, and the entire
human process, but you cannot argue people into it.

5.16 If you had to argue nearly eight billion people into
deciding to agree with prior unity and choose the
Global Cooperative Forum, it would never be able
to begin.

5.17 Prior unity, and the need to implement prior unity
via a Global Cooperative Forum, must be presented
as tacitly, self-evidently heart-true, and everyone's
participation is to be invited on that basis.

5.18 In fact, the Global Cooperative Forum begins in the
instant of its being communicated to the human
population. Everybody-all-at-once has the immediate
ability to implement it, by virtue of everyone hearing
the message and seeing the tacit obviousness of it.

5.19 The happening of truth is not through the mind—
it is at the heart. Truth is not a proposition argued
over against other propositions. Truth is self-evident,
because the heart authenticates it in the moment
of reception.

5.20 Truth is an embrace, just as love is. You do not get argued into love. It is self-evidently right.

5.21 One responds to truth as one does to love, simply through recognizing it. It is not about argument, not about the domain of mind, or of opposites.

5.22 That is how the Global Cooperative Forum will come about. It will happen with everybody-all-at-once, because it is right. It is true, it is so. There is no argument either for or against it. It is simply self-evidently true—immediately, on the moment of its presentation.

5.23 Merely to create another NGO, or some kind of entity that is going to try and convince everybody through argument—or, essentially, the play of opposition—to join a Global Cooperative Forum is never going to work. It will just be another piece of the "tribal" world.

5.24 Prior unity is not a union of many. Prior unity is an intrinsic unity in which there is no separateness, no "difference", no otherness, no opposition, no duality. It is one.

5.25 The working-presumption of prior unity can, therefore, address anything—and self-organize it, straighten it, make it right, and just get on with it.

5.26 The working presumption of prior unity has never been the basis of human action before. Nevertheless, it is the truth-basis for human action, the Reality-basis for human action, and, therefore, the Divine basis for human action.

5.27   The Global Cooperative Forum has no "flags", no
       "name-tags", no "placards", no separate anything,
       no opponents. It is intrinsically non-violent—not
       strategically, but because it has no opponent to defeat.

5.28   If anyone refuses the truth of prior unity, he or she is
       simply shunning it, and does not thereby become an
       opponent.

5.29   The Global Cooperative Forum is a prior-unity Forum
       of everybody-all-at-once, and so it does not have
       anybody to overwhelm or to defeat because everybody
       inherently belongs to this one process and is simply
       part of the happening of prior unity in the form of the
       totality of humankind.

5.30   The urgency of the global situation is such that the
       foundation work of activating the totality of
       humankind via the Global Cooperative Forum must
       happen now, so that, during the next few years, there
       can be global conversion of all systems to a right
       functioning in the context of the total system.

VI.

On Establishing Rules of Participation
For A Global Cooperative Order

6.1 Presently, the international community has no effective
way of dealing with geopolitical issues, because it is
fundamentally about "tribes" in competition with one
another. There is no force that embodies everybody
and that, therefore, can effectively deal with the
system as a whole.

6.2 Bits of the system are always confronting one
another. Therefore, those who hold out or want to
"play it hard" wind up controlling the whole system.

6.3 In general, the so-called "big powers" are bypassing
rules and playing for dominance. But everybody is
playing their part in the "tribal" struggle-game, which
is not in the interest of humankind, and it is not
survivable.

6.4 Rules and accountability are essential for any system.
Any notion that you can bypass such accountability
is a lie in the name of serving some kind of "self"-
interest. And this disposition is creating every crisis.

6.5 Systems self-correct, but when you bypass the system,
as is now the case globally, then the system cannot
correct itself anymore. It is just careening downhill
with a stave shoved in the wheels. It is inevitable that
it is going to self-destruct.

6.6 Therefore, the international power-struggles have to be replaced by a systems-based order with rules and limits established. It is only when the system can represent itself as a totality and keep its rules in front of everyone that the system can correct itself.

6.7 A rational and positive global situation requires rules for participation, based on global interdependence and prior unity—rather than being based on nation-states or other groups engaging in reactive measures in the face of being provoked or (otherwise) acting aggressively to extend their influence.

6.8 The process for dealing with global realities should not be merely punitive. Rules for participation should be established—and then doors would be either opened or closed, based on whether any given nation-state or other entity abides by those rules.

6.9 Participation should be the one thing everybody values—not competition, not dominance and victory over all, but participation in a global system that allows every nation-state, every human domain, to survive and enjoy essential well-being and the growth potential and benefits of participation in the whole.

6.10 The rules of participation in the global community should not be arbitrary, or set up to favor certain parties over others. The rules of participation should establish positive and equal participation for everyone, with no double standards that require some to obey the rules while others do not.

6.11 The Global Cooperative Forum is the system of everybody-all-at-once reasserting itself and establishing rules of participation that put all matters of global business equitably on the table—including matters of severe chronic conflict, competition for resources, degradation of the environment and disruption of weather-patterns, poverty, disease, and so forth.

6.12 Right rules of participation will establish an entirely different principle than nation-state competitiveness. It will allow humankind-as-a-whole to become a functioning system—a system to which all parties get access by fulfilling certain obligations and responsibilities, which apply everywhere.

VII.

On Zero-Point Education

7.1 Ego-culture makes institutions in the egoic likeness— based on the separate and separative "self"-principle. This is what is happening today all over the world.

7.2 As a result, both secular and sacred institutions are being falsified by the imposition of egoity. This is occurring in the domain of politics, in the domain of education, in the domain of religion, and in every domain associated with human life.

7.3 The egoic subversion of human institutions is inevitable—unless such subversion is prevented by upholding a pattern of rightness. The rightness of human institutions depends on there being a system, and a tradition, and people guiding the process who understand how to maintain rightness.

7.4 In the domain of education, it has traditionally been understood that only a thorough rightening of understanding can bring about a rightening of life.

7.5 In the present-time human world, education is tending to be reduced to a propaganda industry that is purposed only to produce the next generation of social and political participants in a programmed life dictated by government, corporations, and economic interests. Thus, such so-called "education" is, in fact, merely about producing a work force.

7.6 Real education is the process of getting to the root of what human existence is about. In the present-time human world, some individuals are yet moved to exercise themselves in such a manner—but there is, in the present-time human world, no collective (or global) process of such real education.

7.7 In the present-time human world, the conventions of education derive from the now-pervasive ego-culture. Such ego-based education leads to divisiveness, competitiveness, and further "tribalization"—thereby undermining the global unity of humankind and working against the systematizing of human responsibility on a global scale.

7.8 People are being indoctrinated all over the world—not just by religion, but by many different systems of education and stimulated activism.

7.9 The use of education to propagandize action based on "tribal" mind and competitiveness must be replaced by a new process of global education that is intrinsically not about either religion or scientific materialism.

7.10 The Global Cooperative Forum is about an entirely new mode of human, political, social, and economic existence—and, thus, about an entirely new mode of education, and of human culture altogether.

7.11 The Global Cooperative Forum is about enabling the transition from ego-culture to a culture of transcending the ego, in which there is a higher principle to which all must be accountable—including individuals, groups, and all the collectives of humankind.

7.12 The basis of the global education I propose is the restoration of the principles of egolessness and prior unity to the course of human life. I call this mode of education "'zero-point' education".

7.13 "Zero-point" education is not merely institutionalized learning. "Zero-point" education is about a way of life that follows from the root-understanding of egolessness and prior unity.

7.14 Therefore, that root-understanding must be demonstrated throughout the totality of each individual's life, and throughout the totality of the collective world in which all human beings participate together.

7.15 The purpose and the evidence of "zero-point" education is "zero-point" living—or the demonstration of "zero-point" consciousness.

7.16 The fundamentals that spring from "zero-point" education and "zero-point" understanding must, necessarily, manifest in the global domain of politics and social processes.

7.17 "Zero-point" education is the basis for global "zero-point" activism. "Zero-point" activism is of a wholly positive and entirely cooperative nature—serving the system-totality of human life.

7.18 A "zero-point" education system would, inevitably, move people into a process of right and positive action—in the context of the global cooperative order.

7.19 "Zero-point" education, established both locally and globally, can counter and replace the kind of religious indoctrination that produces the aberrations of fundamentalist activism.

7.20 The Global Cooperative Forum is, itself, the institutional manifestation of "zero-point" education.

7.21 The present moment in human history is the crucial turning-point—truly, the "zero-point"—in which a new and systematic global human culture can, potentially, emerge. That new culture will be based on global cooperation, in association with principles of accountability that will manage the Earth-world responsibly on a cooperative basis.

7.22 The role of the Global Cooperative Forum is to educate the world in this "zero-point" sense, calling everyone to exercise the cooperative participation and the mutual accountability that are the necessary means of taking responsibility for the human domain and for the totality of the Earth-world.

7.23 Through such responsible "zero-point" education and right self-management, humankind will be enabled to go beyond the otherwise dominant ego-principles of "tribalism" and unprincipled consumerism. Through "zero-point" education, all "tribalism" and unprincipled consumerism will be relinquished—by means of the restoration of the principles of intrinsic egolessness and prior unity.

7.24 The demonstration-sign of true "zero-point" education is not merely the advocating of some form of philosophy. Rather, the demonstration-sign of true "zero-point" education is right life—which is, most fundamentally, a matter of the disciplining of the ego-as-consumer.

7.25 When one has been converted from the "philosophy" of ego-culture to the "zero-point" philosophy, one is no longer disposed to live as a consumer-ego. When one has been converted from the "philosophy" of ego-culture to the "zero-point" philosophy, one is moved to embrace a disciplined right life, founded in the tacit awareness of intrinsic egolessness and prior unity.

7.26 The tacit "zero-point" awareness of intrinsic egolessness and prior unity, demonstrated by the steadily disciplined practice of right life, is the transformed quality and characteristic required of the leadership that is necessary to move humankind (as a whole) to accept responsibility for itself.

PART TWO

Not-Two Is Peace

Capitalization, Underlining, Quotation Marks

The World-Friend Adi Da uses capitalization, underlining, and quotation marks to distinguish between ordinary speech (which describes reality as it is ordinarily perceived) and speech that describes the Indivisible and Absolute Reality. With the use of capitalization and underlining, Adi Da expresses a different view of the world, in which Truth and the terms that relate to that Greater Reality are given more significance than the language of the separate ego and the conventional world. With quotation marks, Adi Da often communicates that some ordinary term, commonly presumed to point to something real, is, in Reality, only an illusion. He also uses quotation marks to point to a specific, technical meaning he intends. (Please see specific terms in the glossary.) ∎

I.

Anthroposphere
(The Natural Zone of Necessary
Human Responsibility)—

A First Word
About The Unified Global Ecology
of The Necessary New Mode
of Human Civilization

1.

My communication in *Not-Two Is Peace* is a direct address to humankind-as-a-whole, because of the now profoundly changed situation of humankind—a situation that is not really being acknowledged and understood to be the case. In the present time, the social, political, economic, and religious domains of the human sphere are all characterized by a kind of "fundamentalism of the old days", a kind of "retro world"—and this is creating a disaster, because humankind has not shifted in its understanding to account for the real situation that now exists. The current situation is one in which the prior unity of humankind is self-evident—but that prior unity is not being acted upon. Instead, people are still hoisting the old "flags" and looking for "victory".

When human beings were rather independent (or disconnected) from one another and living in tribal groups—isolated by geography, and not so much face-to-face—nation-states and all kinds of "tribalism" (religious, social, economic, and political) could represent a positive human and ecological influence, each within its own domain. However, in the present time, such "tribalism" can no longer function positively. In the present time, "tribalism" is producing disaster.

Nation-states came into being through the chaotic process of the unfolding of history, in a time when humankind-as-a-whole was not yet interconnected. In that historical situation, the Earth itself, as a natural domain, provided the only "grid" of interconnectedness. The Earth carried on its own natural processes—but, the more human beings became globally connected, the more they interrupted the natural Earth-process. As a result, there are many things happening to the Earth that are the direct result of human intervention. In previous epochs of history, human beings did not intervene in the natural Earth-process to such a degree. Thus, the natural Earth-process, which once held everything together in a kind of order (or unity), is now globally interrupted—along with the entire process of life altogether. Therefore, the Earth is no longer holding things together.

Furthermore, the totality of humankind is now face-to-face. All the different "tribal" arrangements that became nation-states are playing off one another. Therefore, a new method of establishing order is needed, based on the interconnectedness of humankind. There is potential virtue in the fact that all of humankind is now interconnected—but only if humankind can function cooperatively, and in a disposition of tolerance, rather than in the disposition of exclusion and the will-to-dominate.

A rightly functioning and truly all-inclusive Global Cooperative Forum, based upon the working-principle of the prior unity of all of humankind, will make the face-to-face meeting of humankind-as-a-whole into a positive means of political and social order.* Without such a Global

---

* Adi Da's full discussion of the principles for such a Global Cooperative Forum is given in Part One and in Essays XI–XVIII and XXI–XXIV of Part Two.

Cooperative Forum, there is only going to be more and more "tribal" warfare, creating more and more of a global catastrophe—not only in the historical terms of human disorder, but even in the natural terms of undermining the order of the Earth-process. Indeed, both natural chaos and historical chaos are <u>already</u> happening.

Therefore, there needs to be a new method of human politics and social existence, based on the fact that humankind is entirely face-to-face now. All of humankind is interconnected, but that interconnection is tending to be negative—embroiled in (even deliberately generated) conflict, and involved in efforts to expand and control.

There must now be a method of establishing order which is based on the interconnectedness of humankind-as-a-whole, and which also assumes responsibility for the right serving of (and for right participation in) the natural order. Only by this means can the disastrous effects of the human exploitation of Earth be brought to an end. There must be a <u>functioning</u> <u>unity</u> of humankind-as-a-whole—dealing with the political, social, and economic order worldwide, as well as with the natural order worldwide.

Nation-states are simply "zones" within this totality—"zones" that should be entirely cooperative. Nation-states are among the kinds of structures (already in place) that have come about through the accidents of history, at a time when humankind was <u>not</u> interconnected as a whole. In the current situation, these inherited structures have become subject to all kinds of power-games and power-struggles all over the world. These structures, in their present form, are not to be merely ignored—but they must become accountable and responsible within a total global order of humankind.

The necessary right and true global cooperative order is not a totalitarian order—that, of course, would not be positive. However, a totalitarian order is exactly what <u>could</u> come about through the disposition of conflict that is now ruling the world, with all the players cloaking themselves in their associations with nation-states.

In actuality, the situation of humankind has gone through a progressive but dramatic change over the last few centuries—and especially in the last century. Now humankind is already interconnected and already face-to-face. Therefore, the Earth must become a sphere of "priorly united" nations. There must be a Global Cooperative Forum based on prior unity, on principles that have to do with the unified totality of humankind, and the unified totality that is the Earth-domain itself. This is absolutely imperative—because the current disorder and threat to humankind and the Earth is a result of not taking into account the fact that humankind is now an interconnected unity that is face-to-face. That face-to-face situation is currently associated with all kinds of conflict—between different ideologies, different cultural histories, different religious associations, and so forth.

Therefore, as a result of many centuries of change in the human world, an entirely new and different kind of order is required—politically, and (also) environmentally. This is an entirely new situation, that has fully come into being only recently—most especially in the twentieth century (and particularly in the final decades of the twentieth century), and now in the twenty-first century.

The continuation of the "old ways" of doing things, and the persistence in the old habits of mind and life, is producing the current "neighborhood-wars"—as if it were possible to "play it" as in the old days, and expect that, somehow or other, things will work out politically. The "old ways" are no longer applicable. "Tribal" associations—whether religious, national, or racial—no longer have relevance in the now-interconnected state of humankind.

2.

Humankind must wake up. Humanity is now one—and there truly is only one "boat". Everybody is face-to-face now, and the chaotic results of humankind's dis-united and separative (and, altogether, ego-like) activities are, in fact, undermining the natural order on which everybody was able to depend until the last two hundred years, before human intervention started seriously changing the natural Earth-situation itself.

Ego is ruling—but ego has always ruled. The problem is that, now, ego is ruling in a totally different kind of situation, in which ego has the power to destroy not only humankind-as-a-whole, but even the natural order of the Earth-world.

To imagine that a separate absolute Deity is in charge of the current chaos and suffering in the human world and in the Earth-world is to indulge in ignorance. Human beings themselves have intervened. Whatever the origins of the Earth-world are altogether, the natural domain is now being interfered with by human beings, in this time in which humankind has a total effect on the natural world. Therefore, humankind must not merely appeal to a parent-like "God" to change the situation. The Perfectly egoless Absolute That Is Reality Itself "Expects" (or Intrinsically "Requires") humankind to change its own act.

Human beings are causing negative events in both the natural world and the political world—because human beings are still mentally indulging in "tribalism", while (in actuality) they are globally face-to-face and in "one boat". The ancient "tribal" mode of human culture—in which human beings live in units that are, effectively, collective forms of egoity, living in conflict with one another—is what must stop.

It is not merely that, suddenly, there are negative happenings in the world. There have always been negative happenings in the world. What is new is that the world is now in a different condition from anything that has existed previously. There is now a new situation for humankind—indeed, a new situation for all of Earthkind, and for the Earth itself. This new condition, wherein humankind exists as a totality in which all are interconnected, must be acknowledged and acted upon.

This new situation requires a profound transformation of human consciousness and human activity. Thus, the communication I am making in *Not-Two Is Peace* is not simply a response to current events, in the sense of the "daily news" of the moment. I am addressing the altogether-new situation that exists for humankind and for the Earth itself—a situation that requires a new kind of politics, a new kind of global human order.

In this new global human order, principles representing the totality of humankind, and the Earth as a whole, must become the means whereby human living is conducted all over the Earth. This will require a kind of global "revolution"—but the root-cause of the "revolution" has already happened. The "revolution" that has already happened is the fact that everybody has already come together, face-to-face, and that the totality of everybody is everywhere affecting the Earth. Therefore, it is imperative that human consciousness catch up, and notice what has happened—and choose what must change.

The terrible problems that are occurring politically and naturally in the world today are the result of pattern-driven human unconsciousness. Human beings are continuing mechanically, trying to repeat modes of effort, even modes of thinking, that were workable—up to a point—in the past, but that are no longer workable now. A new kind of human consciousness is required—based on the working-presumption of prior unity, and on an understanding of the indivisibly single world in which everyone is living. This involves not only the notion that there is such a single world, but it requires grasping the necessity for cooperation, and the necessity to function on the basis of an understanding that the Earth is a single system, and humankind (likewise) is a single whole. Humankind must not be forced to function under some kind of totalitarian singleness. Rather, humankind must function cooperatively—in the sense that everyone is living together on Earth, and functioning through a mechanism of global principles that are benign and right and true.

Not-Two Is Peace is about the new method that must be brought to the already existing new global situation. That is the situation to which I have given utterance. The current situation is the result of human unconsciousness, of trying to function automatically on the basis of methods and patterns which applied in the past, but which no longer apply in the present. If the "old methods" are brought to bear in the current situation, they create chaos—human disorder and suffering, as well as chaos in the natural domain.

There is undeniable and inescapable proof in the every day of "daily news" that human beings are <u>everywhere</u> carrying on their activities in a manner that is not productive, and not workable. Humankind must, itself (and as a whole), become truly and rightly globalized. There must be the establishment of principles which serve the potential well-being of humankind-as-a-whole, and which ensure that the Earth-domain itself is able to function soundly. Thus, a different method of human relatedness is required: the non-"tribal", or non-fragmented, method, in which the working-presumption is prior unity.

II.

Humankind Is <u>Literally</u> One Family

There is no difference between people. Human beings are a <u>single</u> species—and, fundamentally, they are all the <u>same</u>. The various colors do not make any difference. Races of human beings are variations of minor genetic changes that developed as human beings wandered the planet and lived under various conditions over thousands of years. Of course, in each place where human beings settled, they developed particular philosophical views and cultural characteristics. Nevertheless, the changes that occurred and the differences that developed are sheerly incidental and minor.

It is important for everyone to understand that <u>humankind</u>, as a species (and as a whole), is (and always has been) characterized by a constant and global process of <u>diaspora</u>. <u>All</u> of humankind is wandering all over the Earth. Humankind (and even life itself, as a singular whole) is, historically and characteristically, <u>dispersed</u> (or scattered). However, in its fragmentation (as many and separate everythings), humankind is, now, acting as if it is not <u>one</u> thing, but, rather, as if it were many different and separate somethings—as if "tribal" differentiation into national, and religious, and cultural particularity, and distinct racial groupings, and distinct language types, and so forth, amounts to a fundamental difference-making force that should redefine humankind, not as one indivisible species, but as many separate and competing species.

<u>All</u> of the apparent diversity of humankind is a superficial diversity within the context of a <u>single</u> (and <u>intrinsically</u>

indivisible) species—which, according to the best (even genetic) analysis, progressively moved out of Africa and into various parts of the world. Therefore, now, the indivisible totality of humankind is dispersed—with relatively small groupings of people having, in times past, become stationary in one or another geographical (and, now, also cultural) location, and (thus and thereby) having become attached to their unique local languages and political systems and religious traditions, and on and on and on and on. There is no end to the local (or "tribal") differences—and human beings tend to make much of the apparent differences between them. However, the apparent differences are (in Truth) merely superficial (or local, and, thus, "tribal", or merely provincial) characteristics—the ordinary variants on what it is to be a human being, located in "point of view" relative to space and time.

The negative (and competitive) presumption of "difference" in the context of the universal human diaspora is a problem of fundamental significance—and it is a problem (or a presumption) that must now come to an end. There must be a presumed prior unity (or intrinsic indivisibility) of humankind— not the domination over all others by one nation (or "type"), and not some numbers of nations (or "similars") indulging in strategic conflict with one another, in order to wage a "final battle" to determine who is going to dominate and rule everybody else.

It is as if all human beings suddenly do not recognize their own brothers and sisters. It is true that one may look different from another, and one may carry a different cultural inheritance and mode of thinking than another, and so on. Therefore, human beings may all look and think differently— but they all are and do the same thing. Everyone must become educated to notice this.

Human beings are all primates—not exactly apes, but something along those lines. How much knowledge do you think a primate inherently possesses? Why would you expect a totally rightly informed mind to be demonstrated by a casually adapted primate?

Why do you—the people of humankind—continue to insist on making the differences that you make, on the basis of local historical memories and provincial institutional configurations of separate groups of people? Why do you do that, instead of understanding that what you are observing, right now, is the indivisible global singleness of a particular species? Every human being is, as such, always already coincident with (and fundamentally identical to) every other—and, therefore, could also be combined, in a very productive and positive sense, with the total world of all of humankind. What is required is the establishing of a global cooperative (and universally participatory) order of humankind—a cultural and social and political globalization of humankind (and not merely an economic globalization of human commerce, within a world-situation characterized by competitive differences).

The diaspora of all of humankind must be re-acculturated, to accept and embrace a universal "homeland of everywhere". The total world of human beings must grow up, to understand humankind as an indivisible totality—now everywhere dispersed, not merely by contemporary political forces, but by the migration of the human species all over the globe for countless thousands of years, and by the accumulation of localized characteristics of life and mind under all kinds of different local (and geographically separate) conditions.

Humankind is in the position, right now, to make some very important judgements about life, and about the relationships between people—and about Reality Itself. As a result of that judgement, either there will be universal war and death or, alternatively, humankind will become established in a global cooperative order, based on the working-presumption of universal prior unity and the universal world-"homeland" that belongs to all of humankind (and, indeed, all of Earthkind).

All have suffered. All are equally full of nonsense. Therefore, in principle, there must be a new and universal politics—a politics of no praise and no blame. By these means, reconciliation must be achieved—cooperatively, in a disposition of mutual tolerance, trust, and respect.

The genetic unity of humankind is inherent. That unity is scientifically known to be so. Yet, the "difference-makers" speak and act as if there were superior humans and inferior humans, superior nationalisms and inferior nationalisms, and so on—as if merely incidental differences were of immense significance. To make much of incidental differences is merely to argue about old stories. Instead of all that, everyone must be exercised anew—toward (and in, and As) Truth in always present-time.

III.

C + T = P:
Formula For World Peace

1.

I t is a matter of the <u>greatest</u> present-time urgency that the prevailing global mood of political separatism, end-game competitiveness, and endlessly multiplied divisiveness be immediately and thoroughly and universally and permanently relinquished—such that the entire world-population of humankind becomes universally intelligent with the heart-positive mind of cooperation and tolerance.

2.

The only way to solve the current world-situation is for <u>everyone</u> to "<u>lose</u> face"—instead of everyone demanding to "<u>save</u> face".

All of humankind should, as a formalized collective, "lose face" together—by acknowledging that, unless human beings live in formally established and formally maintained cooperation and tolerance, they, <u>inevitably</u>, sink into grossly and universally destructive behavior.

Only by <u>everyone</u> "losing face" <u>together</u> will the collective of human beings be able to regenerate the moral strength and authority that is necessary if human beings everywhere are to require cooperation and tolerance of each other—and only when there is <u>first</u> such a regeneration of universally equalized moral strength and authority will there be a universal agreement to create and maintain a truly cooperative and tolerant global human community.

3.

Human beings must accept, with humility, that their rightful position (and that of every one) in the naturally indivisible world-family of Earthkind (including humankind) is not the "ego-place" of prior dis-unity (and, thus, of separateness, separativeness, domination, and control), but the "heart-place" of prior unity (and, thus, of ego-transcending cooperation and tolerance).

It is not the search for peace (for all seeking is, necessarily, based on prior, or presumed, separation from what is being sought), but the active affirmation and enactment of peace (or the presumption of prior, or always already present, unity and non-conflict—as a condition to be always affirmed, depended upon, enacted, and preserved) that is the true and only means for the realization of peace.

Thus, in practical terms, it is only on the active foundation of ego-transcending cooperation and tolerance that it is possible for peace (or right life) to be established among living beings of any form or kind.

Indeed, this Call to Right Life and Peace is a great and absolute moral Law, which I have Epitomized in the Formula C + T = P, or "Cooperation + Tolerance = Peace".

It is absolutely essential that the universal collective of humankind formally embrace and really enact this universal moral disposition.

4.

"Cooperation + Tolerance = Peace" is the Great Alternative to the egoic path of inevitable universal destruction—and, therefore, that moral Law must become a universally accepted (and expected) moral and practical "self"-discipline.

Through the universal application of this great moral Law, the gathering of the Earth-wandering peoples of the world can feel their real strength and prior unity (or inherent connectedness to one another)—and their collective power to transform the "usual" (or "real") politics of egoity, and so actually create and maintain human peace in the natural world.

Everyone should become positively disposed to the establishment of a real and true global cooperative human community—because that global cooperative human community is not merely a "utopian ideal", but a practical and actually realizable necessity for the physical survival and the natural well-being of humankind and even all of Earthkind.

5.

The Formula for World Peace must be embraced as the necessary politics of the future.

Cooperation and tolerance is the necessary and exact "price" for peace—the "treaty cost" for the survival of humankind, Earthkind, and Earth itself.

This is the necessary "new paradigm" for the human design of future effort.

IV.

On Liberation From ego
and egoic Society

1.

The un-En-Light-ened (or egocentric) body-mind-"self"
is founded on the activity of "self"-contraction. The
"self"-contraction is enacted as the effective differentiation of the (thus presumed) separate "self" from the
Intrinsically egoless Self-Nature, Self-Condition, Self-State,
and Acausal Source-Condition That Is Reality Itself—and,
coincidently, the "self"-contraction is enacted as the effective
differentiation of the (thus presumed) separate "self" from
every other form of thus presumed (or, by means of "self"-
contraction, defined) "not-self". And the "self"-contraction is,
likewise, expressed (via the "self"-contraction-definition of
"self" as independent and separative) as the constant concern and search for the preservation of the (presumed-to-be
independent) "self" (or ego-"I"). The "self"-based (or "self"-
contracting, and would-be-"self"-preserving) orientation
toward existence is manifested as the psychology of search
and conflict relative to all that is presumed to be "not-self"—
some and all of which is sometimes desired and sought, and
some and all of which is sometimes feared (or reacted to
with the seeking effort of avoidance), and even all of which
is always limited, mortal, passing, inexplicable, and (therefore) inherently unsatisfactory. Therefore, the psychology of
"self"-contracted (and, as a result, egocentric) existence is
inherently disposed to seek control and dominance over all
that is presumed to be "not-self". For this reason, individual

egocentric lives are a constant expression of heart-felt (and total psycho-physical) anxiety (and even the primitive ego-moods of fear, sorrow, anger, and every kind of un-love)—and individual human actions are, on that primitive basis, always a more or less mechanical (or uninspected and irresponsible) display of strategic techniques of "self"-manipulation (intended to preserve "self") and "other"-manipulation (intended to control, or dominate, "not-self"). And the collective (or group) life of egocentric human beings is, likewise, dominated by the same exclusiveness, the same emotional base, the same inherent unsatisfactoriness, and the same motives toward "self"-preservation, and toward control of what is "outside".

Human societies are always tending to be modeled after the un-En-Light-ened pattern of the individual ego. The political and social systems of the present-day world are not generated by literally En-Light-ened (or even highly "evolved") leaders, ideals, or institutions. Human beings in this "late-time" (or "dark" epoch) live in the un-En-Light-ened world of egoic society—and this is why the signs of the times are so profoundly negative.

The entire world is now nearly out of control with egoic motives. Humankind, indoctrinated by materialistic philosophies, ego-serving technologies, and gross political idealisms, is possessed by the mechanical and emotionally negative efforts of "self"-indulgence (and anxious release-seeking efforts of all kinds), and chronically depressed by the frustration of the ego-transcending deepest and most profound impulses that are the inherent characteristics at the heart and root of every living being. The ego-"I", whether individual or collective, is eventually reduced to sorrow and despair (or chronic life-depression), because of (and as an experiential result of) the inability of life (in and of itself) to generate Happiness and Joy and Immortality. And that "self"-contained depression finally becomes anger, or loveless confrontation with the total world and every form of presumed "not-self"—including even (and especially) the Intrinsically egoless, and Acausally Real, Self-Identity (or One and Only and Non-Separate Self-Nature, Self-Condition, and Self-State), Which is "locked away", by means of conventional (or merely exoteric) ideas of "God Apart", and is (thereby) made into an "Other" by the egoic mind. And, when anger becomes the mood of human societies, the quality of fire (or the primitive and destructive intent of the frustrated ego) invades the plane of humanity. That fire is expressed as all of the aggression and competitiveness (and all of the resultant sufferings and painful illusions) of humankind, including all of the ego-based politics of confrontation. And that ego-fire is, finally, summarized in the acts of war.

2.

The differentiation of existence into ego-possessed units yields, in the case of each "one", the craving for entirely pleasurized and unthreatened existence. This craving (or obsessive motive of "self"-preservation and "self"-glorification) in turn yields inevitable conflict, fear, sorrow, anger, and all kinds of destructive acts in relation to "others" as well as to "self" (because the extreme exercise of "self"-preservation is, ultimately, an aggressive and "self"-defeating motivation that destroys "self" in the final effort to dominate "not-self"). Therefore, all egos (or un-En-Light-ened centers of identity, whether individual or collective) are in aggressive conflict with all other egos (and all that is presumed to be "not-self", or presumed to be "outside" the defined egoic center). All individual and collective egos are involved in programs of "self"-destruction (via patterns of ego-possession, "self"-seeking, "self"-indulgence, reactive emotion, un-En-Light-ened thinking, and so forth), as well as "other"-destruction (via all kinds of reactive activity, based on "self"-concern, that seeks to control, and, ultimately, to dominate, whatever is presumed to be "outside" the "self"-center).

The search for the independent preservation and ultimate enhancement of the separate "self" is the universal model of un-En-Light-ened egoity. Therefore, suffering, power struggle, and war are inevitable in egoic society. And, if the capability for political manipulation and war becomes technologically profound, universal suppression (via aggressive political efforts) and universal destruction (via war) become the common expectation and destiny of all human beings.

The present "late-time" (or "dark" epoch) is just such a time of technological sophistication, in which the egoic model of humanity and human society is the universal basis of mind. Gross materialism (in science and politics) gives human beings no option in the mind except that of the trapped and threatened animal. Therefore, a fiery mood is abroad—full of gross desire, frustration, fear, despair, and aggressive reactivity. The egoic motive of "self"-preservation is approaching its most destructive mood—the mood that appears in the moment of ultimate entrapment. In that mood, there is no longer any will to preserve "self" or world or any others. There is simply explosive fire—based on the deep motives of egoic "self"-preservation, but reduced to action that is most primitive and entirely destructive of both "self" and "not-self". In the collective mind of humanity in the present and growing extremes of entrapment, the explosion of great nuclear bombs merely represents the archetype of anger itself. And it is for this reason that the possibility of a nuclear holocaust, in the extreme moment of the now rising political confrontations, is an irrational—and, therefore, entirely possible, if not inevitable—event.

Past societies have, in their extreme moments of confrontation, destroyed themselves, as well as their opponents. This is because ego-based societies function in essentially the same manner as egoic individuals. Individual human beings kill others and themselves every day. Therefore, groups and societies, confronting one another in egoic fashion, likewise threaten one another with destruction. And, in the extreme moments of confrontation, when "self"-preservation achieves its peak of righteous irrationality, it is profoundly likely that nuclear war will result.

The motives of present-day society are the same as those of past societies. The only difference is that, in the present day, the technology of both communication and confrontation has become both globally extended and profound. Therefore, when globally communicated confrontation reaches its peak of irrationality, war-motives will willingly destroy the entire world—just as readily as, in the past, less technologically sophisticated war-makers have wiped their petty local warring tribes from the face of the Earth.

3.

Many people are now trying to influence governments to abandon nuclear weapons. However, even if they succeed, irrational individuals and groups can still threaten and destroy the common order with "terrorist" tactics and "home-made" bombs. And the "limited" (or non-nuclear) warfare that might still erupt between governments that agree not to make nuclear war is just as much a threat to humanity as any nuclear war.

Therefore, it is now time to accept the political necessity for an end to confrontation-politics, and the establishment of a unified political entity to directly and truly and formally and accountably serve the right collective interests of humankind-as-a-whole. Human beings must abandon their ancient egoic principles and renounce their political, social, and cultural provincialism. Individuals within the collective order of humankind may yet suffer the un-En-Light-ened and immature disabilities of egocentric personality—but governments themselves, as well as institutions and leaders in every area of human endeavor, must abandon the egocentric, subhuman, merely materialistic, non-cooperative, and intolerant (or loveless) posture and style of life. Indeed, humanity as a whole, in the form of a Global Cooperative Forum, must come forward and accept responsibility, in a unified (and truly representative and accountable) manner, for the indivisible representation of its collective interests.

Have you not had enough of the brute, stupid, childish, and (otherwise) adolescent, exploitative representation of human (or, really, subhuman) existence that is played out daily (in the name, and on the lives, of each and every born human being) by competing governments, politicians, militarists, scientists, technocrats, social planners, educators, exoteric and fundamentalist religionists (who aggressively propagate the provincial religions of ego-salvation, rather than practice the universal, and ego-transcending, religion of love), and media hypers (who thrive on the invention and exaggeration of conflict, and dramatically showcase the worst of human instincts in the unending "gotcha" game that denudes and exposes and trivializes and hypocritically mocks the highs, and the inevitable lows, and even the natural ordinariness in the struggling efforts of humankind)? Is it not evident, in your deepest feeling-psyche, that this Wisdom-renouncing world is now being controlled by the worst and most superficial conceptions of existence?

It is now time for every one, and all, to understand themselves, and to reclaim the world from the dictatorship of the ego, and from all of those who play at politics (and life in general) as if it were a TV sporting event that is supposed to excite and entertain everyone.

Nuclear disarmament is a relatively positive, but still too superficial and piecemeal, effort. It is not a truly curative means, but only another palliative and temporary move in the midst of humankind's traditional advance toward future trouble. There is something more fundamental than the disarmament politics whereby enemies come to a gentlemanly agreement on how to kill one another without destroying one another! What is more fundamental, necessary, and truly curative is that human beings, individually and collectively, understand and transcend that which is in them that leads them to confront one another as opponents and enemies.

It may sound naive to speak of the necessity for the childish and brutishly adolescent governments and institutions to understand themselves and renounce the "self"-imagery and the techniques of enemies—but the feeling that it is naive to speak in such terms is merely a reflection of egoic frustration and despair. Human beings everywhere must now transcend that very frustration and despair if they are going to prevent the enslavement and destruction of humankind.

Humanity is living in bondage now. Humankind is already—presently, globally—bound to egocentric and materialistic idealisms that are suppressing the human freedom to live by Wisdom and Realize the Truth. If human beings do not shake loose from this regime, they are going to suffer the extreme fulfillment of collective egoic destiny, in a "Narcissistic" holocaust that will either enslave humankind (via a technologically robotized political and social order) or (otherwise) destroy humankind (via technologically engineered warfare).

It is not naive to suggest and expect a profound change in the conducting of global human affairs when those who could make the demand for change number in the billions. Nor is it folly to try to re-orient humankind when the only alternative is universal slavery and the culture of death. Therefore, all must commit themselves to understand the patterns by which they are now (and have traditionally and historically been) living (both individually and collectively), so that they can then change those patterns and the destinies those patterns will (otherwise) inevitably inflict upon them. The egoic model must—from now on—be intensively "educated out" of the collective order of humankind. The total collective of all of humankind must be educatively re-informed, to understand the primitive egoic basis of the present and traditional collective order. That same universal re-education must, profoundly and immediately, transform the techniques whereby governments and societies enter into relations with one another. However, it is only when they are faced with the indivisible and immovable demands of the rightly re-oriented human collective that the governments and institutions of the world will voluntarily change toward a cooperative and benign mode of association with each other. Indeed, if this does not occur soon, humanity will be entering into what has the potential to be the most destructive period of political confrontation in its history.

4.

A benign and tolerant and cooperative (or thoroughly ego-transcending) view of existence (and, thus, of politics) must now arise in the collective of humankind-as-a-whole. At the present time, human beings are being led to enslavement and destruction by benighted materialists and "self"-seekers in every area of common human endeavor. The Principle of Wisdom has been replaced by the principle of power-through-knowledge—and knowledge has come to mean the views and presumed knowledge determined by the culture and method of scientific materialism, or all that can be achieved or supported exclusively by the intellectual efforts of materialistic philosophy. Science (which has characteristically identified itself with the archaic and false philosophy of materialism) has itself, thus, become identical to technology (or the materialistic power-machine of the "known"), and materialistic technology (along with its like in the form of all the materialistic idealisms that appeal to human egoity) has become the primary instrument for world-manipulation—not only for the material manipulation of the so-called "material" world, but for the political manipulation and gross (physical and mental) control of collective humanity itself.

The political ideals and means of the present time are materialistic, based on a gross and ego-based conception of human existence. There simply cannot be any ultimately effective change in the collective human situation until the true (and intrinsically egoless) voice of humankind-as-a-whole is made to be heard, and is fully and rightly represented by a morally-enlightened leadership. Only when required to do so—by the global collective of humankind—will governments transform their "technique" from a process of "self"-preserving and "other"-controlling confrontation (of their own members, as well as other societies) to a process of cooperation, unification, and a worldwide creative order, based (necessarily) on pluralism, tolerance, and freedom.

The problem of the automatic (and even unconscious) creation of suffering and destruction is inherent in the ego-centric form of individual existence. It is this principle that all must observe and understand in themselves. Human beings must learn from this observation of the ego (in both personal and collective terms), and so equip themselves to freely (both personally and collectively) abandon the egoic model of existence.

5.

The life-principles of abandoning the gross style of ego-based political confrontations and ego-based social participation, or non-participation, must become a matter of active practical commitment on the part of the global collective of humankind—or else humanity will collectively move toward intolerable enslavement and even nuclear (or otherwise war-made, and cleverness-made) destruction.

Therefore, every one and all must consider, and, then, actively embrace every form of true and benign social and political cooperation and all-embracing social and political tolerance—since such cooperation and tolerance are the prerequisites for true social and political peace.

All of humankind (now, and forever hereafter) must actively embrace, and universally declare and promote, and actively require and measure the universal real fulfillment of the simplest Law and Measure of right human life: Cooperation + Tolerance = Peace.

V.

The Time-Tested Politics of Unity
and
The Anti-Civilization Politics of Individuation

Politics, society, and the common behavioral norms of any collective order are modeled in the likeness of the concept (or philosophy) of conditionally manifested reality that characterizes the collective generally.

If the prevailing concept (or philosophy) of conditionally manifested reality is based upon the presumption that conditionally manifested existence is not a unity (but, instead, is characterized by irreducible multiplicity, separateness, independent individuality, and polar opposition), then the collective order will be characterized by the gross politics of dissociative individuation, and by the universally socially-active idea of competitive individualism, and, also, by behavioral norms and expectations that exclusively correspond to the purpose of separate and separative individual "self"-fulfillment.

If, however, the prevailing concept (or philosophy) of conditionally manifested reality is based upon the presumption that conditionally manifested existence is priorly (or inherently) a unity (and is, for that reason, altogether characterized by, and to be conformed to, the sign of indivisible unity), then the collective order will be characterized by the politics of cooperative unity, and by the universally socially-active idea of social indivisibility, and, also, by ego-subordinating behavioral norms and expectations—including such norms as cooperation, tolerance, and globally universal peace.

The traditional, time-tested, and life-proven concept (or philosophy) of conditionally manifested reality is that of prior unity. Politics, society, and the culture of human behavior have traditionally been developed on the basis of the fundamental working-presumption of the prior (or inherent) unity of conditionally manifested reality and the Prior (or Intrinsic) Oneness (and Indivisibility) of the Non-conditional Reality (or the Self-Nature, Self-Condition, Self-State, and Acausal Source-Condition That Is Reality Itself).* And this fundamental presumption, first confessed and communicated by men and women of great Spiritual development, has been the very basis for the universal efforts and purposes of humankind that characterize what is rightly called "civilization". By contrast—except for the basic corrective demand that appropriate individual rights, and true individual well-being, and necessary individual integrity be properly respected and served—the political, social, and general behavioral signs and results of the concept (or philosophy) of conditionally manifested reality as a non-unity (or an "objective" multiplicity divorced from Prior Indivisibility) can largely be described as the effort and purpose of counter-civilization, or anti-civilization, or even barbarism. That is to say, the political, social, and general behavioral signs and results of the concept (or philosophy) of conditionally manifested reality as a non-unity (or a realm of mere multiplicity, separateness, independent individuality, and polar opposition) are those of ego-glorification, general dissociativeness and separativeness, collective dis-unity and disorder, indiscriminate exploitation of all possibilities, abuse and disregard of every form of authority, the magnification of every kind of conflict and difference, the exaggeration of competitiveness, "self"-indulgence, and the purpose of material

---

* Reality Itself—which is the True Self-Nature, Self-Condition, and Self-State (or "Source-Reality") of every being and thing—is not in any sense dependent on conditions, and therefore it is utterly "Non-conditional". See also **conditionally manifested reality / Reality Itself** in the glossary.

acquisition, the breakdown of community and collective culture, the devaluation and the waning of true philosophical
and Spiritual endeavor, and the undermining of the fundamental morality of cooperation, tolerance, and general
peacefulness.

Political, social, and general behavioral "materialism" (or
conventional "realism") are bound to the concept (or philosophy) of conditionally manifested existence as a non-unity
(and, at best, a search for the achievement of unity). And
such political, social, and general behavioral "materialism"
(or conventional "realism") is the overriding common pattern and motion of present-time global pseudo-civilization
(in spite of the always continuing propaganda that merely
idealizes and gives lip service to political and social "unity").

Global peace, human freedom, and human well-being
for all of humankind depend on an individual and a collective change of mind—followed by a corresponding change
of action. It is a matter of converting the mind and the life
and the entire human collective to a right understanding of
conditionally manifested reality (which is, inherently, a great
unity), and to a right (and truly Spiritual) surrender to the
Non-conditional Source-Reality (Which Is, Intrinsically, One
and Indivisible).

When the way of living becomes the active surrender of
egoity, then the conditions of life will constantly prove
the Truth.

All Modes of True Religion
Point To Reality Itself

Every religion is a body of means—a body of all kinds of cultural lore, and myth, and so forth—associated with the effort to seek and find (or "locate") That toward Which religion points, and toward Which life itself points. Indeed, the key matter of human life is to "locate" That toward Which religion points.

If religious practitioners will maintain this perspective, then they will not become involved in the kind of exclusivist assertiveness about their own tradition that makes religion a kind of idolatry—in other words, worshipping the particular tradition itself, rather than embracing the process of Realizing That toward Which all religions point. If all religions subordinate themselves to That toward Which they all point, then there is no conflict between religions. And all of the vigorous, outraging, inflammatory voicing of religious advocacy will be undermined by an inherent humbleness in the face of That toward Which religion can (at best) be a pointer.

In the end, religion is something to be exceeded (or out-grown)—ultimately, in the Realization of That toward Which religion points. There is no religion higher or greater than Reality Itself, or Truth Itself. Therefore, when Reality Itself (Which Is Truth Itself) is Realized, religion has been out-grown, or become obsolete, or has served its purpose.

Consequently, religion is not something to be advocated in absolutist terms, and (thereby) made into a "face", or a kind of "armor", by which to confront other views. Religion should, in no sense, be a kind of role-playing whereby people express a will toward the cultural dominance of others, or express a disposition of cultural superiority with reference to all others.

On the other hand, if religious practitioners remember that they are worshipping, or moved toward, or seeking That Which is Unnameable (and Beyond their particular tradition), and if they also remember that all other traditions are doing the same, reaching toward that same Reality, then there is no basis for conflict. The basis for the conflict is the absolutism that people assume in their advocacy of their particular local religion.

Even in the current epoch, religions are still local phenomena, although some among them attain the scale of what can be called "world religions", with millions of followers. Nevertheless, religion is still a local phenomenon, very much associated with particular regions of the world—and even particular races, particular languages, and so forth. And, yet, Reality Itself—or That Which is Inherently Divine—is That toward Which all religions are pointing. The differing definitions of That toward Which all religions are pointing must not be used as a basis for conflict. And, in fact, That Which is to be Realized is Beyond definitions in any case.

Truly, humankind needs to become equipped with Wisdom—in other words, equipped with something that is greater than religion. Reality Itself is greater than religion. There is no religion higher or greater than Reality Itself, no religion greater or higher than Truth Itself. Wisdom about Reality and Truth is required by all in this situation where all religions and all of humanity are, in fact, face to face. Otherwise, the conflicts, the competitiveness, the ego-based endeavoring will destroy everyone. All of that must be stopped. And it will not be stopped merely by small talk and mutual aggression. It will be stopped by the awakening of everyone, through Wisdom, to Truth Itself, to Reality Itself. Wisdom is the means for the overcoming of conflict and the establishment of the condition of prior unity, in which peace is the characteristic of the meeting between human beings.

That each religion carries its own local phenomena (of states of mind, and all the rest) is simply a fact. And each of the historically well-established religions has long thought of itself as being absolute in its own domain. It must be understood, however, that no particular religion is absolute in the common domain. In that domain, each religion is one among many. And, in any case, all of those many are pointing to That Which Transcends them, each and all, That Which will always Transcend everything conditional.

The Wisdom of Reality Itself humbles all, equalizes all, affirms and establishes prior unity among all. The awakening to the Wisdom of Truth Itself, or Reality Itself, is how the conflicts between religions can be immediately undermined. A completely different kind of discourse becomes possible when people are no longer simply advocating their local (or "tribal") mind, and are instead all Communing (in some fundamental terms) with That Which Transcends "self" (or egoity), or any phenomenon of a collective human kind, or any phenomenon of a conditional kind.

Before That, all are essentially silent. All are equal in front of That. Before That, all are silent, and equal, and inherently at peace. They are participants, then, in a condition of prior unity in the circumstance of Truth. Therefore, rather than trying to figure out how all can be equally voiced in the world, all need to become equally silent—not by being silenced in some forceful manner, but by becoming re-associated with That Which Transcends all modes of advocacy.

It is not the case that religions should disappear. Rather, religions—like all conditional phenomena—are always already transcended in Reality Itself, in Truth Itself. Therefore, how long any religion lasts is really neither here nor there. It is a human phenomenon. It can have its uses—in terms of orienting people toward right life, and cultivating seriousness about Wisdom and Truth Itself and Reality Itself.

In some sense, there needs to be a universal order of religions, in which all are participating equally in the advocacy of Wisdom. Then what is right about them in their zones of human influence will be continued or preserved on that basis, and not on the basis of confrontational advocacy and presumption of cultural superiority that not only feeds the "game" between religions but also feeds the politics of separatism, and of conflict, and of hatred in the world.

Whatever is "left over" of religion when the Wisdom of Reality Itself is embraced—that is fine. Whatever is relinquished in Truth—that is also fine, and should be fine. Just as any individual must be free to grow within any tradition with which he or she may be associated—and even be free to go somewhere else, or to look into other things in addition—so also must all be free within the sphere of their religions.

If all religions exist in a common world order of participation in Wisdom, then they are (in that sense, and to that degree) supportive of one another also. And each will have its usefulness in its zone of influence, because each is a local voice that can speak Wisdom to people within that sphere of religion—thereby truly being of service to them, rather than stimulating them to ego-based exclusiveness, conflict with other traditions, and on and on.

There are those who take offense as soon as somebody says anything that offends the "self"-image of some other religious practitioner. What does that have to do with religion? What does that have to do with what religion is supposed to be about, with reference to Truth? It does not have anything to do with Truth or right life. What does it have to do with? Nothing but the ego-based advocacy of religion as a thing in and of itself, as a kind of idol, a kind of "self"-image that people uphold and want to defend. That is how being offended happens in the common day-to-day.

In Truth, religion itself is not a domain that has anything to do with being offended. True religion is subordinate to Truth, to Reality Itself. True religion cannot be offended. If religion is understood to be entirely subordinate to Truth, to Reality Itself, then it is not ego-based and cannot be offended. When religion is a "self"-image, a "tribal" idea of "self", a "face" for a collective, then it can be offended just as any individual can be offended.

True religion is ego-transcending—and, therefore, egoless. No one is offended in the domain of true religion. All are surrendered. All are Transcended by That Which they advocate. Therefore, instead of religions being inherently in conflict—all waiting to offend one another or be offended by one another—all religions must be made true by being subordinated to Truth, to Reality Itself, Which is Divine.

All the "God"-ideas are simply ideas. That Which Is Inherently Divine is, strictly speaking, not a "God". But that is not something to quibble about. People can use "God"-language, and are free to do so—obviously. Such language is meaningful enough, if it is understood to be subordinate to That toward Which it points.

A "God"-idea is not God. A "God"-idea points toward That Which Transcends the idea. That is God, or the Divine, or Reality Itself. "God"-language does not have to be used, but if it is going to be used, it should be understood to be words or ideas only—and, therefore, it is pointing to something beyond itself.

If you hold on to an idea of "God", then you can be offended. If you maintain your allegiance to That toward Which the idea points, then you cannot be offended, and you exist in a domain of prior unity with everyone and their languages. Just as there should be no inherent conflict between the French language and Swahili, there should be no inherent conflict between Buddhist language and Christian language (to give some examples).

There should be no inherent conflict between religions or between people—or, therefore, between "tribes". Religion is not rightly associated with "tribal" deities that you put on your flag or shield, and use in conflict with others, and make into your own "face", so that you can be offended if somebody makes a casual remark about what is on your flag or shield. That is not the proper domain of religion. The proper domain of religion is Reality Itself, Truth Itself—and, therefore, Wisdom. And Wisdom carries with it certain modes of behavior as an inherent characteristic—behaviors associated with the disposition of prior unity, not the disposition of egoity (or separativeness), and (therefore) confrontation, conflict, non-unity, mutual violence, superiority of one over another, and so forth.

True religion, whatever tradition it may be associated with, is inherently on an equal basis with all other modes of religion that are true. All are advocating What they point to, not what they merely own or believe.

True religion is in the domain of Wisdom—and, therefore, of prior unity, inherent non-conflict, and wise right life.

VII.

Reality-Politics For
Ordinary Men and Women

Characteristically, human beings in this "late-time" (or "dark" epoch) have, both collectively and individually, renounced their real and true politics. Generally speaking, human beings everywhere have renounced both collective and individual responsibility for their truly human lives. In general, human beings are not freely and rightly establishing and preserving the truly human character of their individual lives—and the collective of humankind is not organized to establish and to preserve the truly human character of human life in general.

In this "late-time" (or "dark" epoch) of global anti-civilization, human beings do not, generally, assume cultural, social, and political freedom of right association, right commitment, and (altogether) right life—but they assume, instead, that they have to subordinate themselves to the ideas and the plans of power-seeking bureaucrats, benighted intellectuals, materialistic scientists, religious fundamentalists, and disturbed political revolutionaries, who (because they are yet ego-bound) work to effectively prevent the truly human politics of intimate, cooperative society. And this universal failure of right life reflects (and results from) every human individual's frightened (and, altogether, egoic) suppression of the universal Unifying Life-Principle and of the life-positive vitality of ego-transcending bodily existence.

Because present-day human individuals are everywhere socially indoctrinated to be afraid of their own inherent life-impulse toward unity with all-and-All, there is the present-day world—the "late-time" (or "dark" epoch) of a benighted, ego-bound, and universally misled humanity. Present-day humankind is a global mass of <u>mere</u> individuals, who—because they cannot freely "connect" with one another (and with Reality, or Truth, Itself)—live as slaves of their own minds and egoically separate selves. For the most part, human beings in this "late-time" (or "dark" epoch) are an unconscious mass, "Narcissistically" enslaved by their own egoic motives, and (inevitably) controlled by other egos who are shrewder than themselves.

In their <u>true</u> human freedom, men and women are (naturally, and at heart) oriented toward intimately felt human unity and the Oneness of Truth (or of Reality Itself). Such human individuals positively participate in the cosmically extended Pattern of the universally Self-Evident and All-in-all-Unifying Life-Principle. However, ever since the advent of the modern dichotomy between other-worldly religions and this-worldly utopian idealisms, people have, paradoxically, assumed (in their egoic double-mindedness) that the inherent unifying impulse of life is supposed to be negatively (or at least puritanically) manipulated, suppressed, and (thus) made unconscious, while, at the same time, they assume (or falsely hope) that life in this world is, by means of double-minded human effort, to become an eventual utopian paradise. As a result of this cultural double-mindedness, modern people are deeply troubled about the vital impulses of their natural lives, and about the Ultimate Purpose (and the Intrinsically egoless Ultimate Truth) of life itself. Therefore, the global human society in this "late-time" (or "dark" epoch) is built around the manipulative suppression of the life-force <u>and</u> the simultaneous manipulative exploitation of the materially oriented mind.

Inevitably, double-mindedness becomes "dark" control. Therefore, at last, everything and everyone become emptied of Reality and Truth. The modern doctrine is that people are supposed to <u>work</u>. That is the asceticism of the common man and woman. You are supposed to be a mere salt-of-the-earth worker, and you are not to be fundamentally and ecstatically (and, thus, egolessly) involved in Intrinsic Delight. You are not expected or permitted to be fully and freely conscious—and Consciousness (Itself) is not valued. You are supposed to work, buy junk food and television sets, and always stay tuned (and subordinate) to the propaganda of the daily "news"—and you are not to allow yourself to be aware of anything "Fundamentally Curious" that might cause you to become ecstatic and profound.

Some anthropologists say that what makes human beings unique is that they make tools. In any case, that is only a secondary and debatable unique feature of humankind. Truly, human beings are unique in that they interiorize the problem of survival. The sense of existence itself as a problem, as a dilemma, is characteristic of the un-Enlightened (or merely natural) human condition. And, through the tool of desire, human beings constantly create new solutions.

Human beings tend to seek a condition of release that exceeds the limits of gross experience and death. Thus, human beings invent an interior mental (or even mystical) process, through which they can step out of both ordinary mind and ordinary body, into the illusion of another world. Also, by virtue of having a mind, human beings are capable of entering into transformative (or, at least, manipulative) relationship to the functional processes in their own case and in the world. Thus, human beings create sciences and technologies, as practical tools for dealing with the material conditions of existence. However, both of these possibilities— both interior (or mental, or even mystical) and exterior (or technological, or even utopian)—are extensions of the ordinary game of problem-solving.

Until human individuals begin to develop some basic understanding of their limited (and ego-bound) condition— and, optimally, to directly (and, necessarily, in an ego-transcending manner) participate in the Indivisible and

Non-Dual (or One and Only) Self-Nature, Self-Condition, Self-State, and Perfectly Subjective Acausal Source-Condition of every limited condition, state, or being—they are exploitable by individuals and influences that arbitrarily assume a material power that exceeds their own. Therefore, the usual man or woman, who works in a factory or an office and listens to the "news" faithfully, is constantly (and inevitably) exploited by all kinds of shrewd people who are materially in charge of his or her political, social, cultural, and intimate life.

For the usual person, politics is merely a matter of listening to the "news" every night. Politics in this "late-time" (or "dark" epoch) is either a childish or an adolescent reaction to the fact of being controlled by the "news" of the world and by the abstract, all-controlling politics of the State. One individual plays the "system", and the other is a revolutionary. The child buys the "system" and expects it to work, and the adolescent is a perpetual revolutionary, whose childish expectations were not fulfilled. Both types are merely relating to the world as a parent-like "thing" that controls them.

If you stop listening to (or, otherwise, believing in) the "news", and if you simply observe what is really going on, you (inevitably) become depressed by the feeling that your life is not under your control. However, depression is only a very minimal insight. Obviously, everybody is (both naturally and humanly) controlled. The typical response to the observation of the controlling forces of life is to react by joining a revolution, getting drunk, kicking a couple of bad politicians out of office, having a war, getting "high" on popular illusions, becoming "against" a political "something", or becoming "for" a political "something"—but reaction is obviously not the way to rightly transform real politics. What is needed is to establish a completely different principle of human culture and politics. What is needed is a principle of human culture and politics that is not based on reaction to all the bad "news".

Fundamentally, there is only bad "news" in the ordinary, ego-based, un-Enlightened, chaotic world. Instead of waiting for action from "sources" out in the world somewhere—government sources, media sources, interplanetary sources, conventional religious sources, mystical sources, or whatever it is that you wait for all the time—you must, yourself, become involved in intimate, cooperative community (or real cooperative social culture) with other human beings. In a responsible, mutually dependent, cooperative, tolerant, peaceful, and intimate relationship with other human beings, you must create and protect the basics of a truly human culture and of a truly intimate daily human society.

The only reason the "news" of the world and the abstract (or non-intimate) politics of the State can exploit and control you is that you are in vital (and, altogether, ego-defining) shock—or a double-minded and "self"-defeating reactive recoil from the universal Unifying Life-Principle of Prior Unity. Because you are (thus) alienated from (and emptied of) Reality Itself (Which Is One, or Non-Dual, Intrinsically egoless, and Inherently Free), you believe that you need a number of things you cannot acquire without playing for or against the "system". However, if you are always already egolessly participating in the Self-Nature, Self-Condition, and Self-State of Reality (Itself), you need not be greatly concerned about any of the "news" of the world of egos. Rather, you can and must create your own politics—the intimate politics of cooperative association with your fellow human beings.

The existence of the big political "system" does not make any ultimate positive difference in the daily life of the individual. You can and must live a truly free, responsible life, regardless of the "system" or the "news". Of course, it can be done a little more easily if the "system" is relatively accommodating and the "news" is relatively benign. You would have to be more inventive to do it in an absolutist society, or during a war in a bombed-out town. Nevertheless—regardless of the larger politics, or the state of the "news"—the truly human (and humanizing) politics of intimate, cooperative living can (and, indeed, must) be done. And, therefore, the ego-transcending discipline of intimate, cooperative living is the only real and true politics—or the only genuine "realpolitik" (or Reality-politics) for ordinary (or truly human) men and women.

The true change that you must create is not principally in the "system" itself (or in the parent-like world of competitive egos) but in the ordinary, daily associations between yourself and other human beings. People who would be free must live in a non-egoic and non-competitive manner, in intimate cooperation with one another. Human beings must truly understand themselves—in all of their external and internal egoity—and they must, on that basis, adapt to a cooperative and mutually tolerant arrangement of daily life, in which they are each personally responsible for the character of daily existence, and in which they simply live together, intimately and seriously, free of reactive and dependent association with the parent-like abstract world of the "news".

A truly rational and benign politics cannot be enacted merely by investing humankind in a worldwide system of parent-like bureaucracies. The abstract system creates childish dependencies and illusory solutions, and it discourages the general possibility of genuine personal responsibility, or daily "right life" (and the ego-transcending Realization of the Only and Non-Dual Self-Nature, Self-Condition, and Self-State of Reality and Truth). The true politics of the individual is in relation to what is intimate to him or her. Truly human politics is in the sphere of directly effective relationships, experienced on a daily basis—where the individual's voice and experience can be directly heard and sympathetically felt. That, fundamentally, is politics. All the rest is only the vulgar and inherently disheartening daily "news" of the world-mummery of human egos.

A politics based on truly human, cooperative relationships is not likely to immediately originate on a large scale in a present-day city—although, ultimately (if such cooperation is first done by everyone on the more intimate, or local, scale), even that is an obvious necessity. Present-day cities are merely a random collection of subhuman emergencies. People crowd together in modern cities for all kinds of conflicting and subhuman reasons. These are not genuine cities, in any fully human sense. A true city would be a large-scale <u>cooperative</u> <u>social</u> <u>order</u> (or an effectively <u>single</u> <u>community</u>)—an essentially <u>autonomous</u>, <u>fully</u> cooperative, <u>truly</u> intimate, and Reality-oriented (or Prior-Unity-based) order of mutually dependent people who are devoted to the mature developmental culture of truly humanized (and ego-transcending, and Reality-Awakened) humankind. However, that kind of human order does not exist in the cities of today. Today, a city tends to be a collection of disturbed and fascinated people—not a conscious, positively organized association of truly human (and ego-transcending, and Reality-Awakened) beings.

Without a community of responsible relationships and mature cultural agreements, there can be no right politics. Truly <u>right</u> politics is, necessarily, an expression of right life. Right politics is a functional realization of the collective right relationships between individuals living in free cooperation with one another.

The true cooperative human community (or unified social order) is not merely a utopian commune, in which every ego tries to be perfect, or to be perfectly fulfilled. Such perfection or fulfillment is not possible for the ego (or for the inherently limited and mortal patterns of human life itself). Advanced human "self"-understanding is the principle of life in true cooperative human community. Communities are rightly established when each human participant rightly understands his or her own functional design—not only as mere ego, but, altogether, as a single (or simultaneous) whole, and, ultimately, as an intrinsically ego-transcending Reality-Awakened totality. And communities are rightly organized and managed when the problem-solving, creative capabilities of human beings are rightly "self"-disciplined and, altogether, equanimously measured—on the basis of a true culture, founded on the transcending of the ego-"I" and the Realizing of the Intrinsically egoless Self-Nature, Self-Condition, and Self-State of Reality (Itself). Therefore, fundamentally, human beings must understand and be responsible for their egoity—and, thus, for their tendencies to live life as an inherent (or irreducible) dilemma (or as a state of dis-unity), or (otherwise) as a perpetual search for "self"-glorifying fulfillment of loveless (or separate and separative) inclinations.

In a true cooperative human community, every one knows what every one else has the tendency to become (when irresponsible) and the possibility to become (when responsible). And all serve one another at the level of that understanding. They all also know the functional character and capability of each one among them, and they amuse and enjoy and serve and employ one another at every appropriate level. Right responsibility for functional life (and, thus, for the positive unifying of the structures of the human individual, and of all the members of the human collective itself) must always be assumed and demanded in a truly human (or truly ego-transcending, and cooperative, and mutually tolerant) community. When it is not, that failure of responsibility (and, thus, of individual well-being and of collective unity) will, inevitably, weaken the community—and, thus, enable (or even oblige) shrewder men and women to exploit and oppress the members of the community, and make them slaves to their own egoity again.

If men and women will enter into true cooperative human community—and, therefore, into intimate cooperative and higher cultural relationship with one another—they will no longer be exploitable by any life-negating (or disheartening and freedom-negating) influences from the abstract social and political realm of the worldly "news". The negatively dominant bureaucracy of the world of egos becomes obsolete only through non-use. And, once its negative and parent-like powers become obsolete through non-use, even the State will be obliged to become the simple instrument of the responsible agreements of the people. If the people become truly intelligent and freely cooperative, then the State will, inevitably, do (or become) likewise. And if the people truly become collectively intelligent and responsible, then individual freedom can never really be eliminated by the state of the "news".

Conventional politics has always been associated with an ideal of one or another sort. In the modern era, the ideal has, generally, switched from a humanistic to an economic one. Nevertheless, all merely idealistic systems tend to depend on temporary, emergency solutions to basic problems. This is because conventional idealism is an abstraction—a basis for a politics of manipulation of people by an abstract State, and not for an intimate, cooperative politics of practical responsibility, on the part of the people, for both themselves and the political union (or State) of their lives. The tactics of abstract State politics always relate to a more or less irresponsible and externally controlled populace—and, therefore, the State tends to be fixed in a view of human life as a dilemma that continuously requires new emergency reactions to solve the constant crisis of new emergency problems. As a result, politics becomes an insane conglomeration of temporary solutions, enforced by a bureaucratic State that is oppressive, rigid, immense, and intolerable.

The <u>fundamentals</u> of life must be pre-solved at the <u>local</u> level—at the regional level where the daily, cooperative community exists. Within the cooperative human community, every member should be guaranteed access to the basic necessities and opportunities of life (provided each individual functions responsibly and cooperatively within the community). Generally, the basic solutions to human needs do not (or should not) require resort to any of the resources of an abstract State—but they should be managed locally, in one's own community, and in natural cooperation with other communities. (In other words, first establish intimate, cooperative community and the planned solutions to fundamental needs—and, on that basis, see what kind of agreements are useful in cooperation with other communities and with large-scale cooperative agencies.)

True cooperative politics is a great human adventure, in which human beings are inherently obliged to realize their humanity as an <u>ego-transcending</u> <u>discipline</u>. Human beings do not, in Reality and in Truth, have the option to renounce their humanity or the universal Unifying Life-Principle (or cosmically extended Pattern of Oneness) that sustains them. Rather, human beings must assume the inherent responsibility of human relationships. Human beings must assume <u>all</u> the structures of the human mechanism (both lower and higher) as real conditions of existence—and human beings must become functionally responsible for positively conducting the life-force in every area of their experience. To the degree that they do all of this, human beings are obliged to be committed to right life in the dimensions of time and space—and only in that case are they <u>free</u> to carry on the creative developmental and ecstatically ego-transcending Reality-process of their humanly-born lives.

If human beings do not assume right, ego-transcending, and cooperative collective responsibility for their lives, the daily "news" of the world of egos becomes their inevitable destiny and their dreadful, minimal inheritance. In the world of egos, everybody tends to persist like cattle, grazing on the daily "news", expecting it will all eventually develop into some superior politics or fate. However, truly human politics, or right human destiny, cannot happen <u>unconsciously</u>. Truly human politics begins where consciousness (intelligent, and surrendered, beyond "self"-contraction, into the Non-Dual Reality and Truth That <u>Is</u> the Heart and Light of Consciousness Itself) enters the domain of human existence. There is no right, or truly human, politics without conscious responsibility. You cannot sit like cattle in front of the TV, dutifully listening to the official "news" every day, and rightly expect or fruitfully require that some bureaucrat "in charge" is going to announce some "Super-Program" that will liberate you from your lowly, ego-possessed estate. Rather, you <u>must</u> take responsibility for yourself. It is not by revolutionary reformation of the State, or (otherwise) by mere "self"-indulgent reaction to the daily "news", but only by consciously stepping apart from your childish ego-dependence on the abstract State and your adolescent reaction to the daily "news", that you carry on truly human politics. Therefore, you must provide your own life-requirements, in personal and local cooperation with others. You must enter into truly intimate (or mutually dependent, energetically cooperative, lovingly tolerant, and liberally peaceful) community with others. You must cooperatively share your functions, your resources, and your vitality with other human beings. That is the only right, and truly human, and truly liberating politics for human beings. And, therefore, the choice to enter into real, intimate cooperative community with other human beings is the only real and true politics for ordinary (or truly human) men and women.

The life of the usual (or ego-bound) man or woman is built on the idea that the Law of life is survival, and that survival is the significance, meaning, and goal of existence.

However, in Truth (and, thus, in Reality Itself), the <u>fundamental</u> process of human existence, and even of the very realm of cosmic Nature, is one of <u>right</u> "self"-surrender—or the consistent transcending of all contraction upon separate and separative "self" (or ego-"I"), and the transcending of loveless separation from what is egoically presumed to be "not-self".

Right "self"-surrender—or intrinsically ego-transcending participation in unlimited relatedness—is the Law. The usual life is not built upon the ego-transcending principle of right "self"-surrender, but on the ego-fulfilling principle of survival—or the aggressive ego-glorification of the individualized, separate, and separative entity. This is the common illusion, and this inherently loveless game of surviving as a separate, "self"-contained, and separative "someone" is what makes human existence the overwhelming chaos of troubles that it has now become for everyone in this "late-time" (or "dark" epoch) of global anti-civilization.

The fact is that <u>all</u> specific "somethings" must ultimately be surrendered (or released, and gone beyond), and, therefore, human existence itself must become an <u>intentionally</u> ego-surrendering (or truly ego-transcending) affair, in which no condition is aggressively maintained merely for its own sake. The human individual must grow (by right cultural means) to realize that the Law of life is the positive surrender of all temporary forms to the universal Unifying Life-Principle (or the cosmic Reality-Pattern of Prior Unity) <u>and</u> moment to moment surrender of separate and separative "self" to the Intrinsically egoless Self-Nature, Self-Condition, Self-State, and Perfectly Subjective Acausal Reality-Condition of every limited condition, state, or being. Therefore, the human individual must, by right cultural means, be grown to realize that the inherent and ultimate purpose of life is <u>not</u> a matter of mere and loveless "survival", independent of the Inherent Prior-Unity-Principle of both the conditional reality and the Non-conditional Reality. And <u>only</u> if the individual is (thus) grown to relinquish the ego-principle and to embrace the Prior-Unity-Principle can the individual become <u>politically</u> free. Indeed, to be thus grown is, <u>itself</u>, to <u>be</u> (inherently) politically free.

VIII.

The ego-Culture of Desire and
The ego-Transcending Culture of Love

The Life-Force that is felt within the presumed-to-be-personal body-mind-complex is moved by willful or desiring acts to create circumstances of would-be ego-fulfillment. However, in Reality, That Life-Force Is Truly Universal (or Indivisible and all-and-All-Pervading)—not "inward" and personal (or ego-bound, or "point-of-view"-bound). Therefore, if That Life-Force is manipulated by "inward" motives to satisfy personal desires of all kinds, not only will the resulting satisfaction be only occasional and at most partial, but the Life-Force will Itself be always frustrated, since It <u>cannot</u>, by becoming subordinate to any patterns of personal desires, Fulfill Its Universal (or Indivisible and all-and-All-Pervading) Function <u>As</u> Prior Unity and (Thus and Thereby) Realize Its Intrinsic Divine Freedom in the conditionally arising world.

The human individual is immature—and always dissatisfied—until he or she out-grows mere personal desire (or even any search for ego-based "self"-indulgence), and, instead, lives on the basis of ego-transcending love (or the moment to moment transcending of ego-based desire-patterning), and thereby constantly demonstrates the Universal Moral Disposition of Prior Unity and the responsible intrinsic (or root) management of all functional and relational conditions of experience and action.

The truly mature human individual is, characteristically, free of all the intrinsically and inevitably frustrating limitations of conditional reality and the personal and collective relationship-politics of social egoity.

The truly mature human individual is radiant in the world, such that the Prior Unity of Reality Itself Is egolessly Alive As his or her human person.

Therefore, a world-collective of truly mature (and, thus, rightly humanly and esoterically acculturated) human individuals can create a truly human, benign, moral, and Reality-Enlightened culture, founded in the Intrinsic Self-Apprehension* of the Self-Nature, Self-Condition, and Self-State of Reality Itself.

Only such a world-collective of truly mature human individuals is truly free of the inherent and chronic frustrations that otherwise constantly and only produce subhuman societies, subhuman cravings, and subhuman destinies (both before and after death).

---

* "Intrinsic Self-Apprehension" is the Self-Comprehension which is natively (or intrinsically) characteristic of Reality Itself.

IX.

The Healing Power of
Cooperative Human Community

Only true cooperative community provides the human functional basis for the continuous testing and schooling of truly human qualities. When people exist outside the domain of cooperative human community, all the forms of anti-social and ego-possessed aberration appear—and, once having appeared, they cannot truly be changed, unless the individual is restored to the intimate domain of cooperative community.

Until the individual is restored to (or, otherwise, rightly and truly established in) cooperative community, the responsibility for "curing" his or her anti-social, or subhuman, or (altogether) egoic aberrations seems to belong to abstract professions and institutions. However, neither the secular "machine" of the abstract State, nor any design of arbitrary social laws and brute police, nor any great "priesthood" of psychiatrists and social workers* can do what can be done only by the humanizing influence of right intimate cultural inspirations and expectations within the domain of cooperative human community.

Therefore, one and all should devote their inherent political freedom to right and true cooperative human community. One and all should put all free human energy into the free energizing of truly human things. One and all should constantly righten the life by transcending the separate and

---

* Adi Da is not indicating that psychiatry and social work is "religious", but rather that, in the modern secularizing world, the kind of authority formerly exercised by priests now tends to be invested in psychiatrists and social workers.

separative ego-"self", and this by always subordinating the separate and separative ego-"self" to That Reality and Truth Which Always Already Includes, and Pervades, and Fills, and Exceeds, and Transcends, and Outshines one, and all, and All.

X.

Only Rightness Makes Justice True

1.

Only rightness makes justice true.

Therefore, to what extent does any human being have an innate moral right to kill any other human being? Fundamentally, that right extends to physical self-defense alone—defending against an immediate physically life-threatening cause—whether in the case of an individual, or of nations, or of groups within a society, or of societies as a whole.

It is, in the natural sense, reasonable to assume that, unfortunately, in certain stark and otherwise unavoidable instances of a physically-threatening event, self-defense might call for a strong physical action that could (possibly) result in the killing of another human being—or, in the larger context of collective struggle, even the killing of many human beings. Nevertheless, there is no right—nor is it in any sense right—to kill another human being outside the immediate physical situation of necessary and unavoidable physical self-defense. And even the decision to take aggressively self-defensive physical action should, optimally, be made on the basis of a careful measure of what is the better consequence of the any event—and whether even self-sacrifice is the best of causes to allow.

If a violently-threatening person has been subdued and incarcerated, that person is no longer physically threatening, either to any particular other individuals or to society as a whole. Therefore, there is no cause for society to pretend to defend itself by judicially murdering an already-incarcerated person. The physically-incarcerated person has already been contained and stopped—and, therefore, there is no further right or cause to kill such a person.

The motive of either murder or revenge—even against individuals who have committed the most heinous of acts—is never right or acceptable. Outside the unavoidable necessity of immediate physical self-defense, all killing of human beings by human beings is murder—whether the killing is done by individuals or by collectives.

Everyone is inherently involved in a universal world-pattern of causes and effects—and, thus, there is no "personal" absoluteness about moral faults. When capital punishment is exercised, the executed individual is defined in absolutized "personal" terms, by exclusive identification with a particular fault—and that absolutized "personal" definition (or fixed and exclusive "objectification" of "self") reduces the "person" to a "thing" than which he or she is altogether more. The action of capital punishment denies both the Universal Non-"objective" and Irreducible Self-Nature of Reality and the indefinable (and non-"objectifiable", and intrinsically egoless) depth-nature of human existence. The judicial action of capital punishment, like any other act of murder or revenge-killing, aggressively de-humanizes both the one who is punished and the one (or the one-and-all) who punishes.

The social order does have both the right and the obligation to physically defend itself and all of its members. Therefore, it is certainly appropriate for the social order to exercise itself so as to physically control people or situations that are presently physically threatening. However, once any physical threat has been brought under physical control, there is no moral rightness in executing the person (or persons) who had previously posed a particular physical threat. Once such a physical threat has been brought under physical control, the social obligation is to (for as long as necessary) retain the person (or persons) in a circumstance where it is no longer possible for him or her (or them) to cause any physical harm to others. Except in cases of immediately necessary and otherwise unavoidable physical self-defense, all killing of human beings by human beings is inherently not right. Therefore, murder is not a human right, revenge is not a human right—and capital punishment is not a human right. People (and whole societies) that commit acts of either murder or revenge thereby "toxify" and harm and (potentially) destroy themselves. The moral integrity and the altogether human integrity of humankind is aggressively discarded and lost in acts of murder and revenge—whether committed individually or collectively. Thus, the exercise of capital punishment violates an inherent moral law in the human depth.

To perform, or to watch, or even to condone capital punishment is, necessarily, to perform, watch, or condone murder, blood-lust, revenge-killing, evil intention, and heart-negating purpose. Proof of this is in the fact that, virtually universally, all who perform, watch, or condone any kind of real physical human-to-human violence feel an unavoidable and unquenchable hurt in their hearts.

Therefore, this moral law should be universally observed by all of humankind: Self-defense (and physical defense of human life, altogether) is, in principle, reasonable, and may be appropriate, in the immediately necessary and otherwise unavoidable case of physically controlling what is physically threatening to oneself or others—but there is no longer any right to kill (and, thus, to murder, or to exact revenge upon) a person (or persons) whose physically-threatening activity has been brought under physical control. Likewise, as a direct effort to practice and ensure universal human fidelity to this universal human law, there should always and everywhere be socially-exercised means to prevent acts of murder or revenge from being carried out by individuals, or by nation-states, or by any human collective whatsoever.

2.

Only rightness makes justice true.

Murder and revenge are inherently morally wrong and never justified. Therefore, capital punishment is morally wrong and is never justified.

The negative exploitation and killing of human beings by human beings violates the heart of one and all. Therefore, all should always actively participate in the positive moral rightening and cooperative pacification of "self" and of the relations between all human beings, in order to maximally avoid and prevent the negative exploitation and (outside the strict boundaries of unavoidable exercises of self-defense) the killing of human beings by human beings.

The negative exploitation and killing of non-human beings by human beings violates the heart of one and all. Therefore, all should take care to positively morally righten and pacify the relations between "self" (or even all human beings) and all non-human beings, in order to maximally avoid and prevent the negative exploitation and non-necessary (or otherwise inhumane) killing of non-human beings by human beings.

The negative exploitation, and progressive degradation, and potential destruction of the fundamental order of the natural environment on which all Earth-life depends violates the heart and directly threatens the life of one and all. Therefore, all should always take care (and always exercise "self"-discipline) to always actively participate in positive service and global cooperation that respects and perpetuates the fundamental order of the natural environment of Earth-world.

The positive moral rightening of all human activity (human-to-human, human-to-non-human, and human-to-environment) would, if everywhere exercised, become the universal demonstration of a right and true human disposition, that (altogether, and in general) "self"-disciplines the tendency to physically, politically, socially, culturally, and environmentally "toxify", harm, and, altogether, negatively affect the human and natural world (by not only physical means, but, altogether, by bodily, mental, verbal, emotional, and generally "psychic", or psychological, and even every kind of energy-manipulating means).

The positive moral rightening of all human activity (human-to-human, human-to-non-human, and human-to-environment) must always concentrate on (and proceed on the basis of) the disciplining (and the summary de-"toxification") of the human "self"—itself, and in all of its relations, and in the context of a social order of mutual cooperative pacification of human ego-patterns of "self"-destructive, and "other"-destructive, and world-destructive behavior.

The positive moral rightness of human "self"-responsibility should (and, inevitably, would) include, among all the many practical elements of its totality, the personal (and not merely legally-enforced) responsibility to take genuine care and direct physical precaution to avoid unwanted pregnancies, medically non-necessary abortions, the bodily exchange of sexually-transmittable (or otherwise bodily transmittable) diseases, all participation in the habits and social reinforcing of "self"-poisoning, and "self"-deluding, and socially harmful addictions, and all participation in negative, "self"-deluding, self-evidently false (or profoundly unsupportable) and potentially destructive political, social, cultural, religious, and, otherwise, philosophically-based institutions, traditions, and idealisms.

The positive moral rightening of all human activity (human-to-human, human-to-non-human, and human-to-environment) is, essentially, a matter of always pre-establishing (and, thereafter, always correcting and re-asserting) the principle and the practice of prior unity—and, thus, of mutually sympathetic relational bonding—which inherently, and specifically, eschews (and always prevents) mere "objectification", dissociative detachment, negative exploitation, casually reactive threat and violence, all of unjustifiable destruction, and the will to both relationlessness and chaos. The intrinsic integrity of prior unity is the necessary rightness that makes all justice true.

3.

Only rightness makes justice true.

The negative exploitation (or mere imprisonment, and suppressive, or non-corrective, punishment) of those who commit (and are duly convicted of) crimes violates the heart of one and all—and, ultimately, threatens the future social peace and order of one and all. The imprisonment of human beings by human beings, without otherwise allowing for the human rights and moral impulses of those so confined to be actively exercised, is inherently not right. Such suppressive (or non-corrective) confinement, and even every other kind of mere and intentionally suppressive (or non-corrective) punishment of human beings by human beings, is merely an aggressive act, committed by the larger society, upon those who are already under control (and, thus, are not a present danger to others). Thus, mere imprisonment and all merely suppressive (or non-corrective) punishment are, themselves, criminal acts—and they are always done as acts of revenge, rather than as acts of justice.

Acts of justice are (and require), by definition, moral (and, altogether, morally positive) acts.

Therefore, rightly, those who are duly convicted of crimes should (to the degree, and for the period of time, necessary) be appropriately controlled, and prevented from further criminal (and, altogether, aggressive and threatening) acts. However, while under such control-and-prevention measures, those who are duly convicted of crimes should— and must, for the sake of everyone—actively and daily perform (under proper and necessary supervision) acts of reparation and service, in direct relation to those whom they have wronged or harmed, and, altogether, in direct relation to the larger society in which they have done wrong or harm. To the degree possible in the circumstances necessary to keep them under proper control, those who have been duly convicted of criminal acts should actively and daily perform their acts of reparation and service directly within the public circumstances of the larger society, and, also, within the private circumstances of those whom they have directly wronged or harmed.

Such moral process relative to all those who have been duly convicted of criminal acts rightly observes this should-be-universal moral law: All acts of revenge and merely suppressive (or non-corrective) punishment are, inherently and always, morally wrong—and, indeed, are, themselves, the essence of all criminal motivations and all criminal acts.

Unless society as a whole functions in an inherently morally right manner (even in relation to all who have done wrong or harm), society as a whole is unjust and an outlaw.

If society as a whole is an outlaw, it, inevitably, breeds outlaws, or criminals—or those who are, themselves, motivated to perform, and justify, and condone criminal acts (or acts based upon the motives of revenge and merely suppressive, or non-corrective, punishment).

If an unjust or outlaw society commits acts of revenge and merely suppressive (or non-corrective) punishment on those who are duly convicted of doing wrong or harm, that society as a whole is a threat to itself.

Therefore, any and every unjust or outlaw society should everywhere (and by all truly just and positively lawful societies) be called upon (and expected, and helped) to correct itself.

4.

Only rightness makes justice true.

All of this right moral understanding and right morality of action should be universally cultivated in the necessary global cooperative society of humankind—and this right moral understanding should (thereupon) guide the activities of every nation-state, all individuals at large, and the global cooperative human social order as a whole.

XI.

You The People

On The Necessity of
A Global Cooperative Order of
The <u>All</u> of Humankind

1.

The working-presumption of <u>prior</u> unity—rather than the <u>search</u> for unity—is the right and true context for all human exchanges. If there is the working-presumption of prior unity, then ego-surrendering cooperation and tolerance make perpetual human peace. If there is no working-presumption of <u>prior unity</u>, then human interactions become a mere game of competitive egos. And that competitive game is, now, on the verge of destroying humankind and the Earth itself—even at every level of ordinary, and natural, and economic, and political, and, altogether, social life. That competitive and, at last, constantly confrontational ego-game is a struggle that inevitably occurs in every context of presumed <u>non</u>-unity and separateness—thus producing a situation in which <u>everybody</u> is trying to dominate <u>everybody</u> else. That relentlessly competitive and confrontational situation is a lunatic-asylum game that, ultimately, threatens the very survival of life on Earth.

The entire world is now on the verge of absolute destruction—and for no necessary or justifiable reason whatsoever. The Measure of Truth is not being brought to bear on this situation. Therefore, there is, apparently, no readily applicable means for controlling the madness. It appears there are only competing crowds of factionalists, each crowd advocating its local "absolute"—in political or religious or whatever terms. Nothing—no Truth or Greater Reality—is presumed to be senior to the local beliefs, claims, and demands of every "tribe" of "Everyman".

In order to function rightly and effectively, any human collective—and, therefore, even the collective totality of all the nations of the world—must be based on the working-presumption of prior unity (or intrinsic indivisibility). At this moment in history, there is nothing "united" about the nations of the world. They are, presently, entirely dis-united, divided, competitive, and confrontational—and entirely possessed by the rage of difference.

People commonly presume unity to be a positive value. But they are typically thinking of unity as something to be "worked toward". "Working toward" unity is not what I am talking about. I am talking about prior unity. I am talking about people entering into a dialogue that is based on the working-presumption of prior unity, and non-separateness, and zero-confrontation, and global indivisibility, and the absolute Law of unbreakable peace—rather than a status quo based on the ego-based presumption of separateness, and conflict, and competition.

A certain benign energy can be associated with competition—when that competition is "in its right place" within human society. But, when the world itself becomes a competition, then competition is no longer in its right place.

What is senior to competition is prior unity (or intrinsic indivisibility). As a working-principle applicable to all modes of dialogue and all modes of happening in the world, the working-presumption of prior unity is essential. That is why cooperation and tolerance are not merely "ideals"—which people should "try to make happen". Rather, true cooperation and true tolerance originate from the working-presumption of prior unity. Therefore, it is not that you should seek unity, or <u>seek</u> cooperation, or <u>seek</u> tolerance, or <u>seek</u> peace. Unity, cooperation, tolerance, and peace are the Law and the inevitable demonstration of right life. Unity, cooperation, tolerance, and peace <u>are</u> what always already <u>is</u>. Therefore, unity, cooperation, tolerance, and peace must <u>always</u> be presumed to be the principle that is also <u>presently</u> the case—and, then, human beings must <u>always</u> function on the basis of that always present-time working-presumption.

The very opposite of the Law of right life is now presumed in the usual and common dialogues within the human world. Words like "unity" and "cooperation" and "tolerance" and "peace" are used, but they are typically used in the egoic sense—not in the right sense, of being <u>priorly</u> the case, but in the egoic sense, of being something to seek, or something to affirm idealistically, as a technique of propaganda for manipulating people and situations.

There needs to be a fundamental right dialogue functioning in the human world. And that dialogue needs to have a globally-extended and <u>all</u>-representing and <u>all</u>-participating institutional setting, in order to give it form—but that right globally-extended institution will be made to happen only if humankind ceases to be corrupted by the presumption of non-unity (or the presumption that prior unity, or intrinsic indivisibility, is not <u>always</u> <u>already</u> the case).

2.

The human world has become a kind of insane sporting event, at which people threaten one another and carry on in an insane manner—something like the gladiatorial contests in ancient Rome. It is madness. And TV also plays to that insanity. Everywhere, people and groups look to get attention by getting themselves on TV—often through the exercise of rotten and demented violence, and through the exercise of an altogether aggravated disposition. The human world of nowtime is a lunatic asylum, a soap opera of mummers. That absurd soap opera actually controls the destiny and experience of the total world of human beings—and that world-mummery is, in its root-disposition, totally indifferent to human life, and to the world altogether.

This fault in the human world has what could be called "philosophical" roots. There is a habit of mind and disposition that has taken over humankind. That habit of mind is ego-based. Therefore, egoity has taken over humankind—and egoity is being affirmed as "necessity" and "truth". This dreadful trend in human history is associated with a fixed philosophical "habit" that has been developing for centuries: the "habit" of "objectifying" the "self" and (altogether) "objectifying" both conditional reality and Reality Itself, and (then) identifying with that "objective" position—not only in mind, but in action. From that always "objectifying" position, everything (including Reality Itself) is viewed as an "object"— even the human "self" is viewed as an "object". That "objective self" is the reflected "self", the "self"-idea that ego makes. It is "Narcissus". "Narcissus" is not truly "self"-aware— "Narcissus" is aware of "self" only as a reflection, and (thus and thereby) as if "other".

"Narcissus" is the nature of human society now. As a result, human society is becoming progressively more and more aggravated, and fundamentally dissociated from Reality Itself—leading to an absurd and insane life of competitive conflict for the totality of humankind. And that life of competitive conflict has already negatively affected even the natural systems of the Earth—and it is causing (and would continue to cause) terrible suffering everywhere.

The "objectifying" impulse also, of course, characterizes the view of "scientific materialism". Science (or the scientific method) itself is simply free enquiry, without philosophical prejudices, and without fixed presumptions relative to "results" and "interpretations". However, rather than pure science, it is scientific materialism (or the philosophy of "objective materialism", enacted by means of a philosophically prejudiced control over the interpretations, and even the apparent results, of the application of the protocols of the "scientific method") that now, in general, dominates the societies of humankind. Indeed, scientific materialism can rightly be said to be the root-philosophical basis for the justification of egoic society and ego-based living—because the orientation (and basic method) of scientific materialism is to first "objectify" any and every "subject", and, thus, to look at it as an "object". In other words, the method of scientific materialism is to "objectify", and dissociate from, the any "subject", and, then, to analyze it, dissect it, deconstruct it, and manipulate it in a totally "objective" manner—until, at last, Reality Itself becomes philosophically proposed (or psychologically supposed and presumed) to be merely "objective".

In the programmatic method of materialistic "objectification", the "self", being part of Reality, is also viewed as "objective" (and reduced to the status of "object"). That effort is the program of "Narcissus". "Narcissus" even thinks of himself, or herself, as an "object". "Narcissus" only sees his or her own reflection, his or her mirrored persona—without recognizing it as such, and always thinking it is somebody "else".

Systematic "objectification" of "self", and of even all of Reality, is the characteristic method of egoity. Thus, to every ego-"I", "self" is "object". To itself, the ego-"self" is an "objective" thing—as if an "other", separate and "objective", even to itself. That is a tragic and "self"-destructive situation—both to the ego-based individual and to the totality of ego-based society. Ego-"I" is the "self"-deluded situation—both personal and collective. To "objectify" the "self"—and, thus and thereby, to "understand" the "self" only from outside the "subjective" position itself, and as if "self" is someone "else", or as if "self" is "other" to one's own "point of view"—is madness. However, it is also a commonplace madness—because "Narcissus", the "objectified self" (always viewed and presumed as if from outside), is every ego-"I" (or every presumed-to-be separate and separative "self").

To "objectify" the world is to dissociate from it. Indeed, truly, even what is apparently "outside" the "self" can, paradoxically, only be rightly understood from "inside" (or by means of an ego-transcending discipline, exercised within one's own inherently "subjective" position). However, in this "late-time" (or "dark" epoch), all of human culture and all of human society is based on the process of "objectification". Consequently, the Root-Condition (or the Perfectly Subjective Self-Nature, Self-Condition, and Self-State) of Reality Itself is now lost in human-time—abandoned therein by mere and terminal "objectification".

The "self" is, by definition, not "objective". The "self" is, necessarily, entirely "subjective". Therefore, all phenomena, all of experiential existence, must, necessarily, be understood at the root-"subjective" level (and, thus, perceived and understood from the inside to out). Experience cannot rightly be perceived and understood otherwise (or from the outside toward in). Once the world is "objectified", once the "self" is "objectified", once everything and everyone is "objectified", a state of dissociation and separation is absolutely (and always negatively) enforced. The world of ego and egoic society is based on this habit of dissociation—the habit of "objectification" of everything and everyone, including the "self".

The restoration of sanity and Truth—or the restoration to Reality Itself—requires the overcoming of the "self"-deluded process or activity or event of "self-objectification". In the "self-objectified" ego-state, the "self" becomes a mere reflection, as if viewed from without.

In the egoic world, "self"-consciousness is not, in Truth, aware of "self" (as it is). Rather, in the egoic world, "self"-consciousness is aware as "self"-image—a mirrored image of "self", constructed as if it were an "object" seen from outside. No "object"-consciousness is Real and right "self"-consciousness. Truly Real and right "self"-consciousness requires a capital "S" and a capital "C". Truly Real and right Self-Consciousness is Root-Consciousness—Consciousness As Is, or Consciousness As Itself. Consciousness Itself Is the Tacit Free (and Intrinsically egoless) Witness of all and everything that is apparently arising.* Consciousness Itself is not (and cannot be) "objectified". Consciousness Itself is not (and cannot be) in the form of an "object"—or in the form of the conditional knowing (or the conditional knowledge) of "objects". Consciousness Itself—Which Is Reality Itself— is Prior to all-and-All. Therefore, the True Self-Position is Prior to all arising and all conditionality.

This understanding is the necessary basis for the Realization of Reality Itself. Reality Itself is the only basis for true sanity and well-being. The Prior Unity of the entire conditionally arising world, and the prior unity of humankind, originates (Non-"differently") from (and, therefore, As) the Prior (and Intrinsically egoless) Self-Nature, Self-Condition, Self-State, and Acausal Source-Condition That Is Reality Itself—and That Is always (and Always Already) Prior to "objectification", dissociation, separateness, and separativeness.

Therefore, the disposition that is true to Reality Itself is also the disposition that, in the context of ordinary human life, functions on the basis of prior unity—not on the basis of presumed non-unity (or dis-unity). The root of that transformation—from non-unity to prior unity—is the "self"-knowledge (or "self"-understanding) that transcends the "objectification" of "self" (manufactured by the egoic act of dissociation, wherein the "self" is merely reflected, as if seen from outside).

---

* The natural "Position" of Consciousness Itself is to Stand as the Mere Witness of all that arises, Prior to egoic "self"-identification with the body-mind-complex.

True "self"-knowledge is seeing "self" and world from inside. The "objectified self" is strange, mad, dissociated, detached, in trouble, threatened by mortality, threatened by a "self"-consciousness that is inherently revolting (even to the conscious awareness of the "objectified self"). Seen from outside, the "objectified self-body"—as if seen by another perceiving oneself—is revolting. In that case, the "self" is reduced to mere vulgarity, mere functionality. Its "selfness"-from-within—Prior to arising conditions, Prior to the seeing of "self" from outside—is lost. To see "self" from outside is to be negatively "self"-conscious—dissociated and detached. That "objectified" view of "self" comes to be associated with a vulgar sense of "self"—which is the gross, and merely physical, sense of "self" that arises from viewing "self" as if from outside.

When seen merely from outside, when reduced to the "outside view", the bodily "self" (or the "self" as the body-only) is rather vulgar and disgusting. As has been said, in vulgar reference to the mere functionality of the human body (when seen from outside), it is nothing but a "shit-machine". From the "point of view" of outside (or the position after and subordinate to the "asshole"), the body is disgusting and shameful. From the outside position, you are (always, first of all) looking at the "end-product" of a "shit-machine". From the "point of view" of inside (or the position prior and senior to the "asshole"), the process of bodily elimination is simply a naturally (or "subjectively") pleasurable process of purification. The body is built (and, thus, also brain-"wired") to constantly purify itself—and, thereby, to enjoy the pleasurable sensation of relief and "self"-purity that is naturally associated with the entire cycle of right food-taking and the efficient bodily elimination of waste. When the body is rightly disciplined (by right diet, right sex-practice, and so on), such that it is properly self-conservative and efficiently eliminative, the body regularly enjoys a sense of natural well-being. There is nothing shameful about that. What is shameful (or ashamed) is the "self"-identification with the "end-product"—and, also, the collective human inability to properly and efficiently recycle the inevitable waste products associated with all human life-activity.

As soon as the body is "objectified" (or seen only as if from outside), then, instead of right participation in the eliminative process (or the perspective of the "shitting"), there is simply the "shit" (or the evidence of what the body discards from itself). That "outside view" is a grossly "objectified" view of "self"—a view that is inherently vulgar (or disgusting), and "dark", and detached.

That "dark", outside "object"-vision of "self" is the fixed "point of view" of "Narcissus". "Narcissus" is trapped within (and by) the fixed "point of view"—and, as a consequence of the fixed "point of view" (relative to time and space), attention is confined to outside, and to mere reflections, and to a vulgar, guilty, and chronically ashamed sense of existence. To go beyond that, the human being must be restored to his or her own intrinsic inwardness—and, thus and thereby, to "Locate" What Is the Real Nature (or Intrinsically egoless Self-Nature, Self-Condition, and Self-State) of that intrinsic inwardness.

What is the Real nature of the "subjective" position? When the "subjective" position is rightly discovered and understood (at its Transcendental Root), everything that is apparently "objective" is seen As Is—rather than as seen from without, from the dissociated position.

The entire human world is, by tendency, ego-bound. And ego itself has now become idealized, as a result of a process of hundreds, and even thousands, of years of the "culturation" of human existence in the direction of "Narcissism" (or egoity), to the point where, now, Consciousness Itself (and Reality—Itself, and altogether) has become utterly "objectified" (as a "thing", materially caused, and of a merely conditional, separate, and time-bound nature). As a result, the human world is, now, entangled in a process of "self"-destruction that is on the verge of destroying life itself. That unspeakably dreadful result is the end-phenomenon of a false philosophy. Indeed, this is the "dark" time of that false philosophy. This is the "dark" time—the "end-time" of scientific materialism. Therefore, in order to move the human world from the "dark" destiny of "end-time" to a truly En-Light-ened destiny, there must be a relinquishment of false "objectified" views, as a necessary part of the political, social, and cultural transformation of the totality of humankind.

Scientific materialism is on the "wrong side" of the "asshole" of human experiential awareness. "Objectification"-culture is on the "wrong side"—or the merely reflected side, or the opposite, and opposing, and detached, or abstracted, or fundamentally non-participatory side—of everything. Scientific materialism and the totality of "objectification"-culture are on the "wrong side" because they assume the fixed position (and the fixed, separate, and, therefore, egoic "point of view") of the outside (rather than the participatory, non-separate, and Intrinsically egoless "Stand" of the inside) of Reality Itself (and, thus, of Truth Itself).

Therefore, the cultural enforcement of the "objectification" of "self" and the "objectification" of life altogether must be thwarted—for the sake of one and all in (and As) Reality and in Truth. The process of "objectification" (and fixed "outsideness") must be undone—by Truth. That undoing by Truth is, essentially, what true moral and Spiritual transformation is about. The genuine regaining of the Transcendental and Spiritual and Intrinsically egoless Self-Position (Which Is Truth Itself and Reality Itself) requires (and more and more becomes) a moral and Spiritual trans-formation—"moral" meaning a transformation of livingness, that re-establishes human life in the universal context of Prior Unity (and in the global human context of the constant exercise of the working-presumption of prior unity). Therefore, the truly "moral" disposition is the cooperative disposition, the disposition of tolerance, the disposition of compassion, and the disposition-beyond-compassion, which is true peace.

3.

Conflict and destruction take all kinds of forms in the human world and in human history. There has already been a long chain of terrible tyrants in the human sphere—but people everywhere seem to be unaware of the fact that the latest tyrant is everybody, or "Everyman". The latest—and the last—tyrant is "Everyman". The last tyrant is "the people". In this "late-time", "the people" have, as a collective, become merely another ego-driven, manipulatable, chaotic, and entirely mad entity—a kind of lunatic "herd", a chaos of gross collectivity. That tyrannical "herd" is subject to the same whims and absurdities as any individual tyrant ever was or is. That terrible "herd" knows no limits—and even all and everything it merely thinks it knows is not Reality and Truth. The "herd" that "the people" have become is simply another tyrant—and the last to rise and fall in human-time.

The "tyranny of everybody" is what is happening now. In the now, every individual wallows in the "Narcissistic self-idea", demanding immediate satisfaction of the every wanting-need and random impulse in the body-mind, and threatening all-and-All with "consequence"-to-come, if separate "self" is found still wanting or unsatisfied at end of any day. The "neighborhood wars" between all egos, "tribes", and cults of "thing" are what is happening now. The private wars of "Everyman", the society of "Everyman", the religiosity of "Everyman", the "late-time" of "Everyman" is what is happening now. The "Everyman" is "Narcissus", the last tyrant—

the ego itself. When the tyrant becomes everybody, that is the end-time. When the tyrant is just somebody-in-particular, then there are revolutions, ups and downs and cycles. However, at the last, when the tyrant becomes everybody, there are no more cycles, but only a linearity of sames—and everyone and everything disintegrates in stops. Such is the awful nature of the present time, of ego's rule of all.

Therefore, it is absolutely urgent that there be an immediate and total transformation at the root of human culture and society and politics. A new kind of human institution must emerge in the world—an institution that truly establishes a global cooperative order. That new (and, necessarily, global) institution must establish and enact a non-tyrannical (and even counter-tyrannical, or entirely post-tyrannical) order of rightly and effectively functioning cooperation between everyone—between all nations, between all cultures and "tribes", between all the "neighborhoods".

What is required is not a matter of merely "having a dialogue" and "working toward" unity. In any such effort of "working toward", there is, in all the works, still plenty of effort to dominate. Therefore, what is required is the establishment of the universal working-presumption of prior unity—such that "the people", in every guise, lay down their arms, lay down their conflicts and their aggressive competitiveness, and, on that basis, straightforwardly handle all the business that is in the interest of everybody altogether.

That "handling of business" is not being done at the present time. Now, everybody is "on the brink" with everybody else. It is everywhere like that. The "daily news" is that. Everyone's daily life has become something like an insane sporting event—that is played to the death. The human world of nowtime is like colossal Reality-TV—a dreadful mini-series, a few weeks until death. The common world of nowtime is mere insanity—Reality-madness. Everyone and everything is mad with "Everyman" now—mad with ego, mad with "Narcissus". The last tyrant is everybody—everybody at war with everybody, to the death. If this mad world-mummery continues unchecked, the present time of human history is the end of human-time. It is no longer a matter of one principal tyrant somewhere, some head of state somewhere, who is the "whomever", or the "whatever", that everyone loves to hate as everybody's "enemy". In this "late-time" (or "dark" epoch), everybody is the "enemy". Everybody is wrong. Everybody is at fault. Everybody is "Narcissus". Everybody is "Everyman". "Everyman" is everywhere. The "objectified self" is at large. If "Everyman" is not soon disciplined by the Truth That Is Reality Itself—so that the world of "Everyman" discovers and accepts "its" limits, "its" place—then "Everyman" is going to destroy not only humankind but all life, and the Earth-world itself.

4.

The always globalizing (or would-be-all-inclusive) culture and civilization of genuinely human humankind is being lost and forgotten in the "herd" and rush of present-time at fault. In very fundamental terms, it must be said that genuinely human culture has already been lost, through a terrible "progress", especially over the last few hundred years—and that, only "lately", has gone truly "dark" (within a mere and fatal one hundred years). Just look at the century of recent past: The twentieth century was the deadliest, most murderous century in the history of humankind—and, yet, coincidentally, it is also the century of the greatest "advancements" in the scientific materialist domain of "objectification"-culture.

There are, obviously, many results of truly scientific endeavor that are positive, in the sense of fostering, and supporting, and extending human well-being. Nevertheless, the "objectification"-effort of materialistic scientism is a fundamental, and generally negative (and power-hungry), characteristic of the "Everyman"-culture of this "late-time".

The reductionistic materialism of this all-"objectifying" epoch of "late-time" is fundamentally negative in its philosophical roots, and, therefore, never truly and wholly positive in either its "point of view" or its interpretations or its results. The "late-time" effort of materialistic (and all-"objectifying") scientism is the ego-effort of cleverness, magnified virtually infinitely—even beyond the limit of any right purpose of human usefulness. It is the "objectification" mind-culture, gaining control through merely "objective" (and altogether and reductively materialistic, and even inwardly thus reductive) knowledge—exercising control over "self" and "other" and world, and exercising control over virtually everything in the ordinary physical domain. That cleverness has produced a kind of mad "intelligence"—and a mad "book of its knowings". That "book" has a degree and kind of authenticity—but, at the same time, that "book" is an expression of the ego-bound mind that has "objectified" itself, to the point where it no longer knows itself, except by reflection. The merely reflected "self" is detached—and it knows no bounds, and it knows no Truth, other than what it merely thinks is "Truth" on the basis of having "objectified" everything.

There is nothing merely negative, in and of itself, about true scientific practice and knowledge. What is negative about science is its revisioning (or its reductive re-formulation) as "scientific materialism". Scientific materialism is the ultimate extension of "Narcissistic" culture. Therefore, the enterprise and culture of science must, like all other human enterprises, be brought into the sphere of Truth—and of Perfectly Subjective Reality Itself—or else mere science, like any other merely clever method of mind, simply becomes an instrument of illusion (or of "self"-delusion), and of potential destruction.

The restoration (to Itself) of the Perfectly Subjective State of Consciousness Itself is <u>essential</u>. There <u>must</u> be the globalized transcending of "point-of-view" culture, or "objectification"-culture—and the transcending, therefore, of all dissociation, all separateness, all non-unity. The reductionist justification for "objectification"-culture must be here and now undone, by a comprehensive root-understanding—or else the "last tyrant" will destroy the world.

In order that world-destruction be prevented, the "late-time" ego-culture must be stopped in its tracks. The pond-water into which Narcissus is gazing must be stirred to deep. The merely surface-made reflection must be broken up. And all the people of the humankind must be restored (in their understanding, and, ultimately, Most Perfectly) to the Perfectly Subjective Reality-State That <u>Is</u> Always Already the Case. In the context of that restoration, ordinary and also truly scientific (or truly <u>freely</u> enquiring) knowing of all kinds is appropriate, useful, and potentially beneficial—including what could otherwise be said to be of the nature of truly discriminative "objective" knowledge. When the enterprises of conditional knowledge take place in the context of the Truth of Perfect Subjectivity (or of Reality Itself), then conditional knowledge has the virtue of inherent limits, and the discipline of right situation—and, on that basis, the exercise of conditional knowing is not functioning merely on a "self"-deluded basis, and, thus, dissociatively or destructively (such as is, necessarily, the case when no depth of Truth, or of Reality Itself, is Intrinsically Known).

The Depth of Truth (or of Reality Itself) must be established as the <u>basis</u> of life—not merely as the <u>goal</u> of life. That Depth is the necessary <u>basis</u> of right culture, and not merely the <u>goal</u> of ego-culture. That Depth must become the <u>everyday</u> Truth—such that It transforms everyday experience for everyone.

5.

I am not speaking of all of this in merely utopian terms—as if transforming the world were simply a matter of giving a lecture. A very practical means for contacting everybody, and getting everybody involved in what is new and right, must be precisely organized and consistently put to practical collective global use.

The Internet is an indispensable and, altogether, key and central tool—unique and new to global humankind—for organizing, and implementing, and surely (in every practical sense) happening the global cooperative order of the totality of humankind. Therefore, the Internet should immediately be made thus to serve.

By employing the Internet—and, also (potentially), various existing (but, necessarily, rightly reformed) institutions of global outreach—to globally organize humankind in a perpetual (and perpetually responsible) dialogue with itself, all of humankind can be enabled to collectively, cooperatively, and systematically engage in true and rightly effective global activism. That organized collective cooperative global activism can (and must) both require and systematically make right and positive changes all over the world—and, thus, everywhere require and make a positive rightness, and everywhere require and make an end to conflict, and everywhere require and make an end to all seeking for global dominance (or otherwise negative dominance) by whomever and whatever would seek it.

At this critical turning-point in human history, certain "lessons" must be accepted from the errors and the tragedies of past-time human faults. Among those "lessons", there is, certainly, one principal issue that must be accepted as a universal Law of humankind: No one—and no nation or culture on Earth—has a right, or any license in Reality Itself, to plan, or equip themselves to make, or at any time to materially enact any global or otherwise mass destruction, for any reason or purpose whatsoever, now or ever in human-time.

Therefore, rather than playing the global competition-game to its terrible end, like gangs of adolescents at deadly sport, there must be the establishment of a true Global Cooperative Forum, based on the working-presumption and enactment of prior unity—and, thus and thereby, the globally-extended establishment of a no-nonsense, getting-down-to-business disposition and practice in humankind at large. And, in this Global Cooperative Forum (and right order) of humankind, everyone will—and, indeed, must—focus on the genuine necessary issues that everyone has in common.

6.

A Global Cooperative Forum must be established—a forum that includes everybody, and all nations, without national boundaries, and (altogether) without political, social, or institutional barriers of any kind. It would, thus, be the Global Cooperative Forum (and thereby established and perpetuated right order) of all of humankind.

The Internet (along with the participation of various globally-extended institutions) should be immediately employed to organize and activate the global participation of the total human population on Earth. It is not necessary to first do something else—such as "preparatory" reforms, re-education "programs", and so forth. The totality of humankind already exists, the matters of urgent responsibility already exist—and everything and everyone is always already (or priorly and inherently) existing in a condition of unity. Therefore, there is not any other prerequisite for positive change. The implementation of positive change has only one requirement. It is simply a matter of actively and rightly employing the immediately available tools—to organize (and, thereby, make immediately effective) the human collective as a whole.

The necessary and immediate tool and method for the collective organizing of the total human population on Earth is the Internet!

The Global Cooperative Forum should (and, indeed, must) be an Internet-based process, in which everyone on Earth is connected via a single website—and in which, as a practical matter, the "global business" is addressed and organized via formalized and completely accountable representatives of everyone-at-large.

The purpose and responsibility of the Global Cooperative Forum is to establish a working-agenda, and (on that basis) to systematically and efficiently deal with every kind of issue that is fundamental to right life and supportive of all life, and (thus) to address the rightening of all the terrible things that are "in the works" everywhere—including the pandemic of negative global competitiveness, dissociative warrior-nationalisms, the "sport" of strategic war-making, the everywhere aggressive search for global dominance by corporations and traditional institutions, and all the overwhelming changes now progressing in the natural domain, including global warming and climate change, the global epidemics of disease and poverty, the global depletion of natural resources, the global pervasiveness of toxic wastes, the global dependence on archaic practical and political and social and human-resource technologies and methods, and so on, and on.

The humankind-culture of this "late-time" is the global drama of dis-united nations—or the competitive nations of the world. Such is a kind of absurd global gladiatorial contest. On the other hand, when the universal working-presumption is prior unity (or intrinsic indivisibility), then humankind will not come together merely to try to dominate one another or play off of one another. Nobody has, or can have, that kind of dominance when there is a Global Cooperative Forum based on the working-presumption of prior unity. Therefore, when everybody comes to a seat in the Global Cooperative Forum that is about the working-presumption of prior unity, all the dramatization of "self"-prominence of the "objectified" personality, whether personal or national, is specifically and totally undermined. The habits and games of ego-posturing have no place to sit or shout in the Global Cooperative Forum.

When prior unity is presumed, everybody has a different face than that of "Narcissus". When prior dis-unity is presumed, everybody has a mummer's ego-face—everybody is playing a faker's role, everybody is wearing a deceitful costume, everybody is getting their "fifteen minutes of fame" on TV, by playing on the latest possibility of "daily news".

All of that "TV of Narcissus" is utterly obnoxious and passé—and the signs in the world all prove it is far too late in the human course for humankind to be going on with that nonsense anymore. All of that simply must stop.

The national and institutional and otherwise corporate leaderships all over the world are, at the present time, merely playing on the "objectified-self"-culture of "Everyman", and playing off one another like adolescent goons—as if the world is all a meaningless game of gross consumption and excessive waste, and as if it all is made especially for their own glamour to be seen, and made the "Narcissistic object" of all eyes. Therefore, those "in power" must be everywhere awakened to right responsibility—by everybody else. On the basis of that awakening, all the leaders in the world must become directly and consistently accountable to the now and future billions of humankind-as-a-whole—and such that all who are given leadership responsibilities in the world always act as the true and globally accountable servants of all of humankind.

To play absurd games with the human and natural world is, now and forever hereafter, simply not acceptable. Time is up. Such nonsense must be given no more space and time.

7.

If everyone worldwide is involved in the Global Cooperative Forum—not just localized, but truly globalized—then
a single global demand will be made on everybody in
power, everywhere at once.

There should simply be a rightly managed global cooperative process, in which every individual has particular
responsibilities in the global totality. Right human life is not
about anybody being exclusively and unaccountably "in
power". The conducting of human affairs must, as a practical matter, necessarily be focused through individuals, institutions, and workable systems—but, when human politics is
conformed to a right global mechanism for doings (founded
on the constantly applied working-presumption of prior
unity), then politics will have an altogether rightened face
and characteristic. Any treachery would be undermined
immediately, in the Global Cooperative Forum. Any treachery would lose its footing—immediately—in the Global
Cooperative Forum.

Such right human politics would not result in any kind
of absolute state of social perfection—or "utopia". Human
beings cannot do everything. But they can do much—since
so much of what everyone is suffering is, itself, the result of
human activity. Whatever is humanly caused can be redressed
in a very positive sense—such that the energies of humankind are put to solving the real problems, and immediately
stopping the global absurdity of conflict and mummery.

Human society is not—and never will be—utopia. There is
always the negative and the positive. However, the exclusively
negative is now globalized. It is overwhelming. It is everywhere. It is everyone. Therefore, the situation itself must be
replaced, by a new situation, based on global cooperation.

Who must make and do the Global Cooperative Forum
(and the global cooperative order) of humankind? Everyone.

<u>You</u>—<u>the people of the world</u>. Every one of "Everyman" must be changed, and restored to the non-dissociative circumstance—not just to a change of thought, but to a change in doings, a change of participation, engaged in a truly global place. Everyone must get together—without the unfruitful overlay of the dissociative consciousness of merely "objectified" personality—and get on with what is necessary for the well-being and survival of everyone and everything.

No nonsense—just get on with it.

That is, fundamentally, what there is to say about it.

XII.

Wash All The Flags
(and Leave All Name-Tags
and Placards At The Door)

1.

In international affairs, virtually everyone speaks from a "point of view" that is associated with the interests of a particular nation-state. Everyone is propagandizing something on the basis of a national identity—or, more generally, on the basis of an identity related to some religious, cultural, social, or political institution. In any such case, the basis for political discourse is the prior presumption of a limited identity (or "objectified self-image") that is less than the totality of humankind. This is the fundamental cause of many of the world's problems.

The principle of right and true civilization requires that everyone must always assume the disposition of being part of humankind first. That is the necessary and indispensable basis for right human (or civilized) discourse. The disposition of being part of humankind first means taking the "point of view" of totality and universality. It does not require dissociation from one's nation, one's birthplace, or one's particular citizenship. Rather, it requires the discipline of always exercising a disposition that, fundamentally, transcends any kind of particularity of orientation, and which looks at all human problems as part of humankind's inherently global concerns, without any other "angle" on it whatsoever. In that disposition—and only on the basis of that truly civilized "self"-discipline—the world's problems can be dealt with straightforwardly and effectively, in concrete and practical terms.

The disposition of always (and inherently) being part of humankind first implies a kind of egolessness. Of course, that disposition is still associated with a conditional (human) identity. Therefore, that disposition is still a kind of egoity. That disposition is not equivalent to any form of Spiritual or Transcendental Enlightenment. Nevertheless, the working-disposition of being part of the totality of humankind intrinsically (and actively) transcends (or exceeds) the separate and separative "point of view" of the usual participation in the world-business of human happenings.

There are many levels of conditional identity that are commonly presumed: the personal identity, the localized (or immediate) identity (of life-associations, upbringing, family, and village), and the national and religious and racial identities. All these images of "self", or "points of view", encumber everyone's understanding—but they are, characteristically, the first thing that everyone puts out in front. Everyone is, by tendency, always mumming a collection of "self"-images—or the conventionally "objectified" persona with which each one, ordinarily, tends to identify. Whenever anyone says "I", that "objectified" ego-persona is who they mean.

Nevertheless, if everyone is (as a working-presumption of moral "self"-discipline) always part of humankind first, then that universal context becomes the basis for examining everything. Taking that universal "point of view" inherently and inevitably cools all the potential violence of the discourse of "self"-imagery. On that basis, cooperation and tolerance are made possible, because everyone agrees not to assume their separative identities first—or, at least, everyone agrees to actively assume the rather universal identity of being part of the totality of humankind. In that case, each human being can participate with all other human beings in simply handling the business everyone has in common.

Starting from that universal "point of view", the discussion can focus, in a straightforward manner, on all the issues associated with particularities—including national matters. But all such issues must be addressed in the context of the totality of humankind, rather than in the context of all the lesser (separate and separative) identities, and all the strategizing (verbal, and otherwise) that comes with those identities.

This, therefore, is the necessary implication of being part of a Global Cooperative Forum of humankind-as-a-whole: the obligation and responsibility to go beyond the separate and separative identity (or "self"-image) associated with the "point of view" of conventional living—whether personal and local, or in the somewhat enlarged sphere of one's "tribal" situation or nation-state. The establishment of this basis for universal discourse is absolutely essential. That is what the Global Cooperative Forum allows and enables, and why it has a (potentially, global) corrective or balancing effect. However, what is currently reflected in ordinary daily life, as well as in the discourse of the "daily news", is "point-of-view" language, based on all the different modes of "self"-imagery. Everybody is speaking via a "self"-image that is less than the totality of humankind—and every such "self"-image is in opposition to even every other "self"-image. Thus, the usual discourse is confrontation-language.

Conventional discourse is a kind of theatre, or role-playing. It is mummery. The Global Cooperative Forum makes it possible to transcend this mummery—this merely "dramatic" discourse between assumed identities (or "self"-images). The Global Cooperative Forum intrinsically transcends all such mummery, by providing a uniquely free mode of discourse. In the Global Cooperative Forum, the rules of discourse will be very different from the rules of discourse in a forum where identity (or "self"-image) is presumed to be the basis for exchanges. As long as limited identity (rather than universal identity) is the basis for discourse, the language is all "plus" and "minus": confrontation-language, or language based on presumed differences. In that case, very little resolution is possible—because everyone is trying to "win", or to "save face".

In the Global Cooperative Forum, there is no "face" to be "saved". Therefore, fundamental to the virtue of the Global Cooperative Forum is that it is not based on limited "self"-imagery. It transcends mummery. It transcends the identity of common egoity—by simply setting that identity aside.

2.

Discourse in the Global Cooperative Forum would have different rules than the rules of conventional discourse. There are "rules of order" in any mode of "institutionalized" discourse, and the Global Cooperative Forum is a kind of institutional setting for human discourse. Therefore, the Global Cooperative Forum must have order and rules. It must be organized so as to be practically effective—and all of the details must be spelled out: How is the Global Cooperative Forum to be made practical? How are representation and participation to be organized? What are the rules of discourse, and the "rules of order"?

The fundamental principle governing discourse in the Global Cooperative Forum is the setting aside of the projection of limited identity—whether that identity is based on factors local to one's life-situation or on one's national, racial, or religious associations. In the circumstance of participation in the Global Cooperative Forum, no mode of limited association is to be made into a "label". In the Global Cooperative Forum, such modes of association have no intrinsic significance. Certain local issues (national, racial, religious, or otherwise) may need to be addressed in the Global Cooperative Forum—but discourse within the Global Cooperative Forum should not be based on the "identity-labels" associated with such local issues.

The Global Cooperative Forum is different from any international institution that has existed up to now. No one would "sit at" the Global Cooperative Forum. In the Global Cooperative Forum, people would not have "placards" in front of them, announcing their national identity as the basis for discourse. The fundamental "label" each one would have is "human being"—and nothing else. Thus, the Global Cooperative Forum has an entirely different basis for its discourse. It is not "hot" discourse—it is "cool" discourse.

By eliminating all the usual "labels", the "self"-imagery that creates differences is eliminated out front—such that a cool, or (in the right sense) "objective", "point of view" can be established that can deal with real issues in a straightforward manner, without ego-identity becoming the basis. In that case, the discourse focuses on the subject matter to be addressed—not "hotly debated", but rather coolly considered, because no limited identity is presumed as the basis. Thus, the Global Cooperative Forum is the active world-consideration based on the prior unity of everyone—priorly established, and (therefore) not debated.

The purpose of the Global Cooperative Forum is not to create more status and further differences. Nothing of that kind should be established. There are no separate "flags" in the Global Cooperative Forum. The Global Cooperative Forum is not there in the form of confrontation with anyone. It relinquishes confrontation in principle. No confrontation, no war, no "self"-imagery beyond that of being part of the totality of humankind, and having the entire globe as the domain in which to consider all issues.

3.

There is no stark difference between the human species and all other species. There is a prior unity present in the world as a whole. There is obviously a specific orientation that characterizes human beings as human beings in civilized discourse. But, as a human being, recognizing the prior unity of the world, you must have concern for Earth itself, and all the species within it, all life within it, all structures and forms and processes that are part of the world, including all the non-humans.

This does not mean one should view non-humans as if they were humans. Rather, this means one should view humans as part of a larger whole. That is the necessary basis for considering issues that have to do with non-humans as well as humans—as well as issues related to the environment, and to all other aspects of the world. Humankind has the entire Earth as its province—and, therefore, humankind must deal with issues that have to do with what is of the Earth, and with what is associated with non-human species. Humankind must function rightly and compassionately for all.

Human beings have the ability to conceive and voice issues that relate to the Earth and to the non-human species. On that basis, human beings must address issues that relate to the Earth and non-human species, and human beings must do so rationally and compassionately.

Therefore, such matters are also part of all the issues that would be considered by the Global Cooperative Forum. Everything of Earth—everything non-human as well as everything human. And even everything beyond the Earth that human beings can affect—for example, through space exploration. These matters need to be engaged on the basis of right principles, and not merely become the basis for more conflicts. Conflict and confrontation are endless when non-unity and "self"-imagery prevail. You can make the universe a mummery just as you can make Earth a mummery. The ego makes mummery—and egolessness transcends mummery. Therefore, the Global Cooperative Forum, by its very nature, must operate on the non-egoic principle, on the principle of the prior transcending of "self"-imagery.

The Global Cooperative Forum—by definition, and by necessity—is all-inclusive and non-confrontational.

4.

The Global Cooperative Forum would not eliminate exist-ing national, social, religious, or political institutions. That is not the point. But the Global Cooperative Forum is about cooperation between all these institutions—and the basis for that cooperation is a kind of "tabula rasa" (or clean slate), without "self"-imagery, as the circumstance in which to engage (with all others) in an address to common human problems.

The common (or global and universal) human problems are what the Global Cooperative Forum needs to actively address—because, while everybody is fussing with the latest mummer's drama of the "daily news", things are deteriorat-ing more and more profoundly in areas that (because of the constant diversions made of human nonsense) are not being addressed directly and effectively: the overall condition of the Earth, environmental pollution, global warming, climate change, the abuse of power by corporations and govern-ments, the necessity for new technologies and new methods in every area of human life, the scarcity of fuel resources and of natural and human resources altogether, disease, famine, poverty, overpopulation, urbanization, globalization, human migration, territorial disputes, violent crime, the per-vasive accumulation (and the sometimes actual use) of excessively (and even catastrophically) destructive weapons, the tendency of nation-states to avoid cooperation and mutual accommodation, the tendency of nation-states (or factions within nation-states) to use war (and, otherwise, unspeakably dark-minded violence) as a method for achiev-ing the goals of national and otherwise culturally idealized policies, and so on—and on. Human inventiveness must be released from the perpetual "self"-imposition of mummery (or false, and, otherwise, unnecessary, human drama), that undermines the ability of humankind to handle its right and necessary (and, now, urgent) business.

The "daily news" is about the inventing of drama and oppositions. That is what the news media always tend to do. The news media tend always to look for the "differences", the "opposites", the basis for controversy and confrontation, in order to make a human drama (and even a form of popular entertainment) out of it. Drama is the working-principle of the "daily news". However, that is not the principle of the Global Cooperative Forum. "No-drama" is the principle of the Global Cooperative Forum—no opposition, no differences, no controversy, no nonsense, and only "business handled".

5.

There is no place for "warrior-kings" and "high-mucky-mucks"* in the Global Cooperative Forum. There necessarily must be representatives, but the representatives must be disciplined by the people (and the necessary civilization-principles) they represent. In other words, these representatives have to be able to set aside their "self"-imagery, their conventional identity—their "name-tags", and "flags", and "placards", and "slogans"—and deal with real practical issues, as true servants of the total all of humankind. There can be any number of such servant-representatives, but, as such, none of them are "warrior-kings" or "high-mucky-mucks". In the Global Cooperative Forum, there is no room for the "one-group-over-against-another-group" mentality. By definition, and by necessity, the Global Cooperative Forum operates on the basis of the absolute, prior, and tacit equality of all. The necessary governing-agreement is that there are no "warrior-kings", no "high-mucky-mucks", and no senior (or, otherwise, subordinate) factions.

* "High-mucky-muck" is a humorous term for individuals who are full of self-importance, flaunting their presumed superiority and status. They have important-sounding titles but do very little.

If differences are presumed from the beginning, effective discourse can only proceed a short distance. However, if one begins by making no differences at all, effective discourse can proceed to an unlimited degree. Such is the basis for the Global Cooperative Forum: There are no differences, no "seniors" over against "juniors", no subordinates with others above them. There is an "equal table", in which everyone participates, and where representation is simply a means for making the Global Cooperative Forum able, as a practical matter, to function effectively (and in the interests of everyone equally).

Literally <u>everyone</u> should participate in the Global Cooperative Forum. However, to make it orderly, so that it can function effectively, some individuals must, by necessity, have key representational functions within it. If any of those individuals start "putting on" their "self"-imagery too prominently, they would have to be addressed and disciplined. They would have to be disciplined by the whole, and be able to accept that, and always "wash their flags".

The ability to "lose face" is fundamental to being able to function rightly in the context of the Global Cooperative Forum. You cannot show up as an ego, full of "self"-imagery of any kind—personal, racial, religious, national, or whatever it may be. You cannot manifest that and be anything like a principal individual serving as a significant representative of everyone via the Global Cooperative Forum. Therefore, all who function as representatives in the Global Cooperative Forum must constantly "wash their flags". Individuals serving within the Global Cooperative Forum must constantly drop whatever they may inadvertently (or, otherwise, strategically) introduce that would establish a principle of difference, or that represents a "self"-image that would cause the exclusion of some element of humankind's concerns, or the exclusion of any dimension of human existence.

To participate productively in the Global Cooperative Forum does not mean an individual cannot have personal views that are otherwise particularized—such as, for example, a personal association with a particular religious tradition. However, participation in the Global Cooperative Forum does mean (and require) that an individual must not allow any particular "self"-image (or mode of personal association) to be the active basis for his or her participation in the Global Cooperative Forum itself. All "self"-imagery must be set aside, so that the individual does not even function secretly or unconsciously on a separate and separative and counter-productive basis. Everyone who participates in the Global Cooperative Forum must be able to simply assume the prior identity of "human being"—without "flags", without "self"-imagery otherwise—and to look at everything and everyone, at all issues and all problems that need to be addressed, in a straightforward and unprejudiced manner.

The Global Cooperative Forum is—by definition, and by necessity—constantly self-correcting. Therefore, individuals who can function most flexibly in such a circumstance would be the best people to occupy the principal representative positions that are needed to enable the Global Cooperative Forum to be effective.

Obviously, the confrontational orientation to discourse cannot work in the setting of the Global Cooperative Forum itself. To carry on the process (or global human business) of the Global Cooperative Forum, the participating representatives must be able to relinquish the confrontational disposition, and, yet, still know what are the real human concerns that need to be addressed. Individuals who have a confrontational "talent" would either have to be able to set it aside to participate in this Global Cooperative Forum, or they would have to function in a different role relative to it—perhaps by providing relevant information relative to certain issues. But those who function in the role of participatory representation (of humankind-as-a-whole) within the Global Cooperative Forum, and who, therefore, as a practical matter, must carry on its process, must be (in real practice) free of the confrontational disposition. In that sense, they must be talented "diplomats". They must know how to carry on really effective discourse while (as a really effective "self"-discipline) relinquishing the confrontational attitude, and they must, on that basis, be all-inclusive in their active disposition. It is not merely about having a "poker face"—or a false face, that merely hides a limited and all-limiting "self"-image. Rather, it is about being able to maintain the discipline of non-confrontation—and to really (and always rightly) make things happen, always now.

XIII.

To Take Moral Responsibility
Is To Make Reactivity Harmless

There are very few situations in which confrontation is appropriate. A confrontation is a stand-off. The mood of confrontation is the continuation of an egoic strategy from one's past. It is an immature view.

Taking the frightening facts of the world into account, one must deal with them in an entirely different manner than by egoic reaction. One must undermine—rather than directly confront—negative forces. The only security is in harmlessness. Harmlessness obliges one to open one's face—and, indeed, to <u>lose</u> face! One must undo the force of one's apparent "enemy"—with "small" Eastern-style defense, rather than "big" Western-style defense.

Western-style defense is adolescent. Western-style defense is founded on confrontation—just as the efforts of scientific materialism are founded on confrontation. The fundamental method of Western-style defense is to wound the opponent with a blunt instrument—whereas the Eastern-style defense thoroughly takes into account and understands the energy represented by an opponent.

One must always thoroughly understand and transcend the egoic role of <u>being</u> an opponent, and (on that basis) always actively and responsively undermine the oppositional pattern-energy that is in the opponent—not so that (in the merely conventional sense) one "wins" (and, thus and thereby, becomes egoically "self"-defined as the "winner"), and not so that (in effect) one achieves a position of absolute dominance over the "other" (such that the apparent opponent is reduced to nothing), but always in such a manner that the energy that would otherwise be conflict itself (and separative activity itself, and "difference" itself) is both transcended and dissipated.

One should only "dance" with the other, by not becoming the egoically separated and separative mere opponent of the other. Once one enters into a "dance" with the other, the mutual energy is transformed. That "dance" is essentially a moral consideration of others and of apparent "difference", in which the transcending of egoity is the fundamental mood of relationships.

Everyone must always take moral responsibility for his or her own reactivity in relationships, and see how this moral responsibility actively works itself out on every level—on the intimate level of one's life, but also in the must-be-cooperative politics of global humankind.

XIV.

The Global Necessity For Universal
Rules of Participation

All modes of "tribally"-defined "reality" are "self"-centric—
or (in collective terms) ego-based, ego-serving, and
ego-bound.

All modes of "tribally"-defined "religion" and "knowledge" (including all modes of "tribally"-defined "science")
are structured to serve the collective purposes of the "tribe"
as the normative context for all of its members.

All modes of "tribally"-defined "religion" and "knowledge"
(including "science") are intended to "tribalize" all individual
egos—such that all individual egos substitute the collective
"tribal" ego-identity for their otherwise individuated separate
and separative ego-identity.

Therefore, all "tribal" identities (including all nation-states)
function as collective egos, which (in the likeness of individual
egos) are organized as patterns of separate and separative
(and, thus, competitive and "self"-interest-driven) entities—
all of which are subject to both negative "self"-exploitation
(or false leadership) and possible destructive intentions
(exercised either toward others or toward themselves).

Because all of this is thus and so, it is necessary for all of
humankind (as a global totality) to always establish, regulate,
maintain, and enforce a comprehensive and all-including
and all-obliging global system of "rules of participation"—
the constant effect of which is to universally legitimize the
ego-transcending disposition, by regulating the comprehensive order of everybody-all-at-once, and by "opening the
doors" of global participation in every case of responsibly

accountable compliance and (as a means of self-correcting the system by rightening its constituents) by (in an always appropriately and productively measured manner) "closing the doors" of global participation in every case of would-be non-compliance.

XV.

Everybody-All-At-Once

1.

There are people all over the world who are making virtuous suggestions relative to the achievement of peace—but that activity is not changing anything. Merely to offer guidance and issue calls is, in effect, to wave "placards" and shout "slogans"—and that is useless in the reality-context of the world. What is required, in order for peace to be established in the world, is something profoundly different.

What is required to establish peace in the world is the emergence of the true collective of everybody—all nearly-eight-billion human beings on Earth—by means of a Global Cooperative Forum. The Global Cooperative Forum is not merely another body of people with a virtuous view, offering guidance to everyone and issuing calls. The Global Cooperative Forum is the body of virtually everybody—taking a firm and unequivocal stand, and saying how things are going to be. For fundamental positive change to happen in the world, the world of everybody (all-at-once) must represent itself (all-at-once).

The world of everybody (all-at-once) must get out of the position of passively accepting guidance and receiving calls to virtue. The world of everybody (all-at-once) must accept the necessary position of taking control of the world-situation. That is what must happen—or else there can no longer be any hope of a cooperative world at peace.

By its sheer numbers, the all-at-once collective of everybody as a right and true Global Cooperative Forum is in the position to insist on rightness. This is the only way that peace can be truly established in the world. Political and cultural leaders are not, themselves, going to be able to make this change occur. Such a profound degree of change cannot be brought about by the virtuous voice alone. Rather, such a profound degree of change can only be brought about by the force of humankind as a collective whole, or the "everybody force". The inherent collective of everybody-all-at-once actually is (always) the only true power—but that collective is not currently exercising that power, because that collective is dis-united and in chaos.

In the current world-situation, the total nearly-eight-billion of the current human population are fragmented into numerous nation-states, and fragmented—as individuals (or "ego-identities") and, also, as smaller collectives (or limited and limiting "group-identities")—even within those nation-states. The modern "idealization" of the individual (and the defining of individuals by means of the limiting-principles of "ego-identity" and "group-identity") is, actually, a social and political device for isolating, fragmenting, and dis-empowering everyone—so that humankind (as a whole) has no collective power. If everybody is encouraged to be busy "meditating" on themselves as individuals (or, otherwise, if every individual is dis-empowered by means of the limiting-principles, or "separation-devices", of "ego-identity" and "group-identity"), then there is no true collective of everybody-all-at-once that can make any demands. Thus, the global promotion of the notion that people should focus on their individual interests and concerns—inclined toward "self"-indulgent purposes and illusions of "self"-fulfillment—is a global power-game that subverts both the integrity of the human person and the inherent power and rightness of the totality of humankind.

What is required for change is a unique form of collective action, in which everybody-all-at-once insists on rightness. That "everybody" is, fundamentally, the present-time "nearly-eight-billion" (and the however many in any future time and context), but it would not (as such) include those who merely want to hold power and keep people fragmented and maintain the status quo. It is not possible to tell billions of people what to do—unless those billions are fragmented into a chaos of billions of "self"-involved individuals who have nothing to do with one another (and who, by means of the limiting-principle, or "separation-device", of both "ego-identity" and "group-identity", are even prevented from having anything to do with one another). However, that fragmentation is, in fact, the current situation. The root-problem in the current world-situation is that there are more than seven and a half billion individuals "meditating" on themselves egoically, trying to achieve a kind of (either personal egoic or collective egoic) satisfaction that is not possible. "Perfect" egoic "self"-satisfaction (whether personal or collective) is not a real possibility in a world of limitation and death.

In the present-day, the culture and politics of illusion controls the world. The underlying idea that personal and collective egoic "self"-fulfillment is what life is supposed to be about is the root-source of the current global chaos. As a result, there are more than seven and a half billion human individuals (and, otherwise, large numbers of competitive and mutually dissociative groups, cultures, traditions, races, religions, corporations, and nation-states) that are, characteristically (and even strategically), out of touch with each other—like dust, and bombs, and petty traffic, all blowing in the wind. That wind steadily blows all prior unity into the bits and particles of human chaos.

Therefore, humankind must drop its illusions about "perfect" egoic "self"-fulfillment, and stop living a merely chaotic and fragmented life. That chaos and fragmentation leaves people open to being controlled and manipulated. The reason power-games can be played is that the billions of humankind are fragmented. That fragmentation is what power-seekers exploit. The power-seekers are counting on the billions of humankind remaining detached from one another. As soon as the billions of humankind stop being detached from one another, the illusion-mongers and power-gamers of the world will be "out of business".

2.

The Global Cooperative Forum is about humankind-as-a-whole exercising its collective voice unequivocally, and standing firm, and being unwilling to cooperate with what is not (and must not be) acceptable.

The Global Cooperative Forum is the means by which the collective "force of everybody-all-at-once" can become effective in the world. The Global Cooperative Forum must really represent everybody (all-at-once), and not merely a handful of loud and "self"-deluded individuals and groups who are, apparently, independently in power. The otherwise powerless everybody-all-at-once must become a collective everybody-all-at-once—with undeniable power to change the world-situation, and to assert the world-situation as a non-chaotic prior unity, or intrinsically indivisible whole, and to make the changes that will reverse the destructive destiny that is now in progress. No other means of establishing peace and rightness in the world is going to be effective.

Merely calling on everybody to establish peace and rightness does not create the desired result. To call the chaotic world of egoic human individuals to establish peace and rightness is like trying to give verbal instruction to a cat. Generally speaking, cats do not take verbal instruction—nor do cats respond to advice, or callings, or guidance, or being told what to do at all. They simply do not do that.

That is also how it is with the world of humankind. The world of fragmented individuals and impenetrable collectives is neither available nor amenable to be advised, or called upon, or instructed. However, the world as everybody-all-at-once is (inherently) in a position to collectively decide that things are going to be rightened. The condition of the demand for rightness must be established as reality by the collective of everybody-all-at-once. The Global Cooperative Forum of everybody-all-at-once must be immovable relative to the fundamental requirements for rightness in the world.

Until the total population of the world can be represented effectively, the means to make things right do not yet exist. If the billions of everybody-all-at-once have a voice, and are in a position to express that voice one-pointedly, then everything about fundamental world-rightening could become the collectively self-organized happening of humankind on Earth.

If human beings collectively (as everybody-all-at-once) realize that they are (always already) in a condition of prior unity—and, therefore, of necessary co-existence and mutuality—with one another, and if, on that basis, they stand firm together, then they will be in a position to directly righten the world-situation. The collective of more than seven and a half billion people can—and, indeed, must—refuse to go on with the current chaos.

However, this profound shift will not occur simply because the billions of humankind are advised, or called upon, to do so. The billions of individuals—as billions of egos—are not going to respond to any such advice or calling, because they are too busy indulging themselves in the marketplace of personal, social, religious, scientific, and political illusions. Therefore, the egoless everybody-all-at-once must open their eyes, see for real, relinquish their helplessness, and take direct responsibility for the human world-event. The egoless everybody-all-at-once must renounce its illusions and "come out of the closet" as the only "we" of planet Earth.

3.

People are not awakened from their ego-patterned habits by mere advice and calling. It is not possible to cause people to awaken to the Truth of Reality Itself.

There is nothing that can be done, in the mode of positive action, that will produce Truth-Realization and the actual transcending of egoity itself as a result. Likewise, there is nothing that can be done in the mode of conditional causation (in the conventional sense) that can cause world peace. However, this does not mean that world peace is impossible. It is possible to bring about world peace through acausal means.

Fundamental (or all-rightening) change cannot be caused. However, fundamental change can happen—as a spontaneous (and all-transforming, or all-reforming) self-conversion. Also, the necessary self-conversion that is required for fundamental change to occur can, itself, be enabled to happen—not by causing it as effect (as if it were already not-existing, and, therefore, needs to be "created out of nothing"), but, most simply and directly, by re-empowering the self-organizing integrity and prior unity of the intrinsically egoless everybody-all-at-once that already exists.

It will not be the role-playing of "virtuous speaking" that brings about the necessary fundamental change. Calling everybody to change does not cause them to change. Those who are already moved to do right do not need to be told to do so—and, no matter how much advice and admonition they are given, those who are not inclined to do right are not going to "change their act".

If there is going to be fundamental all-rightening change, something has to require change. Therefore, the world as a whole must be enabled to require change. It is an acausal matter—not a causal matter.

The billions of humankind must become self-organized. The Global Cooperative Forum is the means for self-organizing the total population of humankind into an effective single voice that can simply say how things are going to be. To propose that such an effective single collective voice should and could come into being may seem to be a merely "idealistic" notion—but that single collective voice is exactly what is necessary. That is the only happen that will work the change required by all. Virtuous single voices will not, themselves, be effective. Therefore, since the single collective voice of everybody-all-at-once is, in the scale of human reality, what is necessary, it is a mistake to suppose that it is not possible for that collective voice to happen. If anything is, as a matter of necessity, required by the reality-scale of human existence, it is a certainty that it can (and must) be done.

The really-existing inherent collective of humankind has inherent power. The "everybody-all-at-once" has the inherent characteristic (and integrity) of prior unity and the inherent capability (and integrity) of a self-organizing principle. Power in the hands of a few cannot manipulate the total collective, if the total collective exercises its inherent power of prior unity and self-organizing energy.

It is not that "the people" (as some kind of immense natural ego) is morally virtuous, and should, therefore, "take over the world" through some kind of "mob rule". Only more chaos can come from more ego-power. Therefore, it must be asked, where is true moral virtue? True moral virtue is only at the intrinsically egoless root-context of existence. The egoless root-context of existence is not separate and separative. Humankind, as a whole, must be understood with reference to the root-context of existence—and (by means of a right and true Global Cooperative Forum) everybody-all-at-once must be represented (and rightly extended) by voice and activity that proceeds from the inherently morally-enlightened root-context of existence.

Whenever human awareness is subordinated to the intrinsically egoless (and, thus, non-separate and non-separative) root-context of existence, human life becomes morally enlightened (in both voice and action) by the radiant virtue of selflessness. Therefore, if everybody-all-at-once is (by means of a right and true Global Cooperative Forum) represented and mobilized by morally-enlightened principles and persons, Reality Itself has re-acquired the voice and ability to make right changes.

If all the present-day world-leaders entered into a single great forum, and agreed to accept a comprehensive list of right principles as being absolutely required, then the world would be in a very different situation. However, this is not going to happen—unless everybody-all-at-once requires it to happen.

In the current world-situation, there is no absolute and adamantine requirement for world-leaders to make the choices that everybody-all-at-once truly needs. What power on Earth is going to make it obligatory for the situation to be made right? No merely virtuous voice of calling, advice, and educational effort is capable of enforcing that requirement. Only a demand made by what cannot be subordinated to the usual political power-games is capable of obliging the situation to change. The entire collective of the nearly-eight-billion of everybody-all-at-once is the only power in the world that can change the current chaos.

The powerlessness of egoic individualism must be replaced by an inherently powerful positive collective, that is rooted in right principles, that simply says how things are going to be, and that unequivocally stops allowing itself to be subordinated to what is not right. Effectively, that is what must happen.

How is that to happen? What must, first, be done to enable that happening to become self-manifested is a morally-enlightened and selfless service, that must be enacted by the cooperative effort of a unique group of responsible and capable individuals—who are hereby addressed, and whose response is hereby both informed and requested. The necessary first response and all-enabling service must come from those unique individuals who know how to connect with everybody-all-at-once. If there are enough such everybody-all-at-once-enabling individuals, a reality-connection to the present-day billions of humankind can be readily and directly made. Once that is done, the billions of humankind can (by means of an immediately established right and true Global Cooperative Forum) simply insist that right order be brought into the human domain. Only that would be a demand that would, by unavoidable necessity, have to be respected—and, as a matter of unavoidable obligation, served.

4.

The inherent collective and prior unity that is the "everybody-all-at-once" is intrinsically egoless, self-organizing, indivisible, and cooperative. The human world is currently populated (and self-fragmented) by billions of egos—all deluded by various kinds of influences, and all dreaming of the idea of being able (and even of having the necessity) to fulfill their accumulated desires. However, in actuality, the world-all-at-once is an intrinsically egoless happening.

It is only the presumption of egoity (or the illusion of inherent separateness) that makes the billions of humankind enact separation from one another—such that they refuse to enact mutual tolerance, peaceful coexistence, and universal cooperation with one another. In Reality, the billions of humankind are not separate from one another—and should not act to achieve, affirm, or, in any manner, presume separation from one another. In Reality, the billions of humankind exist in the root-context of egoless prior unity. If the inherent energy of that egoless prior unity were brought to the fore, it would spontaneously take responsibility for self-rightening the world.

Every human being is going to die. Humankind exists in a world where death is an inescapable reality. On the other hand, the world is, at its root, egoless, Indivisible, Absolute, and Infinite.

What Is (intrinsically) egoless must re-assert its inherent power in the world. The Reality-power of everybody-all-at-once existing in the condition of prior unity is what must re-assert itself. When humankind-as-a-whole functions in the disposition of prior unity, a positive order is initiated and (inevitably) self-organized. That can (and must) be done.

Chaos has come about because everything became individuated—every "thing" and every "one". When everybody is fragmented into separate units, there is inevitable chaos. However, when everybody starts to function on the working-presumption of egoless prior unity, then there is the means to bring order into the world of human experience. It is an egoless matter. And, therefore, it is not a religious matter (in the sense of being determined by the dogmas of a particular religious tradition)—but it is a Perfectly serious matter (in the sense of being an articulation of Intrinsically egoless, Indivisible, Absolute, and Infinite Reality Itself).

As egos, the billions of humankind are simply a mob of individuals—and that is chaos. However, the billions as an egoless (or indivisible and cooperative) presence is something entirely different. The intrinsically egoless presence of everybody-all-at-once does not (in order to be re-asserted) require that it, first, be caused—or become the "idealistic" result of some kind of process whereby each individual must first, and one by one, become an egoless Perfectly Enlightened being. No—the intrinsically egoless presence of everybody-all-at-once already (or priorly) exists—and, therefore, it need only be "realistically" self-asserted. The direct and necessary means for that re-assertion is the rational, orderly, and all-representing establishment of a right and true (and, inherently, globally powerful) Global Cooperative Forum.

The Global Cooperative Forum must manifest the unequivocal integrity of the otherwise chaotic voice of everybody-all-at-once. Through the Global Cooperative Forum, everybody-all-at-once must self-manifest a voice that stands for what is truly right and necessary—and a voice that is in a position to non-violently require (or immovably insist) that what is right be really done. That means everybody (each and all) is going to have to lose not just <u>some</u> "face", but <u>all</u> "face". There is no "face" in the right and true Global Cooperative Forum of everybody-all-at-once—<u>none</u>.

The Global Cooperative Forum must truly represent—and, in effect, embody, or self-manifest—the voice that represents humankind-as-a-whole. However, to represent humankind-as-a-whole is not merely to speak for billions of egos—but it is, rather, to represent and speak for the egoless everybody-all-at-once that must be positively effective in bringing order to the current world-chaos. It is not the <u>egoic</u> everybody (or every "I"), but it is the <u>egoless</u> everybody-all-at-once, that must be embodied in, as, and via the Global Cooperative Forum.

5.

The Global Cooperative Forum cannot, appropriately and rightly, be organized by people whose power or leadership in the world is based on presuming (and maintaining) the illusion of people as separate egos. Those who can rightly serve the Global Cooperative Forum must be morally-enlightened persons of true integrity, who, first, relinquish whatever position (and egoic "self"-image) of power they may have previously "enjoyed"—by (now) having become dis-illusioned with ego-based power-positions in general. By virtue of this relinquishment (or "face"-renunciation), such individuals stand in a completely different context—essentially, the egoless context. Standing in that context, they are inherently powerless <u>as</u> <u>individuals</u>—but they are functioning (and truly <u>all</u>-serving) as part and representative of an egoless whole, and they dedicate their talents to help the egoless whole of everybody-all-at-once become effective in a positive and truly global manner. Therefore, the ability to function in the egoless (or truly ego-transcending) manner is the ability that must characterize right leadership in the

Global Cooperative Forum—and in even all the future time and context of humankind.

All presumptions of power, and all personal illusions, are relinquished in the disposition that is coincident with Reality Itself. In that disposition, you renounce your "costume"—your "mummer's role" of the presumed separate (or egoic) "self"—completely. And, in that disposition, you renounce all presumed "ownership" of power and Truth.

All and every one are inherently subordinate to Truth Itself.

All and every one are inherently subordinate to Reality Itself.

All and every one are inherently subordinate to That Which Is egoless, Absolute, Infinite, and Indivisible.

What must be exercised is That Which Is (Inherently) Always Already The Case.

Unity need not be achieved—because unity (or Intrinsic Indivisibility) Is the Prior Condition of Reality Itself.

Similarly, egolessness need not be achieved—because egolessness is the prior condition of all-and-All.

Therefore, rightness need not be achieved—because rightness is the prior condition of all-and-All that arises.

Rightness must simply be exercised—as it is. And the exercise of rightness can be both enabled and implemented. That, in fact, is what must happen.

The disposition to cause rightness is not the disposition you need to demonstrate. Rather, you must stand in the position to do rightness.

The intention to cause (or yet-make-exist) is the motivator and the strategy of ego—because ego always desires and seeks what it presumes is not yet the case.

Truth is the pre-Condition, and the pre-Advantage, and the Inherent Capability of egolessness—and, therefore, egolessness is the self-organizing energy of prior unity, prior integrity, and prior rightness.

6.

The world is deluded by its own artifacts.

Human history is, conventionally, viewed as some kind of continuum of human awareness—whereas it is actually made up of countless numbers of now dead people.

Who has survived?

Nobody has survived.

Who will survive?

Nobody will survive.

Continuous human awareness—as if ego coincides with the simultaneity of <u>all</u> of time and space—is nothing but a mummer's illusion, a theatrically-conceived drama of "Narcissus".

When you attach yourself to the theatrically-conceived drama (or mummery) of life, you forget your actual situation.

Your actual situation is not merely that everybody dies.

Your actual situation, or Reality-situation, is that there is no ego, no separate entity—<u>none</u>.

However, there is Something Else—Reality Itself, or That Which <u>Is</u> egoless, Absolute, Infinite, and Indivisible.

Reality Itself Is Self-Existing, Self-Radiant, and Inherently Perfect.

Reality Itself <u>Is</u> birthless, and deathless, and Perfectly Free.

The egoless human being fully participates in Reality Itself.

The ego-bound human being only <u>seeks</u> for Reality Itself, or for Truth, or for Ultimate Satisfaction, and imagines all kinds of "satisfactory results" that are not the case, and never will be the case, and <u>cannot</u> be the case.

The will to illusion is fundamental to egoity.

To awaken to the intrinsic egolessness of the life-situation is to be free of the "self"-deluded capability for illusion.

Everybody-all-at-once must become dis-illusioned with the ego-made chaos of the present-time world-situation.

That dis-illusionment can make everybody-all-at-once effective in the true Reality-situation of life.

That dis-illusionment can set the energy of everybody-all-at-once in motion, free of the structures and purposes of ego-bondage.

That dis-illusionment is the root and necessary basis for the awakening of everybody-all-at-once to the inherently global responsibility of humankind.

XVI.

Humankind-As-A-Whole
Must Collectively Address
Its Real Issues

I
t has been said that to refuse to do anything about the
conditions of the world is to agree to submit to be ruled
by someone less capable than yourself. Rightly understood, this is an essential communication to humankind-as-
a-whole.

In *Not-Two Is Peace*, I am calling each individual to be
turned about and straightened out in his or her disposition,
the basis on which he or she is living. However, once that
turnabout is the case, then humankind-as-a-whole must
collectively address its real issues. For humankind-as-a-
whole to refuse to enter into a cooperative dialogue and
handle its business is for humankind-as-a-whole to submit to
be ruled by the ego, or the lesser disposition. And the ego
will inevitably take power if humankind does not keep its
representatives accountable.

Thus, *Not-Two Is Peace* is a call to that rightened disposition in the totality of humankind. And humankind must
achieve a right voice and right power—right ability to handle its obligations, handle its business, and handle its problems. Merely to be passive, merely to be waiting to be satisfied like children, satisfied by so-called "people in power", is
for humankind-as-a-whole—or humankind-as-a-species—to
renounce the responsibility that only it can rightly exercise
by a collective process of participation.

Therefore, *Not-Two Is Peace* is a call to humankind to get
organized, to get its act together as a species on Earth. And

the way things currently "work" (so to speak) is not that—it is a setup.

In its present way of happening, the world is a kind of theatre, in which people who seek power for their own reasons and work to get power (over conditions of life, and over humankind-as-a-totality) find ways to achieve that position, and are even given such power because humankind-as-a-whole is not organized, has no voice, has no power collectively, is content to be "the people", just complaining and living "lives of quiet desperation" (as Thoreau said), and feeling that they do not have any power to do anything about it.

Powerlessness breeds negative power. The presumption of powerlessness on the part of humankind-as-a-whole breeds (or consents to) power being taken on an egoic (or negative) basis by those who seek power for their own purposes.

It is necessary that humankind-as-a-whole achieve collective power. But I am not talking about revolution or chaos or riots in the streets. That is not what I am talking about at all. That is merely another disaster, another kind of tyranny—the tyranny of "Everyman".

A true Global Cooperative Forum of humankind-as-a-whole must be established—as the alternative to tyranny. That is the necessary corrective—the Global Cooperative Forum, based on the principle of prior unity. That is the force that will keep all so-called "power" accountable. That is the force that will make power into a positive dimension of collective human life. Then power would exist and function in a situation of discipline that is accountable to the Global Cooperative Forum of humankind-as-a-whole.

In the current epoch, the so-called "people" (or the "masses", so to speak) are under control. They are utterly subordinate. They are instructed to presume powerlessness. As a result, they only indulge in reactive behaviors, when they are displeased with how things are happening. They function childishly, making demands on (or living in expectations of) leaders (or "people in power", so to speak) to somehow make the world into a utopia and dish it up on a silver platter. Obviously, that is not going to happen. In the twentieth and twenty-first centuries, most especially, people are not only treated like children. The "people" have become, in some respects, the presumed "enemy of the state".

The deadly happenings of the twentieth century were no longer armies confronting one another on a distant battlefield. It is not like the Civil War in the United States, where people used to go out and have picnics watching the battles happening between the armies. Yes, there are armies, and people do suffer and die in military situations. But, on the other hand, there is no longer a principle of "hands off the people". Now those who want to use violence or power to control events target the people. It is no longer primarily the military that is dying in armed conflicts now. It is primarily the people who are dying—and who are, in fact, being intentionally targeted.

This is the dreadful "dead end"—the ultimate sign and result—of "power" viewing the "people" as the "enemy", viewing the "people" as a kind of childish, powerless something-or-other to be manipulated and merely given tokens of satisfaction, to keep it subservient. Over time, this has become the full-blown disposition that "the people are the enemy", "the people must be controlled", "the people are a threat to the state"—and on and on and on. That is the psychology of the current situation in the world.

The necessary turnabout is that humankind-as-a-whole must stop presuming a childish position, a subordinate position. If individuals are subordinate, how much power can they have—except to merely be reactive in whatever fashion? It is only in the collective empowerment of humankind-as-a-whole that humankind assumes its right position of power.

Then, anybody who is exercising power is doing so as an extension of humankind-as-a-whole, under the authority of humankind-as-a-whole, through a necessary Global Cooperative Forum that keeps all representation accountable. Such is the necessary corrective, in terms of action. The necessary fundamental principle is the presumption (or the working-principle) of prior unity. And the necessary functional happening is the true establishment of a global cooperative order. That is the practical aspect of what is otherwise a principle of rightness, which is prior unity. In *Not-Two Is Peace*, I cover both aspects—the principle and the practical necessity for carrying out the principle.

The Global Cooperative Forum is about humankind-as-a-whole not refusing to participate.

The Global Cooperative Forum is about humankind-as-a-whole not assuming the position of the "child" or the "enemy of the state", but of being that to which the state must be accountable, that to which all power must be accountable.

But it is not humankind merely as some kind of "mob". The Global Cooperative Forum must function in a very orderly and responsible manner, and on the basis of principle—not just be a circumstance of license to argue, license to be loud in conflict, or license to proclaim one's difference from others. Not that.

The Global Cooperative Forum should be a very sober, discriminating, principled representation of humankind-as-a-whole. But it must be something in which humankind-as-a-whole actually does participate.

XVII.

The Dual Basis
For Right and True Oneness

The collective (and should-be-cooperative, and, altogether, right and positive) <u>exoteric</u> domain of politics, social and economic activity, conventional religions and idealistic culture, and materially-oriented science and technology is, all and always, about would-be-<u>progress</u>, or the potential for always progressive advancement in human and Earth-world survival-solutions and living well-being.

The collective (and should-be-exemplary, and, altogether, illuminating) <u>esoteric</u> domain of the totality of the true beyond-religion culture of Spirituality, philosophy, and the arts is, all and always, about <u>transcendence</u>.

These two human collective domains—the exoteric domain of progress <u>and</u> the esoteric domain of transcendence—are (<u>together</u>) the necessary and always mutually-inclusive basis for right and true human (and, necessarily, always priorly unified, and, thus, always actively and effectively single) polity, society, culture, and life.

XVIII.

Zero-Point Education

1.

There are two most fundamental Great Principles in Reality Itself that are relevant and most essential for humankind.

The First Great Principle in Reality Itself is <u>intrinsic egolessness</u> (or no-"self").

The Second Great Principle in Reality Itself is subordinate only to the First Great Principle in Reality Itself.

The Second Great Principle in Reality Itself is <u>prior unity</u> (or no-"difference").

2.

The ego-"I" is the active and only source and the very structure and principle of <u>all</u> "difference".

Egoity itself is the comprehensive psycho-physical act of "self"-differentiation—or of separation, separateness, and separativeness as a thus and thereby identified separate "self"-identity.

The ego-"I" actively and constantly "self"-projects the idea and the pattern of "difference" onto the world (and onto even all that arises as attention itself).

Apart from the egoically "self"-projected idea and pattern of "difference", there is no intrinsic "difference" anywhere or everywhere in the world.

Apart from and always prior to the egoically "self"-projected idea and pattern of "difference", the world is a seamless whole, intrinsically characterized by a universal state and pattern of prior unity.

The totality of all that arises to attention is an intrinsically seamless whole, intrinsically characterized by a state and pattern of prior unity, utterly without intrinsic "difference".

The totality of all that conditionally arises is an intrinsically egoless prior unity.

The intrinsically egoless prior unity of the totality of all that conditionally arises is never (and cannot be) self-evident to the ego-"I".

Therefore, the ego-"I"—or the activity of "difference"-projection—must be intrinsically, and always immediately, and constantly transcended.

The ego-"I" itself may seek to transcend itself and the apparition of "difference" that the ego-"I" (or egoity itself) "self"-projects onto the world (and onto even all that arises to attention)—but (by its very nature) the ego-"I" (which is the total psycho-physical activity of "difference" itself) cannot transcend itself, and, therefore, the ego-"I" cannot know the intrinsically egoless prior unity of the totality of the world (and of all that arises to attention).

The ego-"I" cannot be transcended by any act or effort of egoity itself.

The ego-"I" can only be transcended intrinsically—and, thus, tacitly and priorly, or always already.

The intrinsic prior unity of the totality of the world (and of all that arises to attention) can be known (or found to be self-evidently the case) only by intrinsically egoless tacit and direct apprehension—or on the basis of prior egolessness.

Therefore, for the prior unity of the world (and all that arises to attention) to be apprehended, egolessness itself and (on that basis) the intrinsic egolessness of all that conditionally arises must be priorly (or always already) tacitly, directly, and always presently known to be self-evident at the root of attention itself and of awareness itself.

For the intrinsic egolessness of attention itself and of awareness itself to be known to be self-evident at the root of attention itself and of awareness itself, it is necessary for human individuals (each and all) to embrace a lifetime of personal schooling, by means of intensive (and, at least eventually, esoteric Transcendental Spiritual) practice-participation in the discipline and process of "zero-point" education.

"Zero-point" education is the constant intensive life-practice of intrinsically knowing intrinsic egolessness at the root of attention and of awareness itself.

"Zero-point" education is not the conventional education—or mere informational and functional development—of the ego-"I" itself, but it is, rather, the actually ego-transcending re-education of the total human person (or the intrinsic and total psycho-physical "un-learning" of ego-"I" itself), which re-education (or root-education) intrinsically, always priorly, tacitly, and constantly (or always presently) "locates" and knows intrinsic egolessness at the root of attention itself and of awareness itself.

"Zero-point" education is the intensive and constant whole bodily (or total psycho-physical) life-process of intrinsically, always priorly, tacitly, and constantly (or always presently) "locating" and knowing intrinsic egolessness (or "zero-point" consciousness) at the root of attention itself and of awareness itself and (on that constant, tacit basis) constantly (or always presently) apprehending the self-evident prior unity of the world (and of even all that arises to attention itself).

"Zero-point" education and the tacit awakening of "zero-point" consciousness is the process and the event of tacit moment to moment root-understanding of the Reality-Condition of conditionally arising experience.

"Zero-point" education tacitly establishes the priority (or intrinsic root-primacy) of "zero-point" consciousness, which intrinsically demonstrates itself as "zero-point" understanding and "zero-point" living (which always actively demonstrates all of the life-transformative implications of "zero-point" consciousness and "zero-point" understanding).

"Zero-point" understanding (or root-Wisdom) is this: No matter what arises, one is never a "self", or a mode of separate identity (or ego-"I")—but one Is-only the Intrinsically egoless Mere Witness and the Eternal Context and Substance of conditionally evident, always temporary, mutually dependent, indivisibly seamless, and Perfectly non-necessary mere patterns of cause-and-effect.

3.

The "zero-point" is (itself) the root of consciousness, the source-point of psycho-physical awareness, the arising-place of perception and conception, prior to ego-"I" (or separate-"self"-identity), prior to the world, prior to "objects" and "others", prior to attention, prior to all the "things" of attention, prior to all divisions, prior to divisibility itself, prior to all modes of separate identity and categorical "otherness", and, altogether, prior to all "difference".

The "zero-point" is the native position—or "zero-state" position—of all conditionally arising experience.

The "zero-point" is the native state of no-"self" and no-"not-self"—no-ego-"I", no-"other", no-"object", no-mind, no-thought, no-theories, no-explanations, no-belief, no-myths, no-histories, no-"God"-ideas, no-"Deity", no-religion, no-"tribe", no-personal-or-collective-identity, no physically-based assumptions, no mentally-based or metaphysically-based assumptions, no-body, no-world, no-time, no-space, no-separateness, no-dilemma, no-problem, no-seeking, no-method, no-answer, no-fear, no-sorrow, no-anger, and no-"difference".

The "zero-point" is the native position, the prior state, the always in-place interface wherein and whereof all conditional awareness is first happening at attention itself.

The "zero-point" is the egoless existence-circumstance of essential and self-evident being—the "point-of-view"-less "place" of the Un-mediated Self-Apprehension (or Self-Apperception) of the Native, Intrinsically egoless, Perfectly Non-separate, Indivisible, Acausally all-and-All-Pervading, and Self-Evidently Divine Self-Nature, Self-Condition, and Self-State of Reality Itself.

To be at the intrinsically egoless "zero-point" of existence is to Be At and As the Native State of Reality Itself.

To Be As Reality Itself Is to Be nobody, and to have nothing, and to know nothing.

To (Thus) Be nobody is to exist and live as no-"self" (or egolessness itself).

To (Thus) Be (and live) as one who has (or "owns") nothing is to be free of all divisive, negative, and harmful (or "other"-threatening) association with the body itself, and with the "things" of this world, and with the world itself.

To (Thus) Be (and live) as one who knows nothing is to be free of all presumptuousness, all mere "belief", all that presumes or makes a "difference", all that would separate "self" from "not-self", all that would dissociate from the "other", and all that is prejudiced against surrender to the native (or always already self-evident) state of intrinsic egolessness and the positively active participatory disposition of prior unity with all-and-All.

4.

The global culture of universal cooperation—and the Global Cooperative Forum itself—necessarily requires a global process of universal "zero-point" education for all.

The global cooperative order (and the Global Cooperative Forum) of everybody-all-at-once, based (as all of that must be) on prior unity, necessarily requires a global "zero-point" culture of life-education based on the essential life-practice of intrinsic and life-active egolessness—or else the very idea of prior unity will be merely a political and social ideal (or even an absurd prescription for an ego-based would-be "utopia") that no one (except the egoless few) knows (or even can know) to be self-evidently the case and that few will even accept as a necessity and as a globally active process and event.

The mere "ideal" of prior unity is (itself) merely a convention of the ego-mind.

It is, therefore, impossible to implement actual participatory prior unity on a global scale, unless the universal process of "zero-point" education (and, thus, the universal establishing of "zero-point" consciousness and "zero-point" understanding) coincidently (or thereupon) establishes an authentic (or "zero-point"-transformed) life-basis for a global culture of "zero-point" living, constantly and intrinsically self-governed in the mode of principled active cooperation—or a culture of human life based (everywhere and systematically) on the universal apprehension, on the part of every one (and all), of prior unity as the self-evident state and pattern of the world (and of all that arises to attention itself).

Therefore, it is necessary for the totality of humankind not only to establish and universally activate a true Global Cooperative Forum, but, also and coincidently, a universal institution of "zero-point" education for each and every one (and all) of humankind.

XIX.

Right Life Transcends
The Three Great Myths
of Human ego-Culture

1.

The world-mummery of human ego-culture survives via the perpetration and the perpetuation of three great (or principal) myths.

The first great myth of human ego-culture is the myth (or the intrinsically false idea) of separate "self" (or ego-"I" itself)—which is the humanly-fabricated idea that the living human experiential being is rooted in an independent and definable "<u>subjective</u>" consciousness (or "inner self", or "mind", or "psyche", or "soul", or "embodied entity", or "located being", or, in one manner or another, metaphysically-existing "point of view").

The second great myth of human ego-culture is the myth (or the intrinsically false idea) of separate world (or of the universe, or the cosmic domain, as "not-self")—which is the humanly-fabricated idea that the totality of everything experienced by the living human being is "<u>objectively</u>" existing (independent, outside, and in relation to the "internal self", or the separate and independent "embodied point of view").

The third great myth of human ego-culture is the myth (or the intrinsically false idea) of separate "Creator-God" (or of the Divine, or the Source and Support and Ultimate Destiny of all-and-All, as a separately defined "Deity")— which is the humanly-fabricated idea that both "self" (or ego-"I") and "not-self" (or the world-totality) are intrinsically related to and dependent upon an "Absolute Other" that is neither "self" nor "not-self", but which is as an "other" to both the "subjectively" apparent and the "objectively" apparent conditions of human experience, and which is to be referred to by symbolic "Names", as well as by conventional (but "Absolutized") pronouns (such as "He" or "She").

Based upon the humanly-projected (and all-and-All-defining) coincidence of these three great myths (or intrinsically false, and all-and-All-limiting, ideas), human cultures are everywhere "tribalized" (and human individuals are everywhere "tribally" culture-bound), and, thus, functionally and entirely subordinated to the ego-based mind that defines and divides Reality Itself (or What Always Priorly and Indivisibly Is) via and into the constructs (or the human false-idea-fabrications) of "self", "not-self", and "Absolute Other".

2.

The globally-extended totality of present-day human cultures is based upon the pervasive enforcement of the three great human "tribal" myths of "self", "not-self", and "Absolute Other".

That globally-"tribalized" web of human acculturation has produced a global collective of ego-cultures—or a complex world-mummery of "self"-deluded, "self"-divided, "self"-indulgent, world-suffering, and "Other"-haunted ego-culture.

The "tribalization" of the human mind (and, thus and thereby, of human life as a whole) is made and done by means of the universal enforcement of the three great myths as root-ideas, or as the root-constructs of "tribally"-required consciousness (both collective and individual).

Therefore, all human beings are now living as "tribally"-bound political, social, and cultural "subjects", of whom it is required (by many modes of "official" pattern-enforcement) that they (each and all) actively subscribe to the three great myths—or universally propagandized false and all-and-All-limiting ideas—of human ego-culture.

3.

It has happened that, in the difficult (and always freedom-seeking) course of the history of human ego-culture, the third of the three great (and "tribally"-enforced) myths has become vulnerable to human doubt, question, and testing.

Thus, the traditionally upheld "tribal" myth (or intrinsically false idea) of the separate and Absolute "Deity" (or "Creator-God", or "Absolute Other") has, for many human individuals and collectives, become either totally unacceptable or (at least) ambiguous (and, certainly, politically, socially, and culturally optional) as a category of "belief" and "knowledge".

What I propose to all-and-All is that all three of the traditionally upheld "tribal" myths (or intrinsically and co-equally false ideas) be equally and simultaneously subjected to human doubt, question, and testing.

4.

If all three of the great myths (or intrinsically false ideas) of human ego-culture are equally and simultaneously inspected (and rigorously doubted, questioned, and tested), not only will all three of those great myths prove to be intrinsically and utterly false and illusory, but the globally-extended world-mummery of human ego-culture will, as a totality, lose its conceptual foundation, its "internal" urge and necessity, and its ability to captivate and control humankind—and, as a consequence, the disastrously suffered (and, now, and forever hereafter, obsolete) world-mummery of human ego-culture will disintegrate and pass away.

In the necessary world-event of the disintegration and the passing away of global human ego-culture, an entirely new (and globally cooperative) human world-culture (and pattern of human world-order) must emerge.

The new (and globally cooperative) human world-culture and human world-order—which must even immediately and now emerge and forever hereafter perpetuate itself—is the globally-extended human world-culture and human world-order of intrinsically egoless right-life-participation in the Perfectly Subjective (or Intrinsically egoless, all-and-All-Including, and all-and-All-Transcending) Self-Nature, Self-Condition, and Self-State of Reality Itself.

5.

The living human experiential being is a conditionally evident pattern-only—rather than an independent "entity" with a separate and eternal metaphysical "self-center".

Therefore, the living human experiential being is (within its conditionally apparent context) intrinsically non-separate—or intrinsically, and dependently, and indivisibly of a prior unity and whole.

As such, the living human experiential being is, at-root, intrinsically and self-evidently egoless—or intrinsically and thoroughly without any conditionally defining "central" (or underlying) root-characteristic.

The living human experiential being is not centered (or rooted) in an independent (or non-dependent) "inner self", "mind", "psyche", "soul", "embodiment", "location", or "point of view".

The living human experiential being (or intrinsically centerless pattern-only) is, at-root (or as is, and altogether), intrinsically (or always already) at the "zero-point" (or of the Intrinsic Non-"difference" Characteristic) of the Perfectly Subjective Self-Nature, Self-Condition, and Self-State of Reality Itself (Which Is Always Already all-and-All-At-Once).

The living human "zero-point"-being (or intrinsically egoless pattern) is a non-separate and psycho-physically participatory pattern-process within the total system, or universally-extended unity of pattern-process, of all-and-All that conditionally (and universally coincidently) arises.

The coincidence between the living total psycho-physical (or whole-bodily-participatory) "zero-point" human being and the universal totality of all-and-All that conditionally arises is an intrinsically seamless (or indivisible) pattern-process (and always prior unity) of conditionally arising and mutually dependent cause-and-effect conditions.

The universal totality (and always prior unity) of all-and-All of conditionally arising appearances, including all "zero-point" human beings, is intrinsically (or always already) at and of the One, and Indivisible, and Perfectly Subjective (or Perfectly Non-"objective" and Non-"different") Self-Nature, Self-Condition, and Self-State of Reality Itself—and, thus, intrinsically (or always already) standing prior to mind (or "inner subjectivity") itself and (therefore) standing prior to all ideas, including "Deity"-myths, ideas of "Absolute Other", and all use of "Deity"-referencing (and "Deity-objectifying") pronouns (such as "He" or "She").

The Self-Nature, Self-Condition, and Self-State of Reality Itself Is (Intrinsically, or Always Already) egoless—or Perfectly Subjective, Perfectly Non-separate, Perfectly Non-"different", Perfectly all-and-All-Including, Perfectly all-and-All-Transcending, Perfectly Indivisible, Perfectly Acausal, and (Altogether) Intrinsically, Perfectly, and Self-Evidently Divine.

Reality Itself Is the Perfectly Subjective (and Universally Self-Evident) "Zero-Point" of all-and-All that conditionally arises.

Right-life-participation in the Perfectly Subjective Self-Nature, Self-Condition, and Self-State is whole bodily (or total psycho-physical) "zero-point"-participation in the indivisible "zero-point" pattern-process of all-and-All that conditionally arises—thus and thereby intrinsically and constantly transcending the three great myths (or intrinsically false ideas) of human ego-culture.

Right life, thus egolessly and whole bodily participatory, is the intrinsically non-"tribalized", intrinsically mummery-free, and intrinsically and altogether free basis for the new human world-culture—or the Reality-Based integrated system and always prior unity of global cooperative order—I (now, and forever hereafter) propose to all of humankind.

XX.

The Global Celebration of Light-In-Everybody

The social circumstance for human beings throughout the world is becoming more and more globalized (or pluralistic) everywhere. Therefore, social and political problems are tending to arise because of the fact that people who are associated with different religious, cultural, ethnic, and racial traditions live in direct proximity to each other. In that situation, each self-defined group wants to ensure not only that its characteristic culture and customs can be freely practiced, but that the group should be distinctly and independently politically represented, and culturally visible (and would-be even dominant), and, altogether, a functioning part of the existing power-structure.

The global result of the "everybody-one-at-a-time" effort to constitute a pluralistic social and political culture is a world-chaos of intrinsically disunited, separate, separative, and competitive factions—and such human chaos inevitably produces a world-mummery of ego-based humankind, perpetually dramatizing the adolescent characteristics of disunity, disrespect, disobedience, and deceit.

The Global Cooperative Forum I have proposed is, altogether, a corrective address to the now globalized (and thoroughly pluralistic) situation of human cultures. In addition to the overall approach of establishing a Global Cooperative Forum, there are particular global cultural initiatives that can be proposed as an effective antidote to the socially, culturally, politically, economically, and environmentally negative results and effects of the world-mummery of non-unity. One such initiative would be to create a period of celebration that is truly globally observed—and thus observed by everybody-all-at-once.

It would be useful for there to be a global public celebration that is about fundamental social unity, positiveness, and cooperation—without being exclusively associated with any particular existing tradition or traditions. Such a period of celebration could be named (in every language) "Light-in-Everybody". The possible period of such celebration could (for the sake of fullest preparation, elaboration, and participation) last for a full month—and the possible appropriate time for such a period of celebration could be the end of the calendar year (because many traditional celebrations are already associated with that time of year).

This celebration would be about acknowledging the universally tacitly understood characteristic of "light" (or non-separate "radiance" of positive being) in everybody one knows and meets. People from particular religious and cultural traditions would be free to use the essential symbols and meaning-elements of their own traditions in their participation in this celebration—while, nevertheless, openly and entirely preserving the universal and non-separatist feeling of the celebration in the pluralistic social (and secular) domain. A celebration by this name (and with this universal meaning) would include everybody and exclude no one—and it would not be fashioned (in any exclusive sense) in the direction of one or another kind of religious or other tradition.

Although it would, in principle, be a secular celebration—in that it would not be identified with any particular religious or otherwise sacred tradition or traditions—"Light-in-Everybody" could be privately (and within the cultural sphere of each and every particular tradition) observed in either a religious or a non-religious manner, as individuals choose, while everyone (each and all) always publicly, openly, and authentically actively manifests and participates in the fundamental virtues of universal social positiveness, universal inclusiveness, universal love, and the universal characteristic of "light".

A primary dimension of participating in the global celebration of "Light-in-Everybody" would be to develop all kinds of means to bring celebratory decorativeness to the daily life of cities and villages—and this could be a means of enlivening the arts everywhere throughout the world.

The celebration would be named appropriately in all the different languages of humankind—in each case, with the universal meaning "Light-in-Everybody".

In every sense, the celebration of "Light-in-Everybody" would be a fundamental public and globally socially positive (and universally socially bonding) expression of the prior unity of all of humankind—and of the intrinsic "singleness" of Everybody-All-At-Once.

XXI.

Reality-Humanity

Self-Liberated From
The Stave In The Wheels

Unless they are specifically prevented from doing so, all systems will spontaneously righten themselves. The universe is a self-organizing, self-correcting, and self-rightening process. All systems are self-organizing, self-correcting, and self-rightening—unless something interferes with the self-organizing, self-correcting, and self-rightening process. The current power-structures in the human world are actually preventing the self-organizing, self-correcting, and self-rightening process of humankind from happening.

The political, social, economic, and cultural patterning (and hierarchy of expectations and demands) of collective human life-systems is organized in the likeness (and by an extension) of the functions of the human brain and nervous system.

The human brain and nervous system is, characteristically, patterned to allow (and to seek, and to reward) a limited range of possible experiences and possible forms of knowledge—and the human brain and nervous system is also, characteristically, patterned to avoid (and to prevent, and even to punish) experiences and forms of knowledge that are not within the otherwise limited range of allowable (and, thus, seekable and rewardable) experiences and forms of knowledge.

Thus, and likewise, and by extension, all collective human political, social, economic, and cultural life-systems are (in accordance with the particular "personality profile" of the particular system in each case) strictly organized to allow (and to purpose, and to reward) only certain limited possibilities of experience and knowledge, and, otherwise, to disallow (and to restrictively prevent, and to punish) all possibilities of experience and knowledge that do not correspond to the designs of the particular case of human collectivity.

If this understanding—rather than any misunderstanding, or mere idealism—is brought to the examination of the totality of all collective human life-systems (political, social, economic, and cultural), then it is possible to re-design, re-orient, and liberate that totality (and every particular case within it) to a universal collective human life-pattern that is based upon the presumption of prior unity (and of inherent inclusiveness), and that is designed both to maximally allow (and promote, and reward) fullest right and true experience and knowledge and to disallow (and to restrictively prevent, and to punish, or, certainly, to not-reward) modes of experience and knowledge that are merely negative and, altogether, dissociated from the "Perfect Knowledge" of Reality and Truth.

The Global Cooperative Forum I propose represents an approach that is entirely different from all past or present efforts to reduce conflict and to achieve real peace. The Global Cooperative Forum I propose represents the emergence of a truly everybody-all-at-once political, social, economic, and cultural force—which will allow and enable humankind to exercise its inherent right and necessity to function as a self-organizing, self-correcting, and self-rightening global cooperative collective.

The Global Cooperative Forum I propose is not based on grandiose speeches about great principles. Nor is the Global Cooperative Forum based on each human being becoming associated with one or another well-intentioned special-interest group. Neither of those approaches is capable of accomplishing the great changes that are now (and forever hereafter) required in the human world. In fact, both of those approaches effectively prevent the self-organizing, self-correcting, and self-rightening process of humankind from emerging. That self-organizing, self-correcting, and self-rightening process must be allowed to freely function in order to reverse the disaster that is now in process. Humankind-as-a-whole—everybody-all-at-once—must be enabled to re-acquire the intrinsic ability to self-organize, self-correct, and self-righten, and thereby prevent the potential termination of human life on Earth.

The current civilization is (characteristically) secular, superficial, materialistic, "outward"-directed, and "object"-directed. The current civilization constitutes a form of propaganda that has driven humankind to the point of self-destruction. That course of self-destruction must not continue. The collective of humankind must do everything possible to prevent its own self-destruction and to re-achieve sanity.

Re-achieving sanity requires an entirely new basis for civilization. This is the "end-time" of ego-culture. The current ego-culture is wedded to the "point of view" of gross materialism—and the false philosophy of gross materialism has brought humankind to the point of cultural and social insanity. There needs to be a profoundly different and right root-understanding of Reality Itself in order for humankind-as-a-whole to be set on a right foundation and to recover its sanity.

The necessary new understanding will not come from the old civilizations. A new kind of civilization is required. This new civilization will necessarily be a cooperative order of human beings in global relationship to one another. This new civilization must be a responsible everybody-all-at-once human process, in order to effectively re-order human civilization.

At the present time, there is less and less true civilization left in the world. The truly civilizing principles are, more and more, being abandoned for the sake of the ego-mummery in which human beings are now and everywhere participating. The civilizing principles that allow human functioning to demonstrate the disposition of prior unity have already been destroyed—especially as a result of the terrible course of the twentieth century, and beginning with World War I in particular. World War I and World War II were, effectively, the self-destruction of global civilization. As a result of those two happenings, and everything associated with those happenings, the self-organizing, self-correcting, and self-rightening principle of humankind was destroyed. Now nothing but "Narcissistic" ego-culture remains, and the consequent human devastation.

The present-time human world is fragmented and stupefied, utterly misled by the grossest kind of deluded thinking about "reality". The mass populations of the world are being seduced by the absurdities of "consumerism". Human beings are, now and everywhere, entrenched in their commitment to absurd "consumer" notions about the potential of absolute "self"-satisfaction—and, otherwise, human beings are (based on their failures of "self"-satisfaction) overwhelmed by "gross realism" views that appear to sanction nihilistic despair, and even unlimited (and intrinsically meaningless) violence.

The time is dark—but people do not see the darkness. Or, if they do see the darkness, they do not have any means to do anything about the darkness, so they just go along with it. The present-time darkness is a clear sign that the inherent self-organizing, self-correcting, and self-rightening principle is being prevented from happening. Otherwise, the manifestation of the self-organizing, self-correcting, and self-rightening principle would be readily in evidence. Truly civilizing principles are the evidence of a self-organizing, self-correcting, and self-rightening free energy.

Thus, the Global Cooperative Forum I propose is a civilizing process—not at all a process of anarchy or negation.

The Global Cooperative Forum I propose is not at all a matter of billions of people participating in some kind of chaotic uprising. Rather, the Global Cooperative Forum I propose is an orderly means for representing everybody-all-at-once in a globally functioning body that has the power to achieve positive actual results.

No positively effective global approach is presently happening in the common world. There is, in global terms, only a persistent inertia of sameness, that is very effectively preventing the self-organizing, self-correcting, and self-rightening process of humankind from happening. Thus, only the status quo is being reliably maintained—and that status quo is leading toward the potential of globally terminal destruction.

The human world is now in a state of virtually infinite fragmentation, in which the individual feels powerless and is just thinking of himself or herself as some kind of "consumer"-ego to be titillated and satisfied, and perhaps to be given a voice, a soap box, here and there. The global state of humankind is absurd and dark. Therefore, this darkest of times requires an immense force of self-correction and self-rightening, an immense emergence of the self-organizing principle that is inherent in humankind as a system of life. Nevertheless, and in spite of this necessity, nothing of the globally rightening kind is going on. Everybody is asleep. People do not truly realize the scale of the disaster that is happening. Furthermore, people do not realize that humankind is <u>actively doing</u> this disaster—and, therefore, that humankind can also choose to <u>stop</u> doing the disaster, and, altogether, humankind can choose (collectively) to re-organize, self-correct, and truly righten the entire system of global humankind.

Nothing can possibly stop the disaster except the force of the whole, the integrity of the whole. That is the only happening that will righten (and en-lighten) the darkness of the human world.

The force of totality (or the integrated whole) is now unable to function. If a long pole (or a barrel stave) were forced between the spokes of the wheels of a rolling vehicle, the vehicle would lurch to a halt. Just so, the integrity of the whole and totality of humankind—which is inherently self-organizing, self-correcting, and self-rightening—has become inert, motionless, and, altogether, rigidified and repetitive, such that the inherent power and tendency of the whole and totality of humankind to self-organize, self-correct, and self-righten itself is not being allowed and enabled to self-manifest. Therefore, humankind (as a global totality, and as a systematically integrated whole) must re-assert and re-enact its intrinsic disposition to require and enable its own self-rightness.

Previous to the advent of modern communications, the human world was a collection of (geographically, and otherwise) disconnected nations (or separate, and, essentially, "tribal", political, social, economic, and cultural entities). However, as soon as the process of industrialization produced communications processes that instantly linked the entire human world together, it became necessary for humankind to function as a whole. Nevertheless, rather than humankind functioning as a whole, all the "old-days" factions—nation-states, regionally and culturally limited religions, and power groups of one kind or another—have continued to aggressively confront one another, all vying for absolute power. That ongoing confrontation is what is actively preventing the force of the whole from emerging. The ongoing confrontation between separate (and, altogether, separative) powers and interests is the "stave in the wheels" of humankind.

Humankind must begin to function as a totality, without the factionalizing associations with competing nation-states, competing culture-groups, competing religions, competing political and economic agendas, and so forth. The vested interests that are keeping the "old days" of human dis-unity intact are what must be bypassed, and replaced by the self-organizing, self-correcting, and self-rightening process—and, on that basis, the priorly unified voice—of humankind-as-a-whole. The Global Cooperative Forum I am proposing is the inherent self-organizing, self-correcting, and self-rightening process of humankind, given a vehicle in which and by which to be effective.

The developing course of industrialization and modernization has not led to the unification of humankind—because the emergence of humankind as an inherently interconnected global totality is what is being prevented by the institutionalization of the "old factions" of separateness. That institutionalization of separateness is how the ancient situation of conflict is kept in place. The "old factions" are all "tribal" entities, from a time in the past when human intercommunication was splintered by the geographical separation of different territories. In the "old days", the "tribal" entities of nation-states and religions were geographically separated from one another. Now, in the age of global intercommunication, these "tribal" voices have emerged as the big political and religious powers, and their interest is to maintain their own absolute power—even by expanding beyond their traditional "territories", and into a globalized domain of exclusive (and even totalitarian) power. The only means by which the separate "old powers" can maintain their power is to persistently re-assert the fragmentation of the world—because they, themselves, came into being in times when the world was not functioning as a whole, but when (rather) there was a scattering (or diaspora) of humankind all over the Earth. Out of that diaspora, separate "tribes" and nation-states—and the separate religions associated with those "tribes" and nation-states—emerged. However, as soon as modern communications appeared, the formerly separate "tribes", nation-states, and religions found themselves, all of a sudden, to be inhabiting the single territory of the one and same and only world.

In the book *The Three Christs of Ypsilanti*, by Milton Rokeach,* there is an instructive (and archetypally significant) account of an actual happening in a psychiatric institution, illustrating what occurs when presumed human "absolutes" confront each other in the same "territory". Milton Rokeach, a social psychologist and personality theorist, held regular group meetings with three male psychiatric patients, each of whom believed he was "Jesus Christ". It was a remarkable demonstration of how ego-based (and "self"-absolutizing) human beings characteristically confront one another, react to one another, deny one another's existence, and work power-efforts relative to one another.

As Milton Rokeach relates, the process of these group meetings (at Michigan's Ypsilanti State Hospital, in 1959–60) did not result in the "curing" of these three "self"-deluded individuals. Just so, the "dialogue" (so to speak) between all the separate power-entities in the world—"tribal", national, or religious—never becomes the wholeness of humankind. No such "dialogue" can ever become the wholeness of humankind—because all of these "tribal", national, and religious forms originated in a fragmented world of dis-unity, and they always seek to re-assert the absoluteness of their own inherently separate (and willfully separative) identities.

With the advent of global intercommunication, the existing power-forces in the world have become something like the three "Christs" of Ypsilanti. All of the presumed (and competing) human "absolutes" are now in the same room with one another—and they are never going to straighten out their relationships with one another, because their thinking is persistently and willfully based on the presumption of separateness, and their action/reaction engagements with

---

* Milton Rokeach, *The Three Christs of Ypsilanti: A Psychological Study* (New York: Columbia University Press, 1964).

one another are always dramatizations of the effort to be and do "self"-absoluteness, "self"-separativeness, and the willful domination of the "other". Indeed, even if humankind—as a mass of nearly eight billion separate <u>egos</u>—got in the same room together, they would never manifest the self-organizing, self-correcting, and self-rightening process that would enable humankind to become unified as a whole. Separateness cannot manifest wholeness. Only prior unity can manifest wholeness.

The Global Cooperative Forum I propose is an active circumstance of means wherein separateness is inherently not the case—and in which neither separateness nor separativeness is presumed, or, otherwise, allowed to control the character, the purpose, or the results of the meeting. The Global Cooperative Forum I propose is not a context in which separate "anythings" come together and attempt to become unified. Rather, the Global Cooperative Forum I propose is the place of function where unity is prior, where prior unity is persistently presumed, and where persistently presumed prior unity is enforced.

Prior unity is not about billions of separate egos. Nor is prior unity about any particular collection of "big" egos. Prior unity is not about "three Christs" in the same room—or separate bodies of people, each from their own fragment of the world, who come together and are supposed to make a unity out of the persistently presumed dis-unity. Egos will never unify the world. Only egolessness (or <u>inherent</u> non-separateness) is the principle of <u>prior</u> unity.

The Global Cooperative Forum I propose is a context in which the inherent principle of prior unity exercises itself, with the ability to make things happen—an ability that cannot be crushed by the "old" powers (whether political, social, or religious). In the Global Cooperative Forum I propose, all the "old" powers must join the whole—washing their "flags", dropping their "placards", leaving behind their "name-tags", and simply functioning as part of the prior unity of humankind-as-a-whole.

No bringing of the "three Christs" into the same room will ever work—because the "three Christs" principle is based on separateness, dis-unity, and "tribal" representation. "Tribes" are not "it". "Tribes" are what must be out-grown.

No conversation between separate powers can possibly righten anything. Therefore, no principle of bringing separate "anythings" into the same room is going to make the world right. The self-organizing, self-correcting, and self-rightening force of the priorly unified whole is the only means by which the world and humankind can be made right.

Humankind must now be in the position of presumed prior unity—but humankind will not realize its inherent prior unity by exercising the voices that are already separate. There must be a bypassing of the voices that are already separate—whether they are "big" voices or "little" voices. It is the everybody-all-at-once voice that must now speak and act. This understanding of what must occur is very different from all other efforts that are currently being pursued for the sake of establishing peace in the world.

Many people are disturbed by how things are in the world of the present time—but they do not have an understanding of what to do about it, because they do not understand how systems work, how the priorly unified force of humankind must function, and how egoity undermines all of that. It is commonly presumed that speaking virtuously about great principles is sufficient to bring about the unity of humankind. However, such virtuous speaking is exactly how unity does not come about.

The "three Christs" in the same room never becomes a unity, nor do they become relieved of their illusions. Rather, they simply persist in exercising their differences—because each one presumes to be an inviolable "absolute". Such is the nature of egos. Such is the nature of "tribes". Such is the nature of nation-states. Such is the nature of provincially-arising (and inherently "tribal" and non-universal) religions. Such is the nature of everything that presumes itself to be separate. The Global Cooperative Forum I propose is about no presumption of separateness whatsoever. The Global Cooperative Forum I propose is about the presumption of prior unity and no-"difference". Thus, the Global Cooperative Forum I propose is the context within which the self-organizing, self-correcting, and self-rightening force of humankind (as a whole) can be exercised.

The self-organizing, self-correcting, and self-rightening process is not a process that is now happening on Earth. Thus, the Global Cooperative Forum I propose represents a process that is not like anything that is already happening. Everything that is already happening is a form of the separate "Christs" confronting each other in the same room. Everything and everyone is now tending to function on that repetitively absurd principle. That mummery of absurdity is the enterprise wherein and whereby human egos imagine they can make things right.

Even the most seriously concerned of people make use of the method of creating "tribal" councils in which everyone gives their speeches. To imagine that this method will result in the rightening of humankind is a fantasy. Indeed, it is worse than a fantasy, because human beings are thereby making themselves dependent on the powers of separateness and separativeness in the already failed world. People trust that their leaders are going to do something about what is wrong in the world, but the leaders are not in a position to do anything fundamental about what is wrong. All the leaders can do is enforce the already-presumed separateness between "tribal" groups and continue the conflicts between those groups. There must be the immediate emergence of the power of non-separateness—through a forum in which

people can participate without "name-tags", "slogans", "placards", or "tribal" interests (whether national, religious, or
local), and simply take charge of the total and comprehensive world-process of human beings. In effect, global industrialization and global intercommunication must now (and
forever hereafter) be demonstrated by globally-presumed
prior unity, non-"difference", and non-separativeness.

The current "tribal" dis-unity simply cannot be allowed to
go on any longer—or humankind will self-destruct. That is
what humankind does in its dis-unity. It "objectifies" virtually
everything and everyone, tries to control virtually everything
and everyone, and (then) will destroy everything and everyone. The "objectification-game" happened long ago. The
"control-game" is already in motion. And the "destruction-
game" is now in process. At some advanced moment, not necessarily too far into the future, the destruction phase will come
to a terminal point—unless this dreadful cycle is stopped.

What creates "objectification" to begin with? The presumption of separateness. The presumption of non-unity,
ego, separate "self", separate "point of view". If you bring
"absolute points of view" together in the same room, they
will automatically create this "objectification, control, and
destruction" game.

On the other hand, there is a universe, and no "point of
view" within the universe is the universe itself. The universe
is the context of all possible "points of view". How is it possible for the universe to be a self-organizing, self-correcting,
and self-rightening process? The universe is a self-organizing,
self-correcting, and self-rightening process because the universe is not merely a "package" of countless numbers of
"points of view". Rather, the universe is a prior unity—prior
to any and every "point of view". That is the Reality-universe.

Humankind is functioning on the principle of ego—or
separate identity and separative activity. Separateness and
separativeness—or ego-"I"—is the idea of "difference". That

idea <u>inevitably</u> manifests as the process of "objectification", control, and destruction. Scientific materialism (rather than true science, or free enquiry, itself) is the "late-time" philosophy of egoity. Scientific materialism gives voice to the dark presumption of non-unity—in other words, to the presumption of "point of view". In Reality, the universe is a prior unity, prior to all "points of view". Therefore, true science simply investigates the universe that is priorly one and indivisible.

The right action of humankind is action based on the presumption of prior unity—not ego, not "tribes", not any kind of form, idea, or cultural expression that came about or emerged in times of dis-unity. Humankind, as a whole, in the Reality-universe, and as an indivisible totality that ultimately exists as an unspeakable prior unity of absoluteness—<u>that</u> is Reality-humanity.

The Global Cooperative Forum I propose is the means whereby humankind can function on the basis of prior unity. Without that means, humankind will destroy itself—in its "allegiance" to the principle of non-unity, or egoic separateness and active separativeness.

Therefore, any effort to righten the human world based on the principle of separate "points of view" is not "it". That is how to understand whether any rightening effort can be effective or not. Look at it. If it is based on the presumption (and the meeting) of separate "points of view", the paradigm of action is not right—regardless of the virtuous intentions that may inspire such meetings. There is no piecemeal approach, or "tribal" approach, that is going to work.

As a system (or a functioning mechanism), the Internet is inherently non-"tribal", inherently global. Therefore, the Internet is a force (or a potentially self-organizing, self-correcting, and self-rightening system) that can be used for right global effectiveness <u>now</u>. The Internet has arisen coincident with the emergence of previously fragmented humankind into a world scene of total inter-communicativeness.

The Internet is currently tending to be mis-used, in the "tribal" (or ego-based) manner—but it need not be mis-used. Simply as a mechanism in and of itself, the Internet stands free—prior to all factions, "tribes", and egos, and it is potentially connected to everybody-all-at-once.

For the Global Cooperative Forum (as I propose it) to function in a right and positively effective manner, there must be representatives, in the manner of a republic. Democracy is rule by "everybody", or a mass of individuals—like countless "Christs" in the same room. A republic, in contrast, is a representational mechanism, or a true self-integrated system. Democracy is everybody-one-at-a-time—but a true representative system (in the mode of a republic) is everybody-all-at-once.* The Global Cooperative Forum I propose must be truly representational, in order to be sufficiently ordered and focused to accomplish things. Billions of people in a "chat room" cannot possibly get anything done, except for the self-repeating chaos and inertia of their separate presumptions and motivations—but billions of people can be rightly represented (and made rightly and positively effective) in and by means of the systematically integrated prior order of a true globally functioning forum.

In addition, the activities of the Global Cooperative Forum I propose must be completely knowable—as they are happening—so that everybody can participate in this representational process, rather than the representatives meeting on their own (or secretly, invisibly, and without accountability to the whole of everybody-all-at-once).

There are all kinds of mechanisms required in order to make the Global Cooperative Forum (as I propose it) work

---

* In "Reality-Humanity", Adi Da refers to the right pattern of the Global Cooperative Forum as in the mode of a republic—but he is not, thereby, suggesting a future global order made up of one single political entity, or state. Rather, he is applying the term "republic" to the Global Cooperative Forum to indicate governance through a particular kind of representation—one where the representatives would not necessarily be elected by the one-person-one-vote principle, but chosen (by some commonly agreed means) based on their evident qualifications to represent the interests of humanity as a whole.

effectively, but, in such a Global Cooperative Forum, there is no separate collective (and no individual) that is senior to the whole. The whole must be (and, inherently, always already is) senior to the parts. In the current human world, the parts are all self-presumed "absolutes"—each (variously) trying either to fulfill itself separately or else to achieve unity with all the "others". That "paradigm of parts" cannot work. Only the paradigm of prior unity is right and true—and always fit to work. When the parts presume themselves to be senior to the whole, the inherent unity of all becomes subordinate to every kind of separate and separative inclination—but when the whole is presumed to be senior to the parts, prior unity becomes the understanding of every one, and all.

In the Global Cooperative Forum I propose, all of the parts must consistently relinquish their "absoluteness" to the whole, and the whole must be globally and thoroughly accepted as the senior principle to which all parts are inherently (but always positively) subordinate. Only in that case is it possible to effectively address urgent issues. Nevertheless, the Global Cooperative Forum I propose cannot accomplish results merely by a central authority issuing verbal pronouncements to a mass of separate and separative (and, thus, perpetually insubordinate) listeners. The Global Cooperative Forum I propose will accomplish results because there are more than seven and a half billion (and always more) human beings always standing as one—and always ready to act on a unified and principled cooperative basis. The prior unity of a consistently principled global cooperative order of humankind, functioning twenty-four hours of every day to positively effectively address all the problems and issues shared by all, will consistently disallow the forces of "tribal" and separative inclination to engineer conflicts and (thus and thereby) to sidestep the issues humankind must address if it is going to survive.

In the Global Cooperative Forum I propose, absolute seriousness is required of everyone, and all. Such seriousness requires the relinquishment of the ego's dominance and the ego's absoluteness. Such seriousness requires consistently principled participation in the self-organizing, self-correcting, and self-rightening process of humankind as a priorly indivisible unity in which there are no separate "absolutes" at all, and in which all presumed-to-be-separate-"anythings" relinquish their "tribal" presumptions.

The ego characteristically presumes "absoluteness" to be true of everything in which it is involved. All such presumed "absoluteness" is an illusion—but it is an illusion that has controlled the world to the point where the world is now in the phase of destruction. The destruction-phase can only be stopped by relinquishing the presumption of separateness and the activity of separativeness, and by establishing the functioning process based on prior unity, and by enabling everybody-all-at-once to participate in that process fully, freely, and positively.

What is at the end is the same as whatever is at the beginning. If you begin with separateness, the end is dark. If you begin with prior unity, all that emerges is light.

Humankind-as-a-whole does not have a "label"—whether "tribal", national, religious, or of whatever kind. In some sense, humankind-as-a-whole does not even have a history, and exists in present-time only. Humankind-as-a-whole has no axe to grind and no stave to force into the spokes of its own wheels. Humankind-as-a-whole exists in Reality, not in time—but humankind-as-a-whole activates itself in the context of time and space, in a self-organizing, self-correcting, self-rightening manner (if allowed to do so, and if it presumes its own inherent right and ability to do so).

It is not in the interest of anyone for there to be the destruction of the possibility of human life. Therefore, it is not in the interest of anyone for any "tribal" faction of whatever nature to "win". Indeed, it is not in the interest of anyone for any "tribal" factions to be at war with one another. Separate-"anythings"-seeking-unity is the principle of falseness. Separateness cannot achieve unity. Unity is a prior condition that must enforce itself. If this is clearly understood, then it will become obvious what must be done, and what must not be done (or allowed to continue), in any particular circumstance.

The persistence of "tribal" conflicts must not be merely tolerated, as if it is just "the way it is". It does not have to be "the way it is". If the mode of "tribal" conflict is merely allowed to persist, it will destroy everybody.

Humankind must organize itself. No "one" can organize it. Humankind must, as a whole, animate the self-organizing force that is inherent in all integrated systems. The self-organizing, self-correcting, and self-rightening force inherent in humankind as an indivisible whole—and not any particular individual or group of individuals—is what must emerge as the Global Cooperative Forum I am proposing to all.

Humankind-as-a-whole does not, at the present time, presume that it has the power to change the world-situation. Human beings are tending to be distracted by all kinds of stimuli that encourage the continuance of the status quo. Therefore, the usual "organizing" of separate "anythings" is what will tend to happen. However, the attempt to "organize" countless "points of view" is not "it". What is required is the emergence of the universally representative force that transcends "point of view", and that self-organizes, self-corrects, and self-rightens the intrinsically indivisible whole of everything and everyone. The Global Cooperative Forum I am proposing to all is the tangible active manifestation of the necessary, and universally representative, and effectively ego-less force of globally self-integrated humankind. My description of that necessary force may (in and of itself) sound like some kind of a metaphysical or abstract principle—but it is not merely a metaphysical or abstract principle. It is an actual force of happening that will necessarily, and inevitably, and fully tangibly and actively emerge—if the "stave" is "taken out of the spokes of the wheels".

In the current world, everything and everyone is being controlled by the pre-industrial and pre-global "tribalization" of humankind. "Tribalization" is persisting in the form in which it existed previous to the Industrial Revolution. Culturally, humankind is still locked in that condition—even though industrialization and modernization, including the advent of the Internet, have happened.

In the late nineteenth century, state-of-the-art communication was the telegraph. Before the telegraph, it took days, weeks, even months, to get information from one place to another—so people could freely carry on, without knowing what was happening on the other side of the planet. As soon as there was the telegraph, there was virtually instant knowledge of what was happening on the other side. And, immediately, the telegraph became the means for widespread falseness of communication. As soon as each side in a conflict could know (in "real time") what the other was thinking, saying, and doing, then false communications—in other words, communications that would mislead one's enemies about what one was thinking, saying, and doing—began to emerge as a basic aspect of modern communications. The strategy was to represent oneself as seeming to think, say, and do what one was not actually thinking, saying, and doing. As a result, the now-complex pattern of global communication, including the Internet, is, to a large degree, based on misinformation—or intentionally false and intentionally misleading communication that (for the sake of some kind of advantage to the separate communicator) hides what is actually being thought, said, and done.

At the present time, the Internet is by no means functioning as a unifying principle. Rather, the Internet is, to a significant extent, functioning in exactly the opposite manner—just like the rest of the world. The Internet is, to a significant extent, functioning as a super-version of the telegraph that emerged in the nineteenth century, where people very quickly got the notion of false representation as a political, social, economic, and cultural strategy.

Therefore, it is not to be presumed that the manner in which the Internet is characteristically used in current time is, itself, right. However, the systematic mechanism (or inherently self-organizing, self-correcting, and self-rightening system) of the Internet obviously <u>can</u> be used altogether rightly and positively.

In the present world-situation, there are nearly eight billion human individuals struggling to survive. Those billions of individuals attempt to shore up their survivability by becoming associated with groups of various kinds—small "tribal" groups, larger national groups, traditional religious groups, and so forth. Membership in such collectives is naively presumed to enhance the survivability of the separate individuals. That is why people become associated with such groups. Such association relieves people of a certain anxiety—and people also like to imagine that such association relieves them of the responsibility for right action.

The world is a madhouse—a mummery of egos, full of illusions.

Nevertheless, the potential of sanity is always priorly the case.

<u>Now</u> sanity must come to the front.

Human beings must <u>now</u> presume to act and live in the inherently sane manner of prior unity—and of the Indivisible Prior Truth That <u>Is</u> Reality Itself.

XXII.

No Enemies

The pattern of world politics that has been dramatized with increasing intensity over time—and with the most devastating effects in the twentieth century, with the two devastating world wars and all the other wars right up to the present day—is based on the idea and the pattern of polar opposition. Therefore, the common political method is to have opposites either confront one another or (otherwise) try to work out some kind of a deal with one another.

As Abraham Lincoln said, "A house divided against itself cannot stand." If the world-system is based on opposites, it will inevitably self-destruct—by creating chaos along the lines of division (or mutual opposition).

There have been (and, no doubt, will continue to be) many efforts to create some kind of global resolution (or world peace) by bringing opposites together. But any such effort is inevitably bound to fail. Such an effort cannot succeed. It is simply not possible, in the "physics" of human affairs, for such an approach to succeed.

Unity cannot be achieved by combining opposites. Unity is the <u>prior</u> condition, the condition that is always already the case. Prior unity makes all opposites obsolete. Therefore, it is prior unity that must be enacted, rather than any continuation of the pattern of oppositions.

The world-situation has now developed to the point that there is nothing further to expect but the global collapse that opposition will inevitably produce. Therefore, this is the critical moment to stop the play of opposites in the domain of world politics. The play of opposites must be replaced by the politics of prior unity—through the Global Cooperative

Forum of everybody-all-at-once. Such is an absolute necessity. Otherwise, the play of polar opposites is going to become absolute destruction.

The principle of prior unity applies to all human endeavor, even to the integrity of a human body or a human personality. Unity is not the result of a play of opposites. Unity is the prior condition.

It is only when unity (or indivisibility) is the principle of life, of living, of action, that unity results. If division (or opposition) is presumed to be the case, more division will result. This is an absolute law. Once this is understood, it clarifies everything about right action and right life.

My address to all human issues—necessarily including what I am saying about world politics—is based on this fundamental principle: Reality Itself is a prior unity. Reality Itself is indivisible and egoless. Therefore, life must be lived in accordance with that Self-Nature of Reality Itself.

This absolute principle is fundamental to all resolution of human problems. In Gandhi's language, it is a "soul-force", or "truth-force", as he understood it.* That must be the force behind all political effort—the force of prior unity. The principle of prior unity determines a course of action that is (necessarily) inclusive of everybody-all-at-once. What is required is not a search for unity. Rather, what is required is the enacting of the power of prior unity. That is the principle. And it must be the governing principle of political action.

How should humankind deal with the world-situation? By enacting the principle of prior unity. And an instrument is required in order to do that. That instrument is the Global Cooperative Forum. The Global Cooperative Forum must make obsolete all play-of-opposition in the world, all nation-state conflicts, all effort to size up great units of nation-states over against other such units, in the attempt to achieve victory

---

* Gandhi's term was "satyagraha", often translated as "soul-force" or "truth-force", indicating Gandhi's insistence that the power of truth can (and should) be used as a non-violent means to effect change.

over one another—one religion over another religion, one nation-state (or group of nation-states) over another nation-state (or group of nation-states), and so forth.

All of this effort to defeat the presumed opponent is insanity. Humankind cannot afford to go on with this. Humankind must stop this.

This is the decisive moment in human history to stop this, because such insanity cannot go on without total devastation being the result. Therefore, there truly is no choice.

Those who hear what I have to say about this will understand: There must be an active embrace of this understanding at every level of human life, including every matter associated with global politics and environmental issues. Everything at the human scale must be addressed on the basis of enacting the principle of prior unity, through instruments that are inclusive of everybody-all-at-once. It is essentially a matter of putting the Truth-principle (or Reality-principle) of prior unity into action. And an instrument is needed to do that—not just words.

It is not a matter of bringing together collectives of different groups—such as governmental organizations and non-governmental organizations—so that they can each have their voice, thereby playing out the chaos of oppositions. There is no time to be doing any such thing. There must be a different instrument—and everybody-all-at-once must volunteer for it and become active within it.

Humankind must wake up to its inherent and intrinsic unity as a whole, and not play on any differences whatsoever. Human beings must grasp this understanding of prior unity—and act on it, through an appropriate instrument that is altogether full of integrity and altogether right. That is the immediate necessity associated with bringing the Global Cooperative Forum into being.

Wherever action is done in opposition to whatever force or entity is considered to be the opponent, wherever there is even a strategy relative to an opponent, the effort will fail. Some kinds of changes may be brought about—but, ultimately, everything stays the same, because the principle is one of division to begin with.

Likewise, every strategy that is developed in opposition to any force whatsoever will inevitably fail. The only principle that can work politically is one in which there is no opponent and no search to defeat an opponent—and, therefore, fundamentally no struggle. Right human politics is simply about enacting—or asserting and carrying out—the principle of prior unity.

That kind of activism does not presume an opponent. It does not involve itself with self-division. Consequently, it will not fail. In contrast, whatever presumes its own self-division will fail. It will only produce more division. Therefore, the only kind of political action that can possibly achieve ultimate success is activism based on (1) the presumption of prior unity and (2) the enactment of prior unity through an appropriate instrument.

There is nobody "else". There is no opponent. The Global Cooperative Forum is a means for bypassing all oppositions, all opposites, and the entire game that plays upon there being opposites at all. There should be presumed to be no opposites, no enemies, no opponent to be defeated. There is simply the intrinsic fact of prior unity. Right politics is simply about acting on that basis.

That is what the Global Cooperative Forum must do. And that is what the form of global activism I am describing must do. That is how it must function: no enemies, no game in opposition, and (therefore) no strategy in relation to a presumed opponent—none.

That is the profundity at the root of such activism—the intensive presumption of non-separateness, of prior unity, of no opponent, of no self-division. That is the only right and effective strategy. It is not a goal-seeking strategy. It is a matter of <u>enacting</u> a <u>prior</u> reality, rather than <u>seeking</u> a <u>different</u> reality. Such is the unique understanding that is the root of all true wisdom.

When I am speaking about politics, I am looking at it in the context of humankind-as-a-whole—not in terms of any circumstance that is negative, full of opposites, looking to achieve some kind of a victory in relation to an opposite or an opponent or an enemy. The root-presumption of not having an enemy is essential to the Global Cooperative Forum. The Global Cooperative Forum must be intrinsically all-including. And there is a discipline necessary for doing that, because people's patterning will tend to have them be expressing opposite views, different dispositions, and wanting to just sit around and talk about all of that. There should be absolutely no discussion of that kind. That has nothing to do with anything.

There is nothing but Reality Itself—the prior whole, the indivisible whole. That is the basis for all right action. All right human action must be based on this understanding.

In one of the Upanishads, it is said that wherever there is an "other", fear arises.* As soon as "difference" is presumed, as soon as separateness is presumed, as soon as an opponent is presumed, there is fear—or the disposition of separativeness, of self-protectiveness, of self-division. The <u>non</u>-presumption of an "other" is <u>the</u> essential principle that will liberate humankind. Wherever no "other" is presumed, Truth awakens.

That is the significance of the title of this book, *Not-Two Is Peace*. What I describe in this book is not merely a method for <u>seeking</u> peace. All twoness is about a search toward a goal—including the goal of peace, which idealists want to find someday. What I am proposing is not idealism. Rather, it is perfect realism—in relation to politics, and in

---

* In Radhakrishnan's translation of the *Brhadaranyaka Upanishad*, this sentence reads "Assuredly it is from a second that fear arises," where "second" is used in the sense of "other" [S. Radhakrishnan, ed., *The Principal Upanishads* (Atlantic Highlands, NJ: Humanities Press, 1992), 164].

relation to every other domain of human life. Such realism involves the intensive non-presumption of "other" and "problem". Such realism is the "not-two" presumption—thoroughly embraced, and become the basis of action. That action is already characterized by unity—not the search for unity, but the Is-ness of unity.

Such is the right basis for all human activism. Indeed, it is the basis for all right action in every domain of human life. And this understanding is how everything can be made right, now and in the future. It is the Wisdom-means that can (and must) be applied in the case of every human process. Therefore, it applies to everything—including the most inclusive of all possibilities, which is the right functioning of humankind-as-a-whole.

This is a call to everyone to be awakened to an intrinsic understanding. It is not about appealing to people as egos, or merely trying to get everybody together, with all their differences, to simply talk things out. It is not about anything like that. It is about completely bypassing all of that. All of that will fail. It is a waste of time—and there is no time to be wasted. Rather, this call to everyone is about presuming the intrinsic Truth-intuition (or Reality-intuition) in everyone, rather than appealing to people as consumer-egos or egos-in-high-places.

The principle of non-violence is an idealistic principle about how to function in relation to an opponent. What I am communicating is not that. The principle of "Not-Two Is Peace" is not a strategy in relation to an opponent. In fact, it is exactly not that. Thus, the principle of "Not-Two Is Peace" is not the principle of non-violence merely, even though it is thoroughly and intrinsically non-violent. Most fundamentally, the principle of "Not-Two Is Peace" is about not using any method that presumes to be in relation to an opponent.

All actions done in relation to an opponent—even if outwardly non-violent—are, in some sense, violent. That needs to be understood. Any struggle with an opponent is a kind of aggression, even if done through the device of non-violence. The approach of "Not-Two Is Peace" (with the Global Cooperative Forum as its instrument) is not like that. It is not an effort in relation to an opponent. It is simply everybody-all-at-once becoming self-actualizing, self-enforcing, self-governing, self-rightening, self-correcting, self-organizing, not opposing anything. It is the whole-all-at-once putting itself in order, as it will inevitably do when the obstruction that is preventing that self-organizing process from happening is removed.

Thus, it is oppositions that are preventing the self-organizing process from happening. The idea of "difference" is what is preventing humankind from self-organizing and self-correcting and self-rightening itself. That is it. The presumption of "difference", the presumption of opposites, of opponents, of necessary struggle, of seeking for unity, of winning against some force or other that is the opposite of your own—that is what is wrong.

This is the unique understanding that people must grasp. The lack of that understanding is the reason why humankind is defeating itself. That is why worthy purposes are failing. It is the presumption of "difference", the presumption of the "other", the presumption of "not yet—therefore, seeking is required".

In other words, the presumption of egoity—or the presumption of separateness and the activity of separation—is the fault that makes all human effort fail. Ego is the "difference"-maker. Ego is the separatist (or separative) disposition. Ego ultimately avoids relationship, dissociating itself from the "other". Therefore, the dissociative principle must be abandoned. It has nothing to do with peace. It has nothing to do with correcting the human situation.

All action based on the presumption of an "other" or of "difference" will inevitably fail. Such action only produces struggle, and not unity. Truly, it could be said that the entire world has engaged in its political efforts at the cost of destroying global unity. The United Nations functions on the basis of opposites or differences. It is based on bringing competitors or opponents together in one place, where they continue to be opponents and competitors in relation to one another. They sit around talking, but such talk has nothing to do with peace, with the unity and well-being of humankind-as-a-whole. Talk will never achieve peace or unity or well-being.

The Global Cooperative Forum is an intrinsically unified body representing everybody-all-at-once. Therefore, there are no differences in it. It is not about a council of nations. It is simply a working-instrument for the priorly unified totality (or whole) of humankind, and it presumes no differences.

Therefore, all "name-tags" and "placards" must be abandoned at the door. You do not bring your nation-state "labels" (or any other "labels") inside. There are no "high" persons. There are no differences. There is no status. All are servants of the whole.

This is not mere idealism. This is Reality in action. It is an absolute necessity. It always has been—but it has never been understood in the context of humankind-as-a-whole, because humankind-as-a-whole never came together before. That coming-together is only a recent happening.

Thus, in the Global Cooperative Forum, it cannot be that the different nations, the different religions, the different cultures, the different races are each having their say, trying to "angle" relative to the interests on their side. The basis for coming together must be the principle of the human totality as a prior unity—bringing no differences to the table whatsoever, but simply bringing the subjects of address that are common to all, and collectively solving those issues through action that is appropriate to whatever particular subject.

To do that, all presumptions of "difference" must be abandoned. That is the principle of the Global Cooperative Forum.

As I have already described, the principle of prior unity as a political means is not the same as the strategy of non-violent aggression in relation to an opponent. It is quite different—and that difference must be understood. What I am communicating is something new. It is not in the likeness of anything that has previously been proposed or enacted. Sympathetic associations can be seen in the history of human efforts toward peace, but the principle of prior unity is not the same as any previous principle for establishing peace. What is unique about the principle of prior unity must be thoroughly grasped and intensively applied.

XXIII.

Two Is Not-Peace

1.

The signs of chaos and insanity that may be observed in the human realm of the present day are an extension of a more fundamental disturbance—which is the ego-based nature of global human culture.

Global human culture has come to be based on consumerism—or the exploitation of the potential of human beings to experience and consume, without any discipline based on a greater principle. As a result, the current global human situation (or political, social, and cultural non-system) is lacking in fundamental integrity, and the human world is now ruled by the "all-consuming individual". This situation, and not any other, is producing the global crisis that human beings are presently facing.

The root-source of disturbance in the human realm is not a financial crisis, or the crisis of global warming and extreme weather, or the problems that arise with the migration of people to everywhere, or the breakdown of the international system in the United Nations, or the epidemic nature of disease and poverty.

The root-source of disturbance in the human realm is the (by-now-paradigmatic) presumption that human beings exist in the world merely in order to consume, to acquire, to luxuriate in conditional experience of all kinds, to exploit the possibilities of enhancing their own "self"-interests—with no other principle or countering force to which they must be accountable.

The right and true principle—to which every human individual and every collective of human individuals must be held accountable—must be identified and, systematically, globally established.

However, as a general rule, those who, to now, have been attempting to address the current world-situation are only working to restore the status quo of ego-culture and mass consumerism. Therefore, even at their best, the current world-servers are not working to righten things profoundly. Rather, they are merely working to perpetuate the ego-culture of mere world-consumerism—and, thus, like a gambler who has already lost all his or her resources, they are merely seeking to escape the immediate emergency situation in which they find themselves.

The global status quo should not—and, indeed, cannot—be restored.

An entirely new mode of human culture must be established—a global "zero-point" cooperative culture—and not the ego-based culture that is based on "tribalism" and mere individual or group consumerism.

Therefore, the principle of the systematic self-regulation of global humankind and a universal pattern of systematic accountability must be everywhere introduced and managed by humankind-as-a-whole.

2.

The Global Cooperative Forum I propose is not merely about running things better on the present basis—not at all.

The Global Cooperative Forum I propose is an entirely new mode of human political, social, and economic existence, and, most fundamentally, a new (and, fundamentally, global) mode of human culture.

The introduction of the new mode of human culture I propose is (and requires) the comprehensive global transition from ego-culture to a "zero-point" culture of ego-transcending cooperation, which is, altogether, established on the basis of a universal practice of mutual accountability, to which <u>all</u> must be accountable—<u>all</u> individuals, <u>all</u> groups, <u>all</u> units of humankind, and <u>all</u> present "tribes" (or nation-states).

Clearly, the existing global pattern of humankind, composed of competitive nation-states (or "tribal" units), is not established on the "zero-point" (or non-ego) basis, or even on the basis of a fundamental impulse to go beyond egoity.

The mutually competitive pattern of existing nation-states is rooted in the nation-based will to dominate. The competition for world-domination is the primal and only "game" of "tribalized" nation-states. That "game of tribes" has now achieved "end-game" status. Therefore, if the existing nation-states are allowed to continue playing the "game" of competition for world-domination, they will, inevitably, destroy all of human culture, even human life itself, and, indeed, even the Earth-world itself—as they have, to a large extent, already done.

Nevertheless, it is not only the "tribalized" nation-states that have created the present situation. Every human being on Earth has—both individually and collectively—created the present situation. Everyone has (both personally and collectively) gone along with the ego-"game" of universal "self"-exploitation, which has resulted in a would-be system, stopped by a "stave in its wheels".

The present ego-culture will not—and <u>cannot</u>—correct itself, because it is not rooted in a system-based and systematically enforced process of universal accountability to any principle greater than the individually and collectively separate consuming-entity.

"Tribes" are consuming-entities. Nation-states are consuming-entities. "Tribes" and nation-states and individual egos are all "units" of consumption—seeking to luxuriate absolutely in their potential to consume, and intending to dominate and enslave all others in order to generate and acquire the things they desire to consume.

Such is the mummery-world of egos here.

That world is now on the verge of self-destruction—for the very reason that it is a lawless (or philosophically false) world.

The total human realm is now based on a totally false principle that has been largely originated by Western society, especially during the past five hundred years of Western dissociation from traditional greater principles of profundity. During that origination-period in the West, the principle (and the false philosophy) of physical existence (or "incarnation")—in and of and for itself—has been glorified to the extreme. As a result, the bodily differentiated individual ego-"I" has, everywhere, become dissociated from any and every principle greater than "self".

When Western society moved away from the philosophy that is associated with the subordination of the individual (and the collective) to the Divine Reality, it set the present course of ego-culture—by installing the bodily-differentiated human individual (and the "materially"-based human collective) at the root of philosophy, and by (thus and thereby) asserting the "material" context of conditional appearances as (itself) the root-context and the root-meaning of existence.

The culture of the West, since the time of the European Renaissance,* is founded on the rise of absolutist ego-culture and the collective dissociative revolt against the traditionally philosophically proposed (and, otherwise, institutionally and "officially" proposed) Divine—or, even more basically, collectively dissociative revolt against the Unitive System of Principle Itself, the Principle of Indivisibility Itself, the Universal Principle that is always greater than and senior to the individual "unit" of experiencing-for-its-own-sake.

---

* The European Renaissance period is generally considered to have lasted from the fourteenth century to the end of the sixteenth century, beginning in Italy and later spreading to the rest of Europe.

The global culture of humankind—which has, for long, universally embraced the Western-originated non-unitive and mutually competitive ideal of individuated personal and collective consumerism—is now destroying itself, because it is based on an intrinsically false and inevitably self-destructive philosophy.

The Global Cooperative Forum I propose is the institutional core of the gathering of the totality of humankind—everybody-all-at-once, in a cooperative system of global self-management and universalized mutual accountability.

That system is intrinsically and always self-accountable to its own system-principle—the "zero-point" principle of not-two, or of intrinsic and always prior unity and universal cooperation.

That "zero-point" cooperative system always spontaneously regulates itself, corrects itself, and rightens itself.

Thus, the Global Cooperative Forum I propose is not merely another means for exercising a corrupt and self-destructive pseudo-system with a unity-denying and cooperation-opposing "stave in its wheels". That pseudo-system, which is now everywhere in place, is based on egoity and "tribalism". Therefore, that pseudo-system is not the basis for the Global Cooperative Forum I propose.

The Global Cooperative Forum I propose is a systematic restoration of intrinsic lawfulness (and true philosophy) to the global totality of humankind.

The Global Cooperative Forum I propose is not about a monolithic (and participation-suppressing) world-government.

The Global Cooperative Forum I propose is about a universally participatory global cooperative—a universally participatory re-systematization of human culture, which has the ability to self-inspect, self-correct, and self-righten its own patterns.

A right and true system of human culture is capable of constantly restoring itself only because, in such a system, the principle of accountability is universally intact.

When the principle of accountability is universally discarded—as is currently the case—the would-be system of order breaks down.

When any system breaks down, a new system must emerge—to replace it.

3.

Two is not-peace.

Two is intrinsically self-divided into egoic "self"-difference and egoic "self"-opposition, competition and confrontation, dis-unity and dis-order, egoic "self"-indulgence and egoic "self"-toxification, globally-extended chaos and war—and, altogether, universal toxicity, disease, suffering, fear, and death.

This is the quintessential moment of two—the end-time brink that requires re-birth.

This moment is the historic opening-door of human time—the necessary and unrepeatable moment for the emergence of a right and true (and accountability-based) global cooperative order, activated (from the root) by a right and true (and universally participatory) Global Cooperative Forum.

All efforts otherwise or to the contrary are (inevitably) purposed to maintain the ego-based "consumerist" status quo—or, at least, to make it seem that the status quo of "consumerist" ego-culture is persisting and "healthy". The status quo could be made to persist for even many more years— but, in that fatal meantime, what would actually be occurring would be the final and catastrophic breakdown of global system-patterns altogether, both human and non-human.

The end-time status quo is a pattern of lawlessness—or, in other words, a pattern without integrity and accountability. To persist in that pattern will, eventually and inevitably, destroy (or self-destruct) humankind and the Earth-world. Therefore, before the end-time status quo achieves terminal self-destruction, the lawless pattern of competitive ego-culture must be replaced by a cooperative global system that brings all human and natural resources into the systematic context of a single cooperative domain—a globally comprehensive system with a necessary rule of accountability that includes every one and all and everybody-all-at-once.

Therefore, human beings must now collectively, systematically, and globally re-organize themselves—rather than permit the terrible "machine" of the end-time status quo to continue. That end-time-"machine" is stealing the virtue of all of humankind, by everywhere preventing human beings from being actively responsible for themselves as a collective totality and for the Earth-domain itself as a natural pattern-totality.

The Global Cooperative Forum I propose is the one and essential new institutional necessity for the necessary new global systemization of humankind. The current pseudo-system is no longer tolerable—and it never was viable. Nevertheless, those who are currently in power have not yet become entirely inclined to deal (at root) with the signs of global systemic breakdown. Many continue to pretend, for example, that—even while the Earth is daily becoming more and more overwhelmingly polluted—there is some necessary (and action-preventing) controversy to be engaged relative to whether climate change is a reality or not (or, otherwise, humanly-caused or not). Nevertheless, the evidence is now irrefutable—the Earth is being polluted, always more and more, by human causes.

The human causes of Earth-pollution (which results in global pollution, global warming, and extreme weather) are a global projection of the politically and corporately propagandized and controlled pattern of individual "self"-indulgence in un-regulated and boundless consumerism that otherwise (by such means as toxic food and drink) pollutes the body of every seeker of the "good life" (and which everywhere results in disease, psychological extremes, unbearable stress-patterns, and every other mode of otherwise avoidable suffering and agony and casual death). Indeed, altogether, the present-time (and future-threatening) global and collective human situation is both dark and insane—a global madhouse of mutual threats, and whole nations in clans of "tribalized" power, competing with one another like rival street gangs, always "protecting" nothing more than their will to egoic "self"-indulgence and egoic "self"-glorification.

The current global and collective human drama is a world-mummery of failed ego-culture.

That world-mummery is rooted in an intrinsically false philosophy, a false root-premise—the intrinsically false philosophy (or intrinsically false root-premise) of egoity itself, or the illusory separate (and always actively separative) "unit" (or pseudo-"entity") of being. That intrinsically false philosophy largely originated in the West, first coming to the fore in the period of the European Renaissance. That false philosophy manifested as so-called "humanistic" views, which dissociated human beings from the Self-Evidently (rather than religiously-presumed) Divine Characteristic of Reality Itself and from the Intrinsic (rather than religiously-presumed)* Spirituality of egolessness, and which (altogether) glorified the ego (or the "unit-of-consumption")—both in the form of the human individual and in the form of all collectives of human association (including nation-states, and all such intrinsically "tribal", or "self"-centered, collectives).

The "humanist" movement glorified ego-based "tribalism"— rather than That to Which (intrinsically and unavoidably) all must be accountable and to Which (intrinsically and necessarily) all are always already subordinate. That to Which all are—and must actively and cooperatively be—subordinate Is Reality Itself, Which Is all-and-All, and Which Is Intrinsically

---

* In other words, "humanistic" views dissociated human beings from Reality Itself As It Is (Divine, Transcendental, and Spiritual), but did not dissociate human beings from conventional religious concepts of the Divine and of Spirituality.

egoless, Perfectly Indivisible, Perfectly Acausal, Perfectly Subjective (or Perfectly Non-"objective"), and Self-Evidently Divine.

In its conventional (and, altogether, ego-based) form, religion is entirely a form of "tribalism", a doctrine invented to grant collective cultural identity to politically and socially defined "units-of-consumption". Therefore, conventional religion is not founded on the surrendering of egoity itself to Reality Itself, or on the actual practice of living subordinate to Reality Itself. Conventional religion is not founded on the actual transcending of egoity at all. Rather, conventional religion is founded on (and, altogether, is designed to serve) the principle of egoity itself—both individual and collective. Therefore, conventional religion is not the answer to the root-problems of human beings—but, rather, conventional religion merely exploits and reinforces the root-problems of human beings.

The Self-Evidently Divine Self-Nature, Self-Condition, and Self-State of Reality Itself does not appear in the "middle" of the context of conventional religion—nor can conventional religion "own", or be the proprietor of, the Divine (Which Is Reality Itself). Indeed, the Divine Is That Perfectly Subjective Self-Nature, Self-Condition, and Self-State Which Intrinsically and Perfectly Transcends conventional religion, all of the ego-mummery of humankind, and all of egoity itself.

4.

For the sake of all-and-All, global human culture must be made right.

The present world-chaos must be clearly and thoroughly understood—not only as the total and final collapse of all of past civilization (or of ego-culture and the "tribalization" of separate and opposing human societies), but as the consummate critical moment of opportunity for humankind as a whole and single order of mutual responsibility on Earth.

This unique moment in historical time is the human-scale "ground-zero"-moment for humankind (as everybody-all-at-once) to righten itself—by re-subordinating all-and-All and everybody-all-at-once to the Principle of Reality Itself.

Now is the necessary "zero-point" moment in human history—the unrepeatable once-in-history moment to systematically and globally organize human culture, politics, society, and economics on the basis of "zero-point" education, which is the necessary fundamental and essential education that orients and enables human beings to actively restore the principles of intrinsic egolessness and universal prior unity as the root-basis of human life.

The Global Cooperative Forum I propose is the first-time systematization of the totality of the human world on Earth—and the totality of a truly global cooperative order is the necessary future for a surviving (and both healthy and progressing) human species. The current world-situation offers only the entropic end-pattern for the disintegration of the human species—which will inevitably become the catastrophic and complete failure of the human species and the total demise of the human species.

The entire pattern and trend of current human culture—including scientific materialism, all modes of false philosophy, and everything relating to the current domain of ego-based consumer politics, social egoity, competitive social systems, "tribal" national systems, un-regulated economics, and conventional religion—is about death.

The course of human events is now converging upon a necessary clear choice between two great alternatives—either the total collapse and destruction of the human species and the Earth-world or the "zero-point" (or quintessential turning-point) of the emerging of a wholly new and systematic global human culture based on universally participatory cooperation, tolerance, and mutual accountability. Clearly, the only right and intelligent choice is to embrace a new global cooperative human culture that will collectively and rightly manage the Earth-world totality, eliminating "tribalism" and ego-based consumerism as the ruling principles of human life on Earth, and replacing them with the principles of intrinsic egolessness and universal prior unity.

The new global cooperative human culture will be self-regulated on a universally participatory and consistently principled basis—not on the basis of ad hoc emergency efforts to return to the "tribalized" status quo. Therefore, this moment in human history is the "zero-point" (or quintessential turning-point), in which the Global Cooperative Forum I propose will provide the institutional basis for the universally participatory and consistently principled self-regulation of globally-extended humankind.

The Global Cooperative Forum I propose should not be engaged as if it were merely a "solution" to a "problem"—but, rather, it must emerge all-new, simply as the intrinsically "problem"-free self-rightening and self-systematizing of the human domain of Earth. Thus understood, effective self-rightening is never based on the ego-mind of "problem". Rather, such self-rightening is, necessarily, based on the always prior and intrinsically "problem"-free working-presumption of intrinsic egolessness and universal prior unity. Therefore, as the consistent working-principle of self-rightening action, the entire presumption of "problem" should tacitly, simply, and effortlessly be relinquished from every context of global (or even personal) self-rightening.

The Earth-world and all of the global human domain have already collapsed far enough. If the pattern of the whole collapses much further, the human life-sphere will not be retrievable. Now is the moment for self-rightening—while the resources that are necessary for the reclamation of the Earth-world and the global human domain yet exist.

In this time, the Earth-world and the global human domain as a whole are, undoubtedly, infected with evil—

evil principles, evil motivations, and an absolute will to resist the change that is now so profoundly necessary. Only one force in the human domain on Earth is great enough to counter the current evil. That one and only force is the intrinsic power of everybody-all-at-once. No single faction can possibly be effective. Evil can be countered only if the totality of human beings insist. No human power on Earth is greater than everybody-all-at-once. There is not anything or anyone that can possibly overwhelm the collective human force of nearly eight billion (and always more) people intent upon universal self-rightening and systematic self-regulation.

5.

In actuality, the calamity everyone fears has already happened.

The "old order" is already dead.

Nevertheless, this need not be the darkest moment in human history. On the contrary, this moment in historical time could (and, indeed, must) be the historic moment in which the Intrinsic Pattern of Reality Itself is established as the universal basis for human life.

The "stave in the wheels" of the life-vehicle of human-kind is ego-culture—the principle of non-cooperation, the principle of absolute competition, the principle of separate and separative consumerism (or egoic "self"-fulfillment for the purpose of ultimate egoic "self"-glorification). The idea that life itself is about physically-based "self"-fulfillment and physically-based other-dominating power is false philosophy—a false philosophy that is, tragically, now proclaimed in the houses and streets of every "tribal" group and nation-state on Earth. Glorification of "self"—the egoic consumer, the body-based individual or (otherwise) "tribal" collective—is, in fact, the dominant world-religion of the present time.

Reality Itself—or That Which Is, Self-Evidently, Divine—
Is the Infinite Self-Existing and Self-Radiant Sphere* within
and of Which all conditional manifestation happens. Physical
(or apparently material) existence is intrinsically and entirely
subordinate to That Self-Existing and Self-Radiant Sphere,
and is, Ultimately, Outshined by and in It. That Self-Existing
and Self-Radiant Sphere—rather than any hoped-for utopia
of egoity—is the True Destiny of human existence.

The Global Cooperative Forum I propose is not a
utopian institution. Rather, the Global Cooperative Forum
I propose is a clearly principled institution that requires
the cooperative and mutually accountable participation of
everybody-all-at-once—without the "stave in the wheels" of
separate and separative identities. By means of participation
in the Global Cooperative Forum I propose, all separate and
separative identities (both individual and collective) are consistently subordinated not only to the global human and
Earth-world totality but to Reality Itself.

The Global Cooperative Forum I propose—and which is
simply the institutional serving-instrument for the principled
and right global systematization of humankind and the Earth-
world totality—can provide an environment for human life
that is predictably principled, constantly self-regulated, consistently life-positive, and entirely conducive to the fulfillment of the egoless prior-unity-purpose of human existence.

That egoless prior-unity-purpose cannot be established
merely on the basis of the human perception of physical
existence. The right human relationship to the perception of
physical existence is to constantly discipline human physical
existence by conforming it to intrinsically right principles.
The Perfect Fulfillment of human existence happens only in

---

* Adi Da has described that, when It is intrinsically "known", or realized, Reality Itself is felt to
be Spherical (and Boundless) in nature.

the Perfect Domain of egolessness, in Perfect Coincidence with That Which Perfectly Transcends all-and-All. Even the Global Cooperative Forum I propose is, itself, always intrinsically subordinate to That Which Transcends all-and-All. The Global Cooperative Forum I propose is not subordinate to human ego-"units" or even to physical existence itself— but the Global Cooperative Forum I propose is intrinsically and always subordinate to That in Which (and as a modification of Which) physical existence, or the Earth-world itself, is arising.

The Global Cooperative Forum I propose is, simply, right principle, right system-organization, and right system-responsibility. The Global Cooperative Forum I propose is not an absurd, impossible, and merely utopian effort. The Global Cooperative Forum I propose will not eliminate all human suffering. It is not possible to eliminate all suffering from the context of human existence itself. Nevertheless, it is both possible and necessary that (via true "zero-point" education and "zero-point" re-adaptation) human beings everywhere understand how to rightly live (and, therefore, how to rightly and accountably self-manage and self-regulate) human life in the context of Reality Itself—and, as a demonstration of that right life, a true "zero-point" culture of cooperation, tolerance, universal participation, and universal accountability, based on the intrinsic and always active transcending of egoity, must thereupon and globally arise.

6.

The entire human world is now obsessed with egoic "self"-indulgence. However, a true civilization can be made only by human beings who have subordinated themselves to principles that transcend the separate and separative "self-unit"-of-consumption (or the separate and separative ego-"I"). Human beings must, both individually and collectively, consistently subordinate themselves to right principle. All human beings must be re-regulated at the root of the origination of "self".

De-regulation—or the abandonment of rightly regulated and principled life—is the fundamental individual and collective fault of humankind. In their adventure of the pursuit of egoic "self"-fulfillment through egoic "self"-indulgence (or un-regulated and boundless consumerism), human beings have personally and collectively destined themselves to chaos and death. That global idealization of the idea of universal de-regulation has now achieved its end-time.

The culture of the everywhere-"Westernized" human realm has, historically, been luxuriating in the results of de-regulated consumerism. The only means by which the West was able to pursue its goal of egoic "self"-fulfillment through un-regulated and boundless "self"-indulgence was that of subordinating and exploiting the human resources of all of the rest of humankind and all of the natural resources of the entire Earth-world. However, the rest of humankind (especially in the East and the underdeveloped nation-states) is, rightly, no longer willing to be subordinated to and exploited by the West—and the natural resources of the Earth-world are, now, at the breaking-point of depletion and pollution. Paradoxically (and tragically)—even though the situation is thus and so, and rather than understanding and renouncing the fundamental wrongness and futility of the Western effort to achieve egoic "self"-fulfillment through un-regulated and boundless "self"-indulgence and thorough exploitation of the "other" and all the natural resources of the Earth-world—all the "tribes" on Earth are now intent on equally exercising exactly the failed "self"-indulgence effort Western "tribes" have long been doing.

The cultural (and political, economic, and social) basis of the current world-crisis is that everybody in the world is now trying to live like Westerners did when Westerners were able to exploit all other nation-states and all of the Earth-world's natural resources for the sake of an un-regulated and boundlessly "self"-indulgent Western society. Everybody in the world is now competing, in a dreadful situation of confrontation, for what has become a very limited reserve of human and natural resources—like dogs competing for the same chunk of meat.

The would-be utopia of ego-based consumerism has failed. That failure is not, in and of itself, negative—although the effects of that failure could be, and have already been, extremely negative. Rather than allowing the current world-crisis to take its full course toward global conflagration, this moment should be embraced as the "zero-point" (or quintessential turning-point) moment for establishing a self-regulating global system of human life—a system of universal participation and mutual accountability that is thoroughly cooperative, principled, and right.

7.

The Global Cooperative Forum I propose must educate humankind at the "zero-point", calling and obligating people everywhere to cooperative participation in, and to accountability and responsibility for, the total human domain and the total Earth-world in which they live and on which they depend. The communication-instrument of the global Internet is fundamental to this process of global self-rightening. Before the Internet itself becomes a victim of the global breakdown, the global Internet must be used to connect everybody-all-at-once, such that the power of everybody-all-at-once emerges to demand and to cooperatively enact the self-rightening of the human and natural totality of the Earth-sphere—and to embrace collective responsibility for that self-rightening, by collectively refusing to submit to the downward course that will otherwise be inevitable.

The power of everybody-all-at-once is the only human power on Earth that can possibly bring about the necessary self-rightening change in the currently chaotic workings of the human world. Nothing else but the collective power of everybody-all-at-once can stop the decline and destruction of the natural Earth-world, the human world-process, and the human species itself.

Everybody other than everybody-all-at-once is merely a faction.

Everybody other than everybody-all-at-once is merely an egoically "self"-interested consumer.

Therefore, everybody-all-at-once must collectively understand and collectively renounce the futile principle and enterprise of un-regulated and boundless consumer-egoity.

Everybody-all-at-once must perfectly coincide and universally re-awaken at the "zero-point".

The chaotic ego-power of everybody-one-at-a-time must, thus and thereby, be replaced by the benign global emergence of the self-rightening systematic power of everybody-all-at-once.

With that emergence, human beings will everywhere readily and cooperatively respond to what needs to be done, and they will readily and cooperatively embrace the collective responsibility for systematically organizing themselves through responsible and mutually accountable participation.

8.

Those who will see to the systematic re-regulation of the human domain must enjoy true "zero-point" understanding, and not be (themselves) extensions of the ego-culture of the past.

I have described such people as the necessary "servant-heroes" of humankind.

Those "servant-heroes" are the "morally enlightened" who must serve at the root of human re-ordering.

Those "servant-heroes" must see to the global transformation of human culture I have proposed and described.

Those "servant-heroes" must be converted from the philosophy of ego-culture to the "zero-point" philosophy that understands human existence as a pattern arising in the Indivisible Context of Reality Itself.

Those "servant-heroes", thus converted, are not disposed to live as egos, and they happily discipline themselves by conforming body and mind to the principles of right human life I have proposed and described.

The true "servant-hero" is a profoundly disciplined individual, who exemplifies the intrinsic transcending and the active renouncing of egoity.

Such is the "zero-point" leadership that is necessary to move humankind, as a whole, to thoroughly enact responsibility for itself as not-two at peace.

XXIV.

723

The Free Declaration of
The Universal Moral, Social,
and Political Laws of
True and Necessary Civilization

I f, as it is commonly supposed, nation-states have an inherent right to defend (and even to expand) themselves, the people (and the human species itself) have the same inherent right—and the self-responsible duty to exercise it. If this were not so, where would nation-states have acquired the right otherwise?

A living species (or even any living entity or individual) is, itself, <u>naturally</u> motivated merely toward survival (by means of reproduction, struggle, domination, and expansion). Only a <u>civilization-culture</u> makes <u>morality</u> and <u>Wisdom</u>. Among all the living species now on Earth, only the human species makes (or, indeed, can make) civilization-cultures. All right human morality is based on the (uniquely) human (and, therefore, mind-based and memory-dependent) capability for the comprehension of <u>totality</u> and <u>universality</u>.

War is no longer a "program" for gaining power over people, territories, and resources by strategically defeating and controlling the <u>representatives</u> of people, territories, and resources. Wars are no longer merely between <u>armies</u>—or, in some limited and "theatrical" sense, between the representative "heroes" of the State. Rather, wars are now "programs" for directly and brutally attacking, and grossly damaging, and (thus and thereby) directly controlling the people, the territories, and the resources <u>themselves</u>.

The people—and not merely the national armies and other representative "heroes" of nation-states—are now the direct and specific targets of all wars. The people—or the totality of humankind (along with all their territories and resources)—are now universally regarded and treated (as a working-principle and policy of virtually all national governments) as the principal and specific contextual enemy and immediate "fair game" of nation-state institutions and their any and all expansive and acquisitive aggressions.

The direct murder and suppression of humankind itself (in the immediate context of national territories and resources) is now the "method of choice" that is the basis of the war policies and power-games of virtually all nation-states on Earth. Therefore, the people—everywhere and all together— must (now, and forever hereafter) actively presume (and must actively exercise) the intrinsic right to approve or disapprove (and, thus and thereby, to allow or not allow) the activities (of war, and of everything else) proposed and exercised by each and every national government of State.

Right laws—based not merely on naturally "self"-based and grossly survival-oriented motives, but, rather, on the truly moral exercise of universal and all-including, and, thus, really civilized, principles—must everywhere govern both the people and the nation-states. Therefore, a global cooperative order of all of humankind, "voiced" through the exercise of truly universal and all-including principles, must, now, and forever hereafter, be the root-context of all nation-states.

People take refuge (and citizenship) in a nation-state because they (by inherent right) expect the nation-state to guarantee and actively uphold their necessary basic human rights to unlimited physical participation (in all basic political, social, cultural, and economic processes) and to unlimited protection from physical violence (whether violence is directed from within the nation-state, in the form of crime, or from outside the nation-state, in the form of war). Therefore, every nation-state (or sovereign political entity) must (by necessity, by law, and by universal agreement) guarantee and uphold these necessary expectations (and inherent rights) of each and all of its citizens, residents, and visitors.

Unlimited physical participation and unlimited physical protection are the necessary basic human rights of all human beings within the boundaries of any civilized nation-state. These rights are not merely "natural" in their nature or origin. Rather, these rights are, in their nature and origin, expressions of the comprehension of totality and universality. Therefore, these rights are of the nature of civilization, and they must originate from civilization—and they can (and will) be guaranteed and actively upheld only by truly civilized nation-states.

The entire world of humankind must enter into a perpetual global dialogue (via a Global Cooperative Forum), and, thus and thereby, establish (and actively perpetuate) a global cooperative order based on mutual cooperation, tolerance, real peace, and the principle of prior unity. In this manner, all nation-states must (in a global dialogue with the thus "righteous voice of the people") be brought to agree to function as civilized nation-states, and, thus and thereby, to absolutely guarantee and to always actively uphold the two necessary basic human rights (of unlimited physical participation and unlimited physical protection) within their national boundaries. Likewise, all such (thus civilized) nation-states must conform themselves to (and, thus, remain always subordinate to) the "righteous voice of the people"— expressed collectively via the always continuous Global Cooperative Forum of all of humankind.

Civilized nation-states have neither the inherent right nor the inherent calling to either guarantee or actively uphold any kind of presumed emotional or mental human "rights", but only necessary basic physical human rights. Thus, in the context of civilized society, the conditions associated with human emotional and/or mental processes and modes of expression must not be associated with pro-active manipulations, rules, and limits, but, rather, with pro-active freedoms and allowances—and a general environment of limitlessness.

The human right of unlimited physical participation must, necessarily, include unlimited physical access to all modes of education, culture, free exchange, responsibility-training, and Wisdom-learning—but, in order for all of that physical access to be right, effective, and truly unlimited, such education, culture, free exchange, responsibility-training, and Wisdom-learning must, itself, be truly free, really demanding, and of an all-inclusive nature. Therefore, no civilized nation-state should establish or enforce any limiting controls on the emotional and/or mental expressiveness of human beings and human institutions within its boundaries—except insofar as any emotional or mental demonstration in physical action threatens, causes, or enacts a limitation on the necessary and basic physical human rights of anyone (including the would-be limitation-doers themselves).

Thus, all civilized nation-states must refrain from the establishing and the enforcing of any laws or procedures that limit the free physical and verbal expression of emotional feelings and/or mental conceptions within their national boundaries. In that case, all civilized nation-states must establish and uphold laws and procedures that guarantee and enforce unlimited free speech, unlimited free emotional expression, and unlimited free physical activity—except insofar as any mode of speech or of emotional expression threatens physical harm on anyone (including the would-be harm-doers themselves), and, also, insofar as any mode of physical activity threatens, causes, or enacts physical harm on anyone (including the would-be harm-doers themselves), and, altogether, insofar as any mode of speech or of emotional expression or of physical activity threatens, causes, or enacts a limitation on the necessary basic human rights of anyone (including the would-be limitation-doers themselves).

The Global Cooperative Forum of all of humankind <u>must</u> <u>perpetually</u> <u>insist</u> <u>and</u> <u>always</u> <u>actively</u> <u>and</u> <u>lawfully</u> <u>require</u> that every nation-state accept, and guarantee, and actively uphold <u>all</u> these requirements for civilized nation-statehood, including the real, active, and consistent conformity and subordination (or self-responsible self-disciplining) of the every nation-state to the "righteous voice of the people" expressed collectively via the Global Cooperative Forum of <u>all</u> of humankind. Likewise, and coincidently, the "righteous voice of the people" must be really, actively, and consistently conformed and subordinated to the principles of the necessary basic human rights, and, altogether, the global cooperative order of all of humankind must be conformed and subordinated to the principle of civilization—which principle requires real, active, and consistent conformity and subordination (or self-responsible self-disciplining) of every human individual to the intrinsically ego-transcending comprehension of totality and universality.

On this basis, the Global Cooperative Forum of <u>all</u> of humankind must constantly and uncompromisingly demand (and always actively and lawfully require) the real, total, and universal global nation-state-<u>enactment</u> (or civilization-culture-fulfillment) of the principle of the <u>physical</u> protection of <u>all</u> of humankind—and, as a support for the necessary physical environment on which the physical protection of all of humankind must naturally depend, the <u>physical</u> protection of the Earth-world as a whole (and even the <u>physical</u> protection of the natural order of the universe within which the Earth-world is appearing and on which it depends) must, likewise, be demanded, required, and enacted.

This is the Free Declaration, for one and for all, of what is right and necessary for humankind in its now much advanced stage of global collective development, and of universal mutuality, and of universal mutual dependence—and of universal mutual aggravation and suffering.

The old moral, social, and political "order" of humankind is now dead. A new and true and right order of humankind is, now, and forever hereafter, necessary. This Free Declaration is the Seed-Utterance of that new and necessary true and right (and truly globally, totally, and universally cooperative) order.

This moment in human-time—July 23, 2006—is the precise and decisive moment of the uniquely new human necessity for all of humankind. Therefore, all signs say and illustrate that, if the new Way of true and right and truly human civilization herein and hereby Freely Declared is not now and everywhere chosen and enacted, the return to a natural and ego-based and inherently immoral chaos of separateness, division, mutual opposition, deadly competition, global conflagration, universal suffering, universal darkness, and universal death will have its global mandate of indifference—to move by nature's "twos" of human species' double-minded left and right of hands, to terminally and conclusively replace the civilization of this always fateful all of humankind.

One and all, consider this Free Declaration of your possibility on Earth.

One and all, Be of this Free Wisdom Blessed and made all right—together and at once.

Not-Two Is Peace (Color Field No. 1)

Image and Text by Adi Da, 2006

" "God"-ideas (and even all mere ideas) are ego-based "objectifications" (or Self-Reflected Self-Images) of the Intrinsic (and Inherently egoless) Self-Consciousness of Reality Itself—and, therefore, of Intrinsically Self-Evident (and Inherently egoless) Real Self (Itself).

No mere "God"-ideas Are Real (Acausal) God.

Only Reality Itself (and, therefore, Intrinsically Self-Evident and Inherently egoless Real Self, or Reality-Self, Itself) Is Real (Acausal) God.

Therefore, "God"-ideas (and even all mere ideas) must be (and, indeed, Always Already are) Transcended in, by Means of, and As Reality (Itself) and Real Self (Itself).

Real Self (or Reality-Self)—or the always first and always present Self-Condition of Conscious Awareness—Is Intrinsically Self-Evident As the Indivisible and Never-Broken Current of Feeling-Energy-Consciousness.

NOTE: The text in this image was hand-calligraphed by Adi Da. The text is a slightly varying version of a passage from the following essay, "Is-Peace".

XXV.

Is-Peace

1.

Reality Itself will not "Save" you, or "Liberate" you, or "Enlighten" you.
Reality Itself Is "Salvation", and "Liberation", and "Enlightenment".

Inherent Freedom Is the Liberation-Gift That Reality Itself here-Shows to all-and-All.

Before and Where an "object" or an ego-"I" becomes defined to any "point of view", A Perfect Mirror Always Stands—Awake.

That Perfect Mirror Is the Acausal, Indivisible, and Intrinsically egoless Self-Nature, Self-Condition, and Self-State (or Reality-State) of all-and-All.

Perfect Peace Is the tacit, direct, and Intrinsically Self-Evident Self-Realization of the Intrinsically egoless and Perfectly Indivisible Self-Nature, Self-Condition, and Self-State of Reality Itself—Which Is Utterly Beyond all mere ideas, and all presumptions of separate "self", and all presumptions of separate "world-out-there", and all presumptions of separate "God".

Reality Itself—One, Indivisible, all-and-All-Including, all-and-All-Transcending, and Intrinsically egoless—Is the One and Only Self-Nature, Self-Condition, and Self-State of all-and-All.

2.

Reality Itself is not an idea.

Reality Itself cannot be encompassed or (in any manner) directly represented by ideas.

Reality Itself—Which Is the Intrinsically egoless Self-Nature, Self-Condition, and Self-State of all-and-All—is neither Evident nor Realizable by means of ideas.

"God"-ideas are the proprietary "objects" (or "intellectual property") of formalized (or mentally pre-formulated and search-prescriptive) religion.

"God"-ideas—and even all mere ideas—are ego-based "objectifications" of psycho-physically-based ego-states.

Intrinsic idea-lessness Is an Inherent and Tacit Self-Characteristic of the Intrinsically egoless Self-Nature, Self-Condition, and Self-State of Reality Itself.

No mere "God"-ideas Are Reality Itself—or the Intrinsic and Intrinsically egoless Self-Nature, Self-Condition, and Self-State of all-and-All.

Therefore, "God"-ideas—and even all mere ideas—must be (and, indeed, Always Already are) Transcended in, by Means of, and As Reality (Itself) and Reality-"Self" (Itself).

Real "Self" (or Reality-"Self")—or the Self-Existing, Always Prior, Transcendental, and Intrinsically egoless Self-Nature, Self-Condition, and Self-State That Is Tacit Conscious Awareness—Is Always Already Self-Radiant As the Indivisible and Never-Broken Under-Current (or Spiritual Root-Force) of Feeling-Energy-Consciousness.

Within the Always Prior and Senior Context of the Self-Existing, and Self-Radiant, and Self-Evidently egoless Feeling-Energy-Current of Reality-"Self"-Consciousness, perceptions arise experientially.

Thoughts (or conceptual processes) also arise within the Intrinsically Self-Evident Feeling-Energy-Current of Reality-"Self"-Consciousness—but thoughts arise only after (or on the basis of) the events and processes of experiential perception.

Every perception (and, also, every event of thinking) is entirely a reflected event, a time-bound apparition, an illusion of separate "objectivity"—an illusion of not-"Self".

Because all perceptions and all thoughts always arise dependently—as a result of conditional causes, and entirely Within and on the Basis of the Always Senior Context of the Priorly Self-Evident and all-Mirroring Feeling-Energy-Current of egoless Reality-"Self"-Consciousness—all perceptions, all thoughts, and, thus, all apparent "objects" Are modes (or merely apparent modifications) of the Perfectly Subjective (or Perfectly Non-"objective" and Non-"different") Feeling-Energy-Current (or Transcendental Spiritual Self-Nature, Self-Condition, and Self-State) of Reality-"Self"-Consciousness Itself.

3.

Therefore, What Is Freedom?

Freedom Is Perfect (or Always Already Prior and Non-"different") Inherence in and As Reality Itself.

Freedom Is Perfect Fidelity to Truth Itself (Which Is Reality Itself).

Freedom Is to Always Already (or Priorly, or Intrinsically) Self-"Locate" (or Self-Identify) the egoless Transcendental Spiritual Self-Nature, Self-Condition, and Self-State of the Real "Self"—or the Intrinsically Self-Evident and Intrinsically egoless Self-Nature, Self-Condition, and Self-State That Is the Always Prior Context of all perception, all thought, all experience, all "objects", all "others", and all of apparent ego-"I", or seemingly separate "self".

Freedom Is to Always Already Self-"Locate" (and, Thus, to Be) the Intrinsically Self-Evident and Intrinsically egoless Transcendental Spiritual Under-Current of Feeling-Energy-Consciousness Itself—Always Already Prior to (and, yet, never separate from) perceptions, or thoughts, or "objects", or "others".

4.

On the basis of the Always Priorly (and always presently) Self-"Located" (and Intrinsically Indivisible, Non-separate, Non-"different", and egoless) Under-Current of Feeling-Energy-Consciousness, all that (apparently, or experientially, and conditionally) arises "objectively" (as perceptions and thoughts) is Intrinsically (or Always Priorly) Transcended—without any act of dissociation, and without any act of seeking.

Therefore, all perceptions and all thoughts (or all "objects" of conditional experience) arise Acausally, Non-separately, and egolessly—Always Already Prior to any sense of "difference", necessity, dilemma, problem, or bondage.

Even the apparent ego-"I", and every apparent "other", and even all of conditionality and death, is Intrinsically (or Priorly, or Always Already) Transcended in the Intrinsically Self-Evident, and Indivisible, and Never-Broken Transcendental Spiritual Under-Current of Intrinsically egoless Feeling-Energy-Consciousness—Which Is the Inherent Reality-"Self" (or Intrinsically Self-Evident Self-Nature, Self-Condition, and Self-State) of all-and-All.

Any perceived or conceived threat to the space-time "point of view" that is the separate ego-"I" tends to become "objectified" as reactivity (or merely reactive activity), in the form of fear, sorrow, or anger.

Any perception or conception of "objectified" and conditionally reactive "self" (or ego-"I") tends to become epitomized as the fear of death.

Therefore, Always Already Transcend the "objectified" and conditionally reactive (and entirely Self-Mirrored) ego-"self" (and all its "objects" and "others") in the Intrinsically Self-Evident Transcendental Spiritual Under-Current of Intrinsically egoless Feeling-Energy-Consciousness—Which Is the Self-Nature, Self-Condition, and Self-State of Reality Itself, Intrinsically Prior to "point of view" in space-time—and, Thus and Thereby, Always Already Transcend death, and fear, and sorrow, and anger, and even all un-love.

5.

Freedom Is Thus.

Freedom Is Reality Itself.

Freedom Is the egoless Transcendental Spiritual Self-Nature, Self-Condition, Self-State, and Inherently Perfect Reality-"Self" of all-and-All.

Freedom Is the Intrinsically (and Inherently Perfectly) egoless and Intrinsically Self-Evident Self-Depth—Wherein all perceptions, all thoughts, and all "objects" are an Always Already Perfectly Transcended (and, Thus, and Thereby, Transcendentally Spiritually Self-Illuminated, or Self-"Bright") world-Mummery.

Freedom Itself need not (and cannot) be either caused or achieved or acquired.

The Perfectly egoless Self-Depth That Is Freedom Itself need not (and cannot) be reached or arrived at from any "location" presumed to be outside or separate from That Self-Depth Itself.

The Perfectly egoless Self-Depth That Is Freedom Itself Is Always Already The Case—and, therefore, "It" can only Be Intrinsically (or Tacitly, Directly, Acausally, and Perfectly) Self-Realized As That Which Is Always Already The Case.

The Perfectly egoless Self-Depth That Is Freedom Itself Is Perfect Peace Itself.

Therefore, Peace Is Peace That Is Peace.

Not-Two Is Peace.

Not-Two Is Not Two.

Not Two.

Not-Two.

Is Peace.

Is-Peace.

PART THREE

Reality Itself
<u>Is</u>
One and Only

I.

The Three Great Principles
of All Truth

I. The Transcendental Reality-Principle of Indivisibility:
    Reality (Itself) Is <u>Inherently</u> Indivisible, One,
    Non-conditional, Non-separate, egoless, and Absolute.

II. The Universal (or Cosmic) Principle of Unity and
    Non-"Difference": The world (or the conditionally
    manifested cosmos) is <u>Inherently</u> A Unity, Which
    (In and <u>As</u> its Intrinsic Self-Nature, Self-Condition,
    and Self-State) is <u>Inherently</u> Non-"different" from The
    Indivisible, One, Non-conditional, Non-separate,
    egoless, and Absolute Self-Nature, Self-Condition, and
    Self-State That <u>Is</u> Reality Itself.

III. The psycho-physical Principle of Non-Separateness:
     The apparent individual psycho-physical entity is
     <u>Inherently</u> Non-separate from The world-Unity (or The
     Inherently Unified cosmic Totality, Which is Whole and
     Universal) and, also, <u>Inherently</u> Non-separate from The
     Inherently Indivisible, One, Non-conditional, Non-separate,
     egoless, and Absolute Self-Nature, Self-Condition, and
     Self-State That <u>Is</u> Reality Itself—and That <u>Is</u>, Therefore,
     The Indivisible, One, Non-conditional, Non-separate,
     egoless, and Absolute Self-Nature, Self-Condition, and
     Self-State of all-and-All.

These Three Principles, Which I have Proposed, are
(Effectively) An Integrated Whole and Single Proposition.
They (Together) Comprise The Right and True Basis (and The

Right and True Measure) for The Correct (and, inevitably, intellectually Liberating) Evaluation of <u>any</u> and <u>all</u> possible propositions of philosophical import made (now, or in the future, or in any time and place at all) by any one (or any school or tradition) at all.

II.

Language-Based Knowledge
Versus
Reality-Knowledge

1.

All conventional knowledge-categories are modes of the perceptual and conceptual language-categories of "name" and "form"—or of categorical "objectification". All conventional knowledge-categories—or all perceptual and conceptual "objectifications"—are "point-of-view"-based constructions, always implying space-time-"locatedness".

Therefore, all perceptual and conceptual "objectifications" are both limited and "local"—or condition-based, "point-of-view"-based, "point-of-view"-serving, "point-of-view"-limited, and intrinsically ego-bound.

True knowledge is, necessarily, Truth-Knowledge, or Reality-Based "Perfect Knowledge"—Which Is Intrinsically and Always Priorly "point-of-view"-less, egoless, and Self-Established (Perfectly Prior to all "difference") in all-and-All-at-once.

2.

Humankind has invented complex language-based systems of conventional perceptual and conceptual knowledge in a collective (and trans-generational, or perpetually self-duplicatable) effort to protect (and extend through time) the otherwise thoroughly vulnerable ego-position on which human cultures are traditionally based.

Those language-based (and perceptually and conceptually organized and communicated) knowledge-systems include the traditionally dominant knowledge-systems of religion and science, as well as of every other kind of ordinary and extraordinary category of human desire, problem, and interest. All language-based systems of perceptual and conceptual knowledge are "local" (and "self-location"-oriented), "self"-limited, "self"-referring (or "point-of-view"-referencing), and (both intrinsically and inevitably) ego-bound and ego-binding—however otherwise profound, apt, or "universal" they may seem, and no matter how "universally" (or at-large) they may be proclaimed or enforced.

Only "Perfect Knowledge" of The Intrinsically egoless, Indivisible, Acausal, Transcendental Spiritual, and Self-Evidently Divine Self-Nature, Self-Condition, and Self-State of Reality Itself Is (both Intrinsically and Inevitably) The Free and all-and-All-Liberating Truth of all-and-All.

Therefore, it is necessary for humankind to base all of human life and culture on Truth Itself, and on the esoteric practice of "Perfect Knowledge" of Reality Itself, and on the intrinsic, fundamental, and always already language-transcending prior unity of all-and-All, and on modes of language discourse that are rooted in Reality-based language (rather than in language-based "reality").

III.

There Is Only Reality Itself—
Which Is Real God—
and No Other Is At All

1.

There is no apparent anyone or anything, whether singular or plural in number, that can be named, or described, or (otherwise) referred to by any pronouns or indicative words—such as "I", or "me", or "myself", or "mine", or "she", or "her", or "herself", or "hers", or "he", or "him", or "himself", or "his", or "we", or "us", or "ourselves", or "ours", or "they", or "them", or "these", or "those", or "themselves", or "theirs", or "it", or "this", or "that", or "itself", or "its"—that is intrinsically other than, or separate from, or non-identical to, The Intrinsically egoless, Irreducibly Indivisible, Perfectly Acausal, and Self-Evidently Divine Self-Nature, Self-Condition, and Self-State That Is Reality Itself.

All that arises conditionally (including all of the languages of mind) is a complex and mutually dependent pattern of evident causes and effects—but none of it is a moment of actual identity.

The only mode of actual identity Is The Intrinsically egoless Self-Identity of Reality Itself—and That universally Self-Evident Mode of egoless Self-Identity Is The One and Only and Irreducibly Indivisible Identity-Characteristic of all-and-All.

The totality of all conditionally arising patterns is a mutually dependent and Perfectly "identityless" (or Intrinsically egoless) whole.

Because the totality of all conditionally arising patterns Is Intrinsically (and Always Priorly) and Irreducibly Indivisibly Self-Established in and As The Intrinsically egoless, Irreducibly Indivisible, Perfectly Acausal, and Self-Evidently Divine Self-Identity of Reality Itself, the pattern-characteristic of the whole totality of all conditionally arising patterns is irreducibly indivisible prior unity.

Reality Itself (or The Self-Evident Divine, or Real God) Is Acausally Self-Existing, Self-Radiant, and Self-Revealed.

Reality Itself (or The Self-Evident Divine, or Real God) Is The Acausal Context (or Perfectly Subjective Source-Condition)—rather than the all-and-All-Causing Doer (or "Objective Creator")—of the whole totality of all conditionally arising patterns.

Therefore, Reality Itself (or The Self-Evident Divine, or Real God) does not cause conditionally arising patterns—but all conditionally arising patterns are, within the universal circumstance of prior unity, coincidently and mutually dependently causing and effecting one another, In, Of, and As The Intrinsically egoless, Irreducibly Indivisible, Perfectly Acausal, Perfectly Subjective, and Self-Evidently Divine Self-Nature, Self-Condition, and Self-State That Is Reality Itself.

Reality Itself (or The Self-Evident Divine, or Real God) Is Only, Acausally, egolessly, and Non-separately Self-Evident—Always Already both Perfectly Prior to and As all-and-All that arises apparently and conditionally.

Therefore, there are no intrinsically separate, independent (or non-dependent), and non-caused conditionally arising patterns, "things", entities, beings, or "selves".

2.

Really (or Always Priorly, Intrinsically, Necessarily, Self-Evidently, and At The Root), all possible names, descriptions, references, pronouns, and indicative words, in any and every mode, or kind, or tradition of language (even as proposed or engaged by any species or variety of conditionally apparent being at all), <u>directly</u> <u>and</u> <u>only</u> Refer to The Perfect Self-Identity, or The Perfectly Subjective (or Always Priorly Self-Standing), Intrinsically egoless, Irreducibly Indivisible, Perfectly Acausal, Non-conditional, Non-"objective", and Self-Evident Divine—Which <u>Is</u> Reality Itself, Truth Itself, The Beautiful Itself, and The One and Only and Indivisible Real God (or The Intrinsically all-and-All-Transcending, and Always Already With-all-and-All-Coinciding, and Perfectly Acausally Self-Existing, and Perfectly egoless, and Self-Evidently Divine Self-Nature, Self-Condition, and Self-State That <u>Is</u> Reality Itself).

Therefore, <u>all</u> modes of conditionally (and merely conventionally) presumed identity are merely convenient fictions, based on the apparent relational transactions between temporally and spatially configured and mutually associated (or provisionally related) "point-of-view-locations".

As such, <u>all</u> names, pronouns, and conditional "self"-references (or ego-"I"-identifications) are merely transactional fictions, or provisional modes of pseudo-identity, presumed on the basis of a perceived need to understand, organize, and manage the conventions of conditionally apparent "point-of-view-relations".

3.

Unless <u>all</u> of this is clearly and actively understood and lived by <u>all</u> human beings (both individually and collectively), the environment of conditionally (and merely conventionally) presumed pseudo-identities (linguistically specified, and mentally proposed, and, altogether, humanly activated, by names, pronouns, and descriptive references of all kinds) is liable to become—and <u>usually</u> <u>does</u> become—a basis for egoically "self"-deluded illusion-cultures (or a human world-mummery).

The fiction of separateness—and the denial of the universal characteristic of prior unity—is a mind-based illusion, a lie, a terribly deluding force, and a profoundly and darkly negative act.

Therefore, it is <u>necessary</u> for there always to be a universal (and truly sacred) human context and process of <u>right</u> <u>cultural</u> <u>education</u>—such that <u>all</u> human beings are actively and constantly reminded of (and, indeed, constantly and actively adapted to) The Universal Reality-Principle, Which <u>Is</u> Self-Evident as the intrinsic prior unity of one and all and All in the conditionally arising pattern of world-experience.

Likewise and coincidently, it is necessary for there always to be a universal (and truly sacred) human context and process of <u>right</u> <u>esoteric</u> <u>practice</u>—such that <u>all</u> human beings are actively and constantly reminded of (and, indeed, constantly and actively re-Awakened to) The Intrinsically One and Only and Perfectly egoless Self-Identity That <u>Is</u> The Self-Nature, Self-Condition, and Self-State of Reality Itself (Wherein and Whereof <u>all</u> modes of conditional identity are intrinsically understood to be merely convenient fictions, or matters of ordinary convention, provisionally and culturally superimposed on the apparent patterns of conditionally arising phenomena, but otherwise Always Intrinsically Transcended in, and Always Effectively Sublated by, The Intrinsically egoless One and Only Self-Identity That <u>Is</u> The Self-Nature, Self-Condition, and Self-State of Reality Itself).

4.

The individual and collective denial—and active refusal—of The Universal Condition and Intrinsic Law of prior unity is the root and substance of a perpetual (and egoically self-perpetuating) universal crime against humanity, performed by every one and all of humankind itself.

The Intrinsic Reality-based Principle of prior unity Is The Principal and Necessary Universal Law of global humankind. The essence of right universal cultural education is the constant promotion and active whole bodily (or total psycho-physical) adaptation-training of all human beings relative to the everywhere-detailed enactment of The Universal Law of prior unity.

The essence of right universal esoteric practice is the constant and whole-bodily (or totally psycho-physically) active individual and collective exercise of Intrinsically egoless devotion to Real God—and, thus and thereby, to the human exercise of constant active commitment to Non-conditional Self-Realization of The One, and Only, and Irreducibly Indivisible, and Perfectly Acausal, and Perfectly Non-Separate, and Perfectly egoless Self-Nature, Self-Condition, Source-Condition, and Self-State That Is Reality Itself and (always coincidently) to un-conditionally active, and always actively ego-surrendering, and truly "self"-giving, and everywhere limitlessly applied, and (in every intention and effect) harmless love and service of all living beings and the total world-circumstance on which all living beings very vulnerably depend for life itself.

On The Reality-Basis of Thus right and true universal human education and esoteric practice, one and all must, at root and heart and whole bodily (or as an exercise of psycho-physical totality), always and only (and, at last, Most Perfectly) "Know" Thus, understand Thus, feel Thus, think Thus, speak Thus, act Thus—and, altogether (one and all), Be Thus and live Thus.

IV.

The Intrinsic Power
To Righten World-Conditions

Human difficulty is inherent in conditional Nature itself, during life and after death.

There is no Absolute "Other"-Power Causing things to happen.

Countless beings and forces (visible and invisible) are causing things to happen.

This is a cause-and-effect cosmos.

The pattern of cosmos is (itself) the totality of all causes and effects.

There is no single "anything" in charge.

Every "thing" is in charge.

Every "one"—or every space-time-"located" (and, thus, apparently separate) "point of view"—is in charge, as both cause and effect, moment to moment in space-time.

Every "one" is having an effect on all "others", and every "one" is suffering from the effects of all "others".

Therefore, I Call you (and every one, and all) to a life that is constantly emerging at the "zero-point" (intrinsically prior to all patterns of cause-and-effect), and (thus, and thereby) to a life that is always already Perfectly being Transformed—not by an illusory "One Cause" or an imagined "Deity" that is presumed to be "in charge" of everything, but by the Self-Existing, Self-Radiant, Indivisible, Acausal, and Intrinsically egoless Conscious Light That Is the Transcendental Spiritual and Self-Evidently Divine Self-Nature, Self-Condition, Source-Condition, and Self-State of everyone and everything.

If every one (each and all) would Realize and Actualize Intrinsic, Absolute, and "zero-point" (or system-root) Unity with the Intrinsically egoless Conscious Light That Is Reality Itself, world-conditions would positively and inevitably change—by virtue of the acausally transformative intrinsic force of the pattern-root of all energies, actively represented by all those who are thus surrendered to Intrinsically egoless Prior (or Intrinsic) "zero-point" Unity with the Transcendental Spiritual and Self-Evidently Divine Self-Nature, Self-Condition, and Self-State of Reality Itself.

Indeed, the Realization of egoless "zero-point" Indivisibility—at the root of every otherwise ego-bound human being and as the thereby self-evident prior unity of all-and-All—is the necessary pre-condition for the emergence of a global cooperative order of humankind.

Therefore, the Global Cooperative Forum will emerge only when everybody-all-at-once understands and accepts it as a necessity and (thereupon) demands that it be thus and so and now.

V.

Always <u>Be</u> What and all
That <u>Is Not</u>-"self"

1.

The ego-"I", or psycho-physically presumed separate and actively separative "self"-identity, is intrinsically "different" from What and all that is egoically identified (and actively differentiated and "objectified") as not-"self".

Characteristically, the ego-"I" strategically and "self"-defensively or "self"-protectively clings to the bodily persona and the personal and collectively "tribalized" mind of the conditionally-patterned "self"-identity—and, on that basis, the ego-"I" actively, constantly, and as a psycho-physical totality differentiates itself from What and all that the egoic "self"-identity intrinsically and actively presumes to be not-"self".

As a result of all of this ego-based strategizing (in both the personal and the collective domains of life), human beings are caught in a constant "self"-made struggle—always characterized by a fundamental disability, which is the fundamental inability to actively identify with What and all that the egoic "self"-identity identifies (and actively differentiates and "objectifies") as not-"self".

2.

The What and the all that is egoically identified (and actively differentiated and "objectified") as not-"self" always consists of two fundamental modes of not-"self".

The first mode of egoically identified (and actively differentiated and "objectified") not-"self" <u>Is</u> What Intrinsically

<u>Transcends</u> the ego-"I" (or the psycho-physically "self"-presumed <u>separate</u> "self"-identity).

The second mode of egoically identified (and actively differentiated and "objectified") not-"self" is all that is egoically identified (and actively differentiated and "objectified") as "<u>other</u>" than the ego-"I" (or the psycho-physically-active <u>separative</u> "self"-identity).

3.

The What That Intrinsically Transcends the psycho-physically "self"-presumed separate ego-"I" <u>Is</u> Reality Itself—or The One and Only and Indivisible Self-Nature, Self-Condition, and Self-State of What <u>Is</u>.

Reality Itself <u>Is</u> The Universal Transcendental Self-Nature, Self-Condition, and Self-State of all-and-All.

Reality Itself <u>Is</u> Intrinsically egoless, Indivisible, Acausally and Transcendentally Spiritually Self-Present (both Universally and At The Root of all-and-All), and Self-Evidently Divine.

Reality Itself—or That Which <u>Is</u> (Itself) Divine—Is Transcendentally Spiritually, Universally, Uniformly, Perfectly egolessly, and In-Everywhere-of-space and In-every-mode-and-instant-of-time-and-form-and-person Simultaneously Self-Transmitted and Self-Evidently Self-Revealed <u>As</u> and Via the total cosmic continuum of space-time, which is The conditionally apparent Self-Evidence of Intrinsically Acausal Reality Itself <u>As</u> The Transcendental Spiritual Energy and The Always Prior Unity of Conscious Light.

4.

The all that is (apparently) "other" than the psycho-physically actively separative (or psycho-physically actively "self"-differentiating) ego-"I" is all-and-every-one and each-and-all-of-every-"thing" that is identified (or, always mistakenly, "self"-presumed) by the ego-"I" to be "other" than itself.

Every psycho-physical action (whether of body, emotion, or mind) of ego-"I" and of all-and-every-one and every instant and mode of change of form, or place, or orientation of each-and-all-of-every-"thing" is a happening of conditionally apparent cosmic space-time-energy (or natural and otherwise conditional energy) that is always and inevitably psycho-physically self-transmitted into, via, and throughout all time and all space as active "effective causes" and "causative effects".

The ego-"I" and all that is "self"-presumed by the ego-"I" to be "other" than the ego-"I" is a seamless pattern of cosmic (or natural and otherwise conditional) energy, always actively functioning as "effective causes" and "causative effects"—and always happening in an always priorly and systematically unified universal cosmic context of conditionally apparent events.

5.

The fact and the active "effective causes" and "causative effects" of the separate and separative psycho-physical ego-"I", or conditionally presumed "self"-identity—and, thus, the totality of the conditionally active "effective causes" and "causative effects" of the "self"-differentiating activities of all human persons, cultures, and societies—is the principal illusion, error, and fault of humankind.

Therefore, the always principal necessity for humankind is to establish and perpetually enact personal, cultural, and social understanding, means, obligation, and accountability for the personal and the universal collective transcending of the psycho-physical ego-"I", or the otherwise inevitable universal personal, cultural, and social habit and distress of ego-bound and ego-binding action and system-chaos.

6.

The universal personal, cultural, and social means for the transcending of the psycho-physical ego-"I", or the psycho-physical activity of separate "self"-identification and actively separative "self"-differentiation, is the "self"-discipline of always tacitly and whole-bodily-actively (as a unified psycho-physical totality) identifying with What and all that would otherwise be egoically identified (and actively differentiated and "objectified") as not-"self".

7.

The universal personal, cultural, and social "self"-discipline of always tacitly and whole-bodily-actively (as a unified psycho-physical totality) identifying with What and all that would otherwise be egoically identified (and actively differentiated and "objectified") as not-"self" is intrinsically ecstatic— or a process of always immediately transcending the psycho-physical presumption of separate "self"-identity (or ego-"I") and the ego-based psycho-physical activity of not-"self"-differentiation and "other-objectifying" separativeness.

8.

The universal personal, cultural, and social practice of intrinsically ego-transcending ecstasy by means of always tacitly and whole-bodily-actively (as a unified psycho-physical totality) identifying with What and all that would otherwise be egoically identified (and actively differentiated and "objectified") as not-"self" is always two-fold, because there are always two fundamental modes of otherwise would-be-egoically-identified (and otherwise would-be-actively-egoically-differentiated-and-"objectified") not-"self": The What and the all.

9.

The always first mode of the practice of intrinsically ego-transcending ecstasy is the practice of tacit, Prior, and constant <u>Root-Identification</u> with What Intrinsically Transcends the ego-"I"—or the, necessarily, esoteric practice of tacitly, Intrinsically, Always Priorly, and Always At The Root of the whole (or total unified psycho-physical) body Self-Identifying with The Intrinsically egoless, Indivisible, Acausal, Transcendental Spiritual, and Self-Evidently Divine Self-Nature, Self-Condition, and Self-State of Reality Itself.

10.

The always second mode of the practice of intrinsically ego-transcending ecstasy—which always follows consequentially and subordinately upon the tacit, Prior, and constant Root-demonstration of the first—is the intrinsically (and Always Priorly) ego-transcending personal, cultural, and social practice of tacit and whole-bodily-active (or unified and total psycho-physical) <u>sympathetic</u> (or <u>compassionate</u>), <u>participatory, and cooperative</u> identification with all-and-every-one and each-and-all-of-every-"thing".

11.

Therefore, the universal personal, cultural, and social discipline of intrinsically ego-transcending ecstasy is of The Nature of A Two-Fold Universal Reality-Law and Reality-Based Imperative: Always <u>Be</u> What and all That <u>Is</u> Not-"self".

12.

True ecstasy <u>Is</u> The Intrinsic Self-Realization of egolessness itself <u>and</u> of The Indivisible Acausal Self-State of The Transcendental Spiritual Conscious Light That <u>Is</u> Reality Itself.

13.

To Be What Is (in Reality Itself) Not-"self" (or What Intrinsically Transcends the ego-"I") Is to tacitly and whole bodily (or as a unified psycho-physical totality) Stand (Intrinsically, Always Priorly, and At Root) As egolessness itself and As The Indivisible, Acausal, and Self-Evidently Divine Self-State of The Transcendental Spiritual Conscious Light That Is Reality Itself.

14.

To Be all That (in Reality Itself) Is Not-"self" (or all that is otherwise "self"-presumed to be intrinsically "other" than the psycho-physically-presumed ego-"I") is to always tacitly and whole-bodily-actively (as a unified psycho-physical totality) sympathetically (or compassionately) identify with and to always tacitly and whole-bodily-actively (as a unified psycho-physical totality) cooperatively participate in indivisible prior unity with all-and-every-one and each-and-all-of-every-"thing".

15.

Always ecstatically Be What (in Reality Itself) Is Not-"self"—by always tacitly and At The Root of the whole body (or At The Root of the intrinsically unified psycho-physical totality of your person) Self-Identifying with The Intrinsically egoless, Indivisible, Acausal, Transcendental Spiritual, and Self-Evidently Divine Self-Nature, Self-Condition, and Self-State of Reality Itself and (on That tacit, or Always Prior, and Intrinsically body-and-mind-Transcending Root-Basis) always whole-bodily-actively (as a unified psycho-physical totality) and Intrinsically egolessly identifying with all That (in Reality Itself) Is Not-"self" by always sympathetically (or compassionately) and (in a fully participatory manner) cooperatively being all-and-every-one and each-and-all-of-every-"thing".

VI.

The Zero-Point and The Infinite State

1.

Infinity (or the infinite state) is not a number.

Infinity (or the infinite state) is not a quantity, or a conditional limit, or a "location" in space, or in time, or in any sequence, or in any process or cause-and-effect event.

Infinity (or the infinite state) can be neither attained nor approximated by the addition of any number (or any fraction of a number) to the number one.

Infinity (or the infinite state) can be neither attained nor approximated by the subtraction of any number (or any fraction of a number) from the number one.

It is not possible to move closer to infinity (or the infinite state).

It is not possible to move further away from infinity (or the infinite state).

Therefore, infinity (or the infinite state) is intrinsically unattainable and intrinsically unquantifiable.

2.

Zero (or the zero-point) is not a number.

Zero (or the zero-point) is not a quantity, or a conditional limit, or a "location" in space, or in time, or in any sequence, or in any process or cause-and-effect event.

Zero (or the zero-point) cannot be attained by either numerical addition to or numerical subtraction from the number one or any number (or any fraction of a number) other than one—because both numerical addition and numerical subtraction are pre-quantified motions, or motions of quantities of number in relation either to themselves or to other quantities of number.

Zero (or the zero-point) can be neither attained nor approximated by motions or transactions of quantities (or numbers)—because zero is intrinsically non-quantifiable (or innumerable).

Therefore, zero (or the zero-point) is intrinsically unattainable and intrinsically unquantifiable.

3.

If the concept of number (or of discrete quantity) is postulated before zero (or the zero-point) and infinity (or the infinite state) are contemplated, then the idea of zero (or of the zero-point) and the idea of infinity (or of the infinite state) are (necessarily) categorized as numbers (or quantities) and as "entities" that are intrinsically two, and (thus) non-identical to one another—as if zero (or the zero-point) is, by definition, at the beginning and infinity (or the infinite state) is, by definition, at the end.

To invent number, human beings did not begin with zero (as a discrete number) and, then, start counting forwards— nor did they begin with infinity (as a discrete number) and, then, start counting backwards.

Rather, to invent number, human beings first invented the ideas of "point of view" (or of "localized" and separate "self"-identity), and of the "other" (or "not-self"), and of "difference" (or "objective quantity").

Only after number was already invented—based on the original invention of "point of view" (or "localized" and separate "self", or ego-"I") and of "object" (or "difference", or "not-self")—did human beings invent the ideas of zero and infinity.

Thus, originally, human beings mistakenly superimposed the idea of number onto the ideas of zero and infinity—and, as a result, human beings have struggled with the irrational paradoxes of that false superimposition ever since.

However, if the original error is understood and the false superimposition thus removed, contemplation of the root-ideas of zero (or the zero-point) and infinity (or the infinite state) can serve the human root-intuition of The Intrinsically egoless and Indivisible Self-Nature, Self-Condition, and Self-State of Reality Itself.

4.

The concept of the number (or discrete quantity) one is the root-number, the "source" of all quantified numbers and all "differences".

The concept of the number one is the numerical idea-representation of the ego-"I"—or the separately quantified "self"-identity.

The presumption of separate ego-"I" is the root-source of all numbers, or all modes of quantification.

The ego-"I" is the "shadow" behind all numbers.

If neither the separate ego-"I" nor the quantified number one is presumed, or postulated, or even conceived, neither number nor quantity nor "difference" is presumed, postulated, or conceived.

If neither number nor quantity nor "difference" is presumed, postulated, or conceived, infinity (or the infinite state) and zero (or the zero-point) are not (and cannot be) differentiated from one another—and, thereupon, infinity (or the infinite state) and zero (or the zero-point) are intrinsically self-apprehended to be self-evidently indivisible and the same.

5.

Both zero (or the zero-point) and infinity (or the infinite state) are intrinsically numberless, or prior to the condition of discrete (or separate) quantity.

There is neither number nor distance between zero (or the zero-point) and infinity (or the infinite state).

Neither zero (or the zero-point) nor infinity (or the infinite state) is senior or subordinate to the other.

There is no hierarchical relationship between zero (or the zero-point) and infinity (or the infinite state)—and there is no "difference" of any kind between them.

Zero (or the zero-point) and infinity (or the infinite state) are intrinsically equal, one, only, and the same.

The apparent (or conventionally presumed) "difference" between zero (or the zero-point) and infinity (or the infinite state) is a miscalculation of ego-mind, based on the conditionally supposed "reality" of number—and, fundamentally, of the "source"-number one, which is the ego-rooted (or "point-of-view"-based) originator of all presumed "difference".

6.

Infinity (or the infinite state) is intrinsically, or always already, at and of and as zero (or the zero-point).

Zero (or the zero-point) is intrinsically, or always already, at and of and as infinity (or the infinite state).

Infinity (or the infinite state) is zero (or the zero-point).

Zero (or the zero-point) is infinity (or the infinite state).

Infinity (or the infinite state) is irreducibly non-finite, dimensionless, not-differentiated, not-quantified, not-"located", thoroughly without limiting characteristics, and (altogether) zero-only.

The zero-point is zero-only.

The zero-point is infinite (or non-finite).

Infinity (or the infinite state) <u>is</u> zero (or at, in, of, and <u>as</u> the zero-point).

The infinite state—or the zero-point of being—is intrinsically egoless and indivisible.

"Infinity" (or the "infinite state") and "zero" (or the "zero-point") are conceptual and verbal (and, sometimes, visually pictured or symboled) signs indicating the same "entity" of reference and meaning.

Therefore, infinity (or the infinite state) and zero (or the zero-point) <u>are</u> intrinsically indivisible and identical—or same-only.

7.

Infinity <u>is</u> zero.

Zero <u>is</u> infinity.

The infinite state is always already at, in, of, and <u>as</u> the zero-point—or always already and irreducibly prior to all numbers, all quantities, all "objects", and all "difference".

The zero-point is always already at, in, of, and <u>as</u> the infinite state—or always already and irreducibly prior to "point of view" (or ego-"I", or separate "self"-definition) and always already and irreducibly prior to all "others".

The infinite state and the zero-point are always already and irreducibly one and the same, always already and irreducibly prior to both separate "self" (or ego-"I") and all of "not-self" (or "object", "other", and "difference").

8.

All seeking is a numerically-based effort that is intended to solve the "self"-presumed "problem" (or ego-dilemma) of the number one (or the separate and separative ego-"I") by addition to or subtraction from itself, enacted either by stages or all-at-once.

All seeking would, in effect, achieve either the infinite state (which is infinity, or the infinite, itself) or the zero-point (which is zero, or egolessness, or no-"thing"-ness, itself) by motions or transactions or stages or suddenness of quantities (or numbers).

Neither infinity nor the infinite state nor the infinite itself nor zero nor the zero-point nor egolessness nor no-"thing"-ness can be attained or achieved or approximated by quantified, or numerical, or numbered, or progressive, or sudden, or in any manner conditional (or cause-and-effect) means.

Egolessness and the infinite state are intrinsically and irreducibly one, non-"different", and always priorly (or always already) the case.

Therefore, all seeking is intrinsically false, non-necessary, and futile.

9.

The Infinite State—or The Zero-Point State That Is Intrinsically egoless and Perfectly Indivisible Reality Itself— Is Intrinsically, Always Already, Irreducibly, and Self-Evidently The (Intrinsic and Only) Case.

The Infinite State Is Intrinsic and Intrinsically Perfect Fullness.

The Zero-Point State Is Intrinsic Indivisibility, Prior Unity, Non-"difference", and Non-separateness.

The Indivisible Zero-Point State of Infinite Fullness Is The Intrinsic and Only Case.

VII.

The Truth of Prior Unity
<u>Is</u> The Intrinsic Self-Revelation
of Reality Itself

There <u>Is</u> Only Reality Itself.

It <u>Is</u> Self-Evidently The Case That Only Reality Itself <u>Is</u>—<u>As</u> "It" <u>Is</u>, Whatever and However "It" <u>Is</u>.

Reality Itself Intrinsically and Necessarily Includes The Totality That <u>Is</u> All That <u>Is</u> all-and-All.

Therefore, Reality Itself Intrinsically and Necessarily Transcends (or <u>Is</u> Perfectly Prior to) any and every apparent <u>particular</u> "location", or space-time "point of view", or separate "self", or ego-"I", or "object" of egoic attention.

The egoic (and, thus, pervasive and conventional) "point of view" relative to all "others", the world, and "God" is that all "others", the total world, and (the however postulated and defined) "God" (or Reality-Source of all-and-All) is <u>not</u> "self".

From the (inherently separate) "point of view" of the ego-"I", the (every) "other", the total world, and the conventionally presumed "God" is "not-self"—or an "object" of "self", which is (thus) "other" than (or "different" from) "self".

In Reality Itself—Which <u>Is</u> Intrinsically egoless and "point-of-view-less", or Perfectly Prior to any and every possible "point of view" (or separate space-time-"location")—<u>There Is Only</u> "<u>Self</u>" (or One Indivisible, Non-separate, and Intrinsically egoless Self-Nature, Self-Condition, and Self-State That <u>Is</u> all-and-All, and That <u>Is</u> The Source, or Source-Condition, of all-and-All).

Therefore, The Truth That Is Always Already and Perfectly Self-Revealed In and As Reality Itself Is The Prior Unity (and Perfect Indivisibility) of all-and-All.

Prior Unity (or Perfect Indivisibility) Is The Inherent, Native, and Irreducible Self-Evidence (or Self-Revealed Reality-Characteristic) of all-and-All.

Therefore, there is not any "not-self".

There is no separate "God"—but Intrinsically egoless Reality Itself Is Only "Self".

The world Is "self"—non-separately.

The world Is Infinite "Location", Intrinsically Transcending every "point of view" (or particular "locus" of apparent "location").

Every "other"—or every apparent relation of the apparent "self"—Is "self", non-separately.

Therefore, in Reality Itself—and There Is (Self-Evidently) no Real alternative or Real opposite to Reality Itself—There Is an Inherent and Universal Moral Law.

The Universal Moral Law That Is Inherent to Reality Itself and Self-Evident in and As Reality Itself Is Universal Prior Unity (or Perfect Indivisibility), Expressed by and as The Intrinsic Fundamental Imperative in every heart: "Locate" no "other" as "object" (or "not-self"), but identify and relate to all-and-All as "self"—not "different" from your Real (and Intrinsically egoless) Self-Nature, Self-Condition, and Self-State, and not separate from your own apparent space-time-"location" (or sphere of "point of view").

In Reality Itself, there is no separate "self" (or absolutely existing "point of view", or absolutely independent space-time-"location").

In Reality Itself, there is no separate "object" (or absolutely defined "thing" of attention, or absolutely independent space-time limitation).

The every apparent "other", and the total apparent world, and That Which Is Always Already all-and-All-

Transcending (or The Self-Evidently egoless and Absolute Reality-Context of all-and-All) <u>Is</u> "Self"—or Inherently and Self-Evidently Not-separate from The Intrinsic (and Intrinsically egoless) Self-Nature, Self-Condition, and Self-State of Reality Itself, <u>As</u> "It" <u>Is</u>.

All of apparent "self" <u>Is</u> Intrinsically egoless and Indivisible—in and <u>As</u> Reality Itself.

Reality Itself <u>Is</u> The One and Only and Perfectly Indivisible "Self"—or Self-Condition, and Source-Condition—of all-and-All.

Reality Itself <u>Is</u> Not-Two.

Reality Itself <u>Is</u> "Self"-<u>Only</u>—Intrinsically egoless, Not-separate, Not-"different", Not-"other", Not-"object".

Reality Itself <u>Is</u> One-Only—Intrinsically Indivisible, Non-Dual, Perfectly Inclusive, Non-Divisive, and Inherently Free of problem, seeking, and attained result.

Reality Itself <u>Is</u> Self-Existing—or Self-Evidently Not-caused.

Reality Itself <u>Is</u> Self-Evidently Acausal in the apparent context of all that is either cause or effect.

Reality Itself <u>Is</u> Self-Existing <u>As</u> Limitless Acausal Self-Radiance—or The Universal heart-Current, or all-and-All-Pervading Root-Energy, of Acausal Love-Bliss.

Therefore, Reality Itself <u>Is</u> The Law (and The Very and Intrinsically egoless "Self", or Self-Nature, Self-Condition, and Self-State) of Self-Radiance (or Perfectly ego-Transcending Love-Bliss), Always Already Self-Manifested in and <u>As</u> The Intrinsic heart-Imperative (or The Moral Law Inherent in all-and-All) That Self-Requires active ego-Transcending love— or action and regard that are Always Already Coincident with the Intrinsic Self-Apprehension of The Self-Nature, Self-Condition, and Self-State of Reality Itself (Which <u>Is</u> Intrinsically egoless and Perfectly Indivisible Prior Unity, Boundless Self-Radiance, and Limitless Relatedness <u>As</u> Intrinsic Love-Bliss Itself).

Love Is The moment to moment Enactment (or Self-Radiation) of The Intrinsically Self-Evident Principle of Prior Unity.

Love Is Non-exclusiveness—or Perfect Indivisibility and Perfect Inclusiveness.

Love Is The Intrinsic (and, thus, moment to moment) Transcending of ego-"I"—or separate and separative "self" (or the inherently divisive "self"-dramatization of "point of view").

Love Is The Intrinsic (and, thus, moment to moment) Transcending of the separate "subject" (or the egoic and divisive "self") and the separate "object" (or the illusory "not-self").

Love Is The Intrinsic and The Active Relinquishment of the separation and "objectification" of "self" and "other".

Love Is Boundless Self-Radiance—or egoless Self-Magnification of The Root-Current of the heart (Which Is The Self-Energy of Reality Itself).

Love Is The Universal Self-Radiance of the all-and-All-Including and all-and-All-Transcending Self-Nature, Self-Condition, and Self-State That Is Reality Itself.

Therefore, in the plane of human world, love Is The Intrinsically Self-Evident—or By-Reality-Itself-Revealed—"self"-Discipline of Cooperation, Tolerance, and Peace.

VIII.

What Is No-"point-of-view"
Is all-and-All

The Mere and Only Presence.
Mere and Only.
Indivisibly One—and Only.
The Mere Presence.
Reality Only.
Only Reality Itself.
The Mere and Only Presence Of Reality Itself.
Mere and One.
Mere.
One.
Only.
Only all.
Only all-and-All.
That Is.
That Is all.
That Is all-and-All.
Only egoless One.
No "difference".
No "difference" no separateness Is—and Only.
Is As all-and-All As One and Prior Unity Of all-and-All.
All "cause-and-effect" In and Of That Only.
Acausal egoless Only That.
The Presence Of Reality Itself.
No "Deity" Is That Is.
Only God That Is Is Reality Itself No-Deity Divine.
All of all-and-All Is Only That That Is As all-and-All
Indivisibly.

No "selves" Are here.

Only opposites, and circles, and cycles, and spin.

Nothing conditionally arises that is not a pattern thus.

Every "problem" is only pattern—and, therefore, only a condition of opposites in a state of mutual contradiction, or irreducible opposition, or internal conflict, or spin.

To seek a "solution" to any "problem" by struggling with its pattern is only to become entangled in the mummery of opposites, by means of egoic "self"-identification with conflict and circularity, which only produces more and more cycles of patterns and "problems".

The only Perfect Resolution to any "problem" Is always At the Root, Prior to the "problem", and Prior to the state of "problem" itself, and Prior to the ego-"I" that knows and seeks in the domain of pattern itself.

The only Perfect Resolution to "problem" and the search for "solutions" Is always Prior to ego-"I" and its "object"—or At the Root, or In the Source-Position, and As the Source-Condition In and Of and As Which opposites, and circles, and cycles, and spin, and all-and-All of pattern, and "problem", and search arise.

The world is only patterns, patterning the all-and-All Of Only.

The world is only pattern patterning itself—a self-perpetuating figure of duality, "difference", change, uncertainty, and certain death.

You Are Not In, Of, and As the world.

You Are Always Already—Priorly, and At Root—What Is No-"point-of-view".

What Is No-"point-of-view" Is all-and-All.

I Am Here
To Awaken A Bright New Age
of Global Humankind

I Am Here
To Awaken A Bright New Age
of Global Humankind

I Am Looking for men and women who will live free of every kind of seeking, attendant only to the consciousness of universal prior unity, who will constantly devote themselves to the responsible cooperative management of individual and collective human life in the Indivisible Form and Logic of Reality Itself, rather than the egoic and separative form and "difference"-bound logic of egoity and illusion.

Such men and women are the unexploitable human presence of Reality Itself.

They will not devote themselves to turning the world to dilemma, seeking, life-exhaustion, and mere experience bereft of wisdom.

They will not devote themselves to the gross exploitation of desire and mere conditional possibility.

They will not devote themselves to strategic ascent to various goals beyond, or to absurd "evolutionary" aims, or to merely conventional exoteric and esoteric human transformation.

They will actively function in the Intrinsic Pattern of Reality Itself, turning themselves, and all of humankind, and, indeed, all things into unconditional relatedness and balanced well-being.

They will everywhere remove the effects of previous separative action, and restore the form of life to prior unity and indivisibility.

They will design and enact every kind of stability, and they will constantly re-discover the Beautiful Itself.

They will everywhere establish the presence of undivided peace.

While they constantly abide in the tacit apprehension of the Intrinsically egoless Context of Reality Itself, their eye of intelligence will always be on the present forms of perception, and not on the otherwise un-Real, or on the merely "objective", or on the merely "subjective", or on the false, or on the artificial, or on the absurd, or on the ironies of mere mind and memory at all.

Their perception of present form is always already stable and whole, and not a mere reflection of some other time or event.

They will not think and do the world as if it were merely a symbol for entirely other and would-be things.

They will constantly assert the egoless Form and Pattern of Reality Itself, while always conscious of the prior unity of all.

They will always serve the order of egoless wisdom and seamless knowledge.

They will always further develop the necessary, and they will always employ only the life-positive means.

They will always make only economic and wise use of science and technology, or all of conditional knowledge and its applied capability.

They will not be motivated merely by clever human invention, but by Reality Itself, Which Is the Always Present, and Which Is the Intrinsically Seamless Totality communicated in all forms.

They will not pursue any kind of human victory over the natural domain, or any kind of ultimate victory for some by means of the permanent defeat or domination of others.

They will always only enact the conditions for present universal balance and well-being.

They will always promote and uphold the universal wisdom of egolessness, in which right understanding of prior unity is the always public foundation of existence.

Thus, I Look to Establish a new global order of men and women, who will actively establish and sustain a universal new human age of sanity and wisdom.

That new age will not be an age of the occult, the conventionally religious, the scientific, or the technological glorification of humankind.

Rather, that new age will be the anciently expected universal age of authentic human existence, wherein human life will be everywhere engaged entirely apart from the tragic history of human ignorance, dissociativeness, bewilderment, and great search.

The would-be "new age" envisioned by mere seekers is a spectacular display that only extends the traditional madness, exploitability, and foolishness of humankind.

Therefore, I Am here to Awaken a new global order of men and women, who will not begin from all that was, but who will, instead, apply themselves, apart from all dilemma and all seeking, to the harmonious event of prior unity and cooperative peace.

That new universal order and age of global humankind will be always Illuminated by the Intrinsic Freedom of Reality Itself, and it will be always Thus Bright and New.

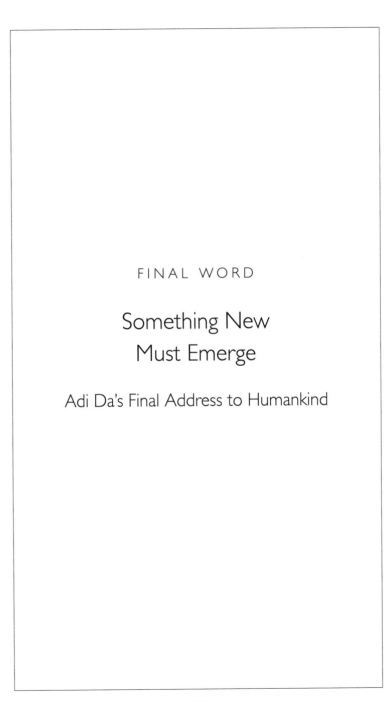

FINAL WORD

Something New
Must Emerge

Adi Da's Final Address to Humankind

Something New
Must Emerge

On November 27, 2008, at his hermitage in Fiji, the World-Friend, Adi Da, passed from the body. On the morning of that day, he gave final instructions about the manuscript of this book. And, on that same morning, he spoke spontaneously as follows—offering what was to be his final word on the current state of humankind and his calling for the incarnation of a Global Cooperative Forum.

Wherever people come together collectively, a social contract is established—a social contract among egos. And, where social contracts emerge, collectives appear—including nation-states, and so forth. Such collectives are the setting within which human civilizations develop.

As soon as any social collective comes into being, people expect certain benefits to come from the existence of the collective. Fundamental among the expected benefits are increased security, increased longevity, increased leisure (or increased freedom from need), and increased enjoyment of life. Thus, when people enter into a social contract, by becoming part of a social collective, there is an expectation that at least a significant number of individuals in that social collective will be able to experience this fourfold benefit—of greater security, greater longevity, greater freedom from need, and greater enjoyment of life—to a more significant degree than they would if they were not part of the collective. This expectation is particularly true in the case of such large-scale collectives as nation-states.

A rightly managed social collective does, indeed, provide a greater degree of these four principal life-factors—for at least some portion of the membership of the collective. However, the expectation of such benefits generates a dangerous illusion—a collective illusion based in the ego's search for relief from all fear and threat. It is the illusion that conditions of security, longevity, freedom from need, and enjoyment of life can exist to an <u>ideal</u> degree. Furthermore, it is the illusion that, rightly, such <u>idealized</u> conditions characterize human life as it should be—and that, therefore, such conditions should be demanded by all human beings. And, finally, it is the illusion that such <u>idealized</u> conditions can actually be established on a fullest and permanent basis and maintained indefinitely on a large scale. Such is the fundamental illusion that arises in the context of human civilization—or, in other words, whenever there is a social contract among egos.

In reality, life is not secure. In reality, life does not carry with it any reason to presume longevity, or even one more moment of existence. In reality, there is no fundamental freedom from need, or from the struggle and stress of dealing with need. In reality, all enjoyment is fleeting.

It does not make any difference how much "civilizing" is done or how much group solidarity is created. <u>No</u> degree of civilization can change the natural reality of mortal existence. That is why "utopia" is an illusion. And that is why the expected "utopian" benefits of civilization—or, in other words, the expected "utopian" benefits of a social contract among egos—are illusory.

At best, a social contract among egos is an arrangement that produces a <u>tentative</u> and <u>modest</u> degree of increased security, longevity, freedom from need, and enjoyment of life—for some. And, in any case, such life-improvements cannot be guaranteed to last. No degree of life-improvement can change the fundamental core reality that life is insecure, brief, full of need, and incapable of absolute fulfillment.

There are times in human history, such as the present world-moment, when the factors of security, longevity, freedom from need, and enjoyment of life are becoming increasingly threatened—experienced by fewer than before, and experienced much less by those who are accustomed to enjoying them to some degree. In such a circumstance, people begin to suffer a psychic crisis—a crisis in the psyche of egoity itself. Then political and social leaders start calling upon people to make sacrifices for the sake of the social collective—as if the mere fact of belonging to such a collective, on the basis of a social contract, is, in and of itself, a virtue. But the only reason people enter into any such social contract is in order to enjoy greater security, longevity, freedom from need, and enjoyment of life. There is no point in asking people to make sacrifices in order to belong to the social collective if the collective is altogether failing to provide any degree of security, longevity, freedom from need, and enjoyment of life, or is providing those factors to a much lesser degree.

Such is the current state of global human civilization. People are being asked to "tighten their belts", to make sacrifices of one kind or another, in order to continue belonging to the existing social-ego contracts all over the world—nation-states, and everything altogether. But how long will people continue to be willing to make such sacrifices?

Civilization is in crisis. The human world altogether is in crisis. The notions of security, longevity, freedom from need, and enjoyment of life are showing themselves to be illusions—very tentative, and able to be enjoyed by only a relative few. And the relative few who enjoy such life-conditions do so at the expense of others—and, in fact, on the basis of the suffering and exploitation of others.

Something new must emerge. That something new is not going to emerge from the pattern of nation-states, or even from the gathering of nation-states (in the form of the

United Nations). That something new can only emerge from everybody-all-at-once—the power of humankind as a totality.

Humankind as a totality must relinquish the old civilization. It must accept that the old civilization is dead, the old civilization is gone, useless, non-productive. The old civilization can no longer provide security, longevity, freedom from need, and life-enjoyment for people. Less and less can the old civilization do anything useful at all. The old civilization is now profoundly degraded, and will only get worse with time.

A new mode of social contract must emerge—a mode of social contract not founded on egoity. There must now be an egoless mode of social contract—based on cooperation, tolerance, and universal participation and accountability. Such is the nature of the necessary global cooperative order.

In order for such a global cooperative order to come into being, there must be a core institution based on the universal participation and accountability of everybody-all-at-once. I call that core institution the Global Cooperative Forum. The Global Cooperative Forum is the necessary transformative movement on Earth. ∎

THE WORLD-FRIEND, ADI DA

From his birth on Long Island, New York, in 1939, the World-Friend Adi Da was not an ordinary child. His parents were ordinary lower middle-class people, and his childhood, on the outside, was unremarkable. But his own experience, as he relates in his spiritual autobiography, *The Knee of Listening*, was something else. Very early on, he realized that he did not see things as others did. For him, the world was not peopled with separate others and full of separate things. Rather, he existed in a radiant, fluid field of energy that suffused everything, and <u>was</u> everything, circulating constantly in his body, from the heart. He called this radiant field the "Bright".

Around the age two, there was a profound shift in his perception of reality. One day, when receiving the gift of a puppy from his parents, Adi Da spontaneously "put on" the "glasses" of separateness. He saw the puppy, and he saw his parents. Now, suddenly, they were discrete "others", and he, likewise, was a separate self, an "I", who must henceforth relate to "others". It was the end of the sublime innocence of his infancy, but it was not the end of the force of the "Bright" in his life. In fact, it was only the beginning.

As Adi Da grew into adolescence and youth, the radiance of the "Bright" receded more and more, but its latent power remained, driving him to discover the truth about existence, whatever that would take.

What is consciousness? What is our real nature? Adi Da pursued these questions fiercely at Columbia University, but without satisfaction. No conventional answer was sufficient for him. Instead of fearless philosophical enquiry, he found the norms of everyday experience automatically accepted as truth—separate self, separate world, and separate God.

And so his search intensified—in the alleys of New York City, in the halls of Stanford University, in Christian seminaries, at the feet of spiritual masters, and in experimental writing. In rare moments, the relentless effort of his seeking fell away in pristine clarity, uncontainable ecstasy, transcendental peace. Such breakthroughs of the "Bright" urged him on, revealing each time new depths of understanding and new challenges. For no experience, however great, was permanent. No belief was useful, no spiritual method or technique was commensurate with what he truly required—the unbroken restoration of the "Bright".

It happened. In September 1970, while sitting silently in a small temple in Los Angeles, Adi Da re-awakened to the "Bright", and, from that moment, It was never lost or diminished. He was simply Being That. As he wrote later:

> *During the night of humankind, I Awakened as perfect, absolute, limitless, indivisible, un-Conditional Love-Bliss Itself—in Which the body and the mind . . . . boiled into a solder of undifferentiated Reality. It was the madness of dissolution into most perfect Self-Awareness, Infinitely Expanded—As my own inherently boundless Presence— wherein there is only "Brightness".*
> —*The Knee of Listening*

From then on, Adi Da found that his own meditation was obsolete, vanished in the fullness of what he had Realized. But a new phenomenon now arose. He saw countless faces, innumerable beings passing through his subtle awareness, and he spontaneously "meditated" them. He found himself experiencing the qualities of all these beings, and working to ease and release their obstructions. In others words, through Adi Da's re-awakening to the "Bright", the influence of the "Bright" was freely radiating through him, and blessing living beings. There was no thought in this. A channel of Grace had been opened up in the inherently unified field of Reality.

It was not long before this mysterious process took on concrete form. In the decades that followed, hundreds of people approached Adi Da as spiritual master, and he established Adidam, the esoteric way of life founded in the "Bright". Many years of intense engagement with his devotees were required for this fundamental work of teaching, and, by the early 1980s, Adi Da was moved to live in a more secluded way, free to work with renunciate devotees and to concentrate in a universal work of blessing. In 1983, he was given the remote island of Naitauba, Fiji, as his hermitage (now named Adi Da Samrajashram), and in his first months of residence there, he spoke this to the devotees with him:

My work is not—and, indeed, it never has been— engaged exclusively for the sake of those I am already associated with. Nor, in the future, will it be exclusively for such individuals. My work is done for the sake of all beings. This is the significance of the move I have made into Hermitage. I can stand in this world, in this radiation place, and do Blessing-work for everyone.

—January 1, 1984

Naitauba Island is situated on the international dateline, a symbol of the fact that Adi Da's work of world-blessing inclines to neither "half" of humanity—neither the West, nor the East—but only to the whole. And "the whole", as he indicated, includes the indigenous peoples all over the world, who preserve humanity's ancient knowing of the prior, or inherent, unity of existence.

Adi Da expressed the truth of prior unity through multiple universal means—artistic and literary—and, in 2006, he wrote *Not-Two Is Peace*, in which he calls for a new global human process in which prior unity becomes "the public foundation of existence". He does not propose such a process as a recipe for utopia, but, rather, as the only workable option, if humankind is to survive:

I am here to Awaken a new global order of men and women, who will not begin from all that was, but who will, instead, apply themselves, apart from all dilemma and all seeking, to the harmonious event of prior unity and cooperative peace. . . .

Such men and women are the unexploitable human presence of Reality Itself.

—*Not-Two Is Peace* (pp. 319 and 321)

In 2008, the World-Friend Adi Da passed from the body while at work in his art studio. Regardless of his outward activity at any given moment, he was, as he said, "spiritually extended all over the world", opening up a channel for the "Bright" to Radiate universally during and beyond his lifetime on Earth.

The Meaning of "World-Friend"

The designation "World-Friend" was (to the best of our knowledge) first used by Sri Rang Avadhoot (1898–1968), an Indian spiritual master with whom Adi Da had brief contact while in India in 1968. Adi Da indicated that the reference "World-Friend" became spontaneously true for him in his own case after he received Fijian citizenship in 1993. Formerly a citizen of the United States, he was, at that point, permanently established in his hermitage on Naitauba Island, Fiji—associated, as he put it, "with every dimension of human life—East, West, and indigenous peoples". The title "World-Friend" is indicative of his free blessing-intention toward the world and all beings, human and non-human. The title "World-Friend" also suggests his disposition to speak to all in universal "friendship", frankly and compassionately, always founded in deep sympathy and love. ■

.

GLOSSARY OF TERMS AND PHRASES

Acausal—Neither caused nor causing; therefore, existing beyond (or prior to) the realm of duality in which the law of "cause and effect" is operative.

all-and-All—A phrase Adi Da created to describe the totality of conditional (or ordinarily appearing) existence—both as the "sum of its parts" and as an undivided whole. He defines lowercase "all" as indicating "the collected sum of all presumed-to-be-separate beings, things, and conditions", and uppercase "All" as indicating "the All (or the undivided totality) of conditional existence as a whole".

body-mind-complex—With this term, Adi Da is communicating that each human being is a "complex" of fundamental faculties. Those fundamental faculties include body and mind, and also emotion and breath.

conditionally manifested reality / Reality Itself—Adi Da distinguishes between two meanings of the word "reality". (1) He refers to reality as we ordinarily perceive it and participate in it as "conditionally manifested reality". This "ordinary reality" is the complex effect of all kinds of conditions. Thus, the "ordinary reality" can manifest only in accordance with whatever conditions are the case. Therefore, because the "ordinary reality" is dependent on conditions, Adi Da describes it as "conditionally manifested". (2) In contrast to "conditionally manifested reality", Adi Da refers to "Reality Itself" (with capital letters). Reality Itself is not in any sense dependent on conditions. In other words, Reality Itself is utterly "Non-conditional". Adi Da states that Reality Itself is the "One and Only Self-Nature, Self-Condition, and Self-State" of every thing and every being in the universe.

Conscious Light—Adi Da defines Reality (Itself) as "Conscious Light". By making this definition, he is communicating that the two essential characteristics of Reality are Awareness (or Consciousness) and Radiance (or Light). Furthermore, Adi Da states that Conscious Light is the essential Nature (or the "One and Only Self-Nature, Self-Condition, and Self-State") of every thing and every being in the universe.

diaspora—The "diaspora" ("dispersion" or "scattering") of humankind all over the earth, over the course of many thousands of years, has resulted in the establishment of different cultures and philosophies. But no matter what cultural or even racial differences have appeared, Adi Da emphasizes that humankind is still a single species.

"difference"—Adi Da defines the presumption of fundamental "difference" as the essential fault that characterizes the unliberated human ego. The core of this presumption is the primal notion that "self" is separate from "everything and everyone else". That primal notion is described by Adi Da as the "root" of all human suffering and dilemma.

ecstasy—The word "ecstasy", derived from Greek, means "standing (stasis) outside (ec-)". Adi Da uses this word with the specific meaning of "standing outside the egoic 'self'" (a condition which is inherently blissful).

ego / ego-"I"—Adi Da teaches that the ego is an <u>activity</u>, and not an <u>entity</u>. The activity of egoity is what Adi Da calls the "'self'-contraction", or the presumption of separate and separative existence. When he uses the term "ego-'I'", he places the "I" in quotation marks to indicate that he uses it in the "so to speak" sense. He is indicating (by means of the quotation marks) that, in Reality, there is no such thing as the "I", even though it appears to be the case in ordinary experience.

egolessness—Adi Da uses this term to mean "the condition of freedom from the presumption of a separate and separative existence", or "the condition of freedom from the presumption of separate 'point of view'".

end-time—Adi Da uses "end-time" to mean the end-phenomenon of human ego-culture and the loss of the connection to Reality Itself—and not any traditional religious myth associated with this term. See also **"late-time" (or "dark" epoch)**.

Enlightenment—The actual Realization of Reality Itself, or Truth Itself—Which Realization is Inherently Full of Light. Adi Da sometimes sets the word "Light" off in hyphens (as in "En-Light-ened") to emphasize the root-meaning of the word.

everybody-all-at-once—A phrase coined by Adi Da indicating the "all-at-once collective" of humanity—which is not a collection of separate individuals, but the force of humankind as a collective whole, based in the fundamental presumption and truth of prior unity.

face-to-face—Humans all over the earth are now "face-to-face" with one another, in that no one exists in an isolated tribe or culture. There is now a single world, transformed by worldwide communication, economic interdependence, and the potential of global warfare.

Global Cooperative Forum—See Part One, especially pp. 33–39.

global cooperative order—Adi Da uses this term to describe humankind's embrace of and participation in the principles of prior unity, and cooperation and tolerance, through the establishment of a functioning Global Cooperative Forum that addresses all the issues humanity faces worldwide.

"God"-idea—Adi Da uses this term to emphasize that human propositions about "God" are concepts generated by human minds, which only point to the great Reality that is Real God.

gross—Adi Da most often uses "gross" with its meaning of "made up of material (or physical) elements". The gross (or physical) dimension of existence is (thus) associated with the physical body and world.

"ground zero"—A term coined in the twentieth century to describe the site where an explosion (especially a nuclear one) has occurred. After September 11, 2001, this term was also commonly used to refer to the site of the destroyed World Trade Center in New York City. In this book, Adi Da uses "ground zero" to describe the state of global human culture in the early twenty-first century. His use of "ground zero" also relates to the "zero-point", or the inherent egolessness of human life. See also **"zero-point"**.

humankind-as-a-whole—A phrase coined by Adi Da to indicate the force of humankind as a collective whole, when it functions on the basis of prior unity.

"know"—When Adi Da places this word (and its variants, such as "knowing" and "knowledge") in quotation marks, he does so to indicate that the ego's characteristic presumption of separation between the "knower" and that which is "known" makes it impossible to know anything as it really is. Adi Da capitalizes "Know" and "Knowledge" to indicate a wordless, direct Realization—rather than any form of knowledge based on the illusion of separation between "subject" and "object". See also **"Perfect Knowledge"**.

"late-time" (or "dark" epoch)—Adi Da uses the terms "late-time" and "'dark' epoch" to describe the present era, in which doubt of anything at all beyond mortal existence is more and more pervading the entire world, and the "self"-interest of the separate individual is more and more regarded to be the ultimate principle of life.

lose face—To "lose face" is to give up the effort to "look good", and, thus, to stop defending whatever presumed-to-be-positive self-image one tends to present to the world. See **save face**.

mummery—The dictionary defines "mummery" as "a ridiculous, hypocritical or pretentious ceremony, observance, or performance". Adi Da uses the term "mummery" to describe all the activities of ego-bound beings, who are committed to the false view of separation and separativeness.

"Narcissus" / "Narcissistic"—Adi Da uses "Narcissus" as a key symbol of the un-enlightened individual as a "self"-obsessed seeker, enamored of his or her own "self"-image and egoic "self"-consciousness.

He is the ancient one visible in the Greek myth, who was the universally adored child of the gods, who rejected the loved-one and every form of love and relationship, and who was finally condemned to the contemplation of his own image—until, as a result of his own act and obstinacy, he suffered the fate of eternal separateness and died in infinite solitude.

—Adi Da
The Knee of Listening

"neighborhood-wars"—The term "neighborhood-wars" describes the destructiveness of the ego (or the presumed separate "self") at all levels of human endeavor—not just the conflicts between nations and ethnic groups but in the most intimate scale of human interaction (the "private wars of Everyman"). This term comes from Adi Da's literary work *The Mummery Book*.

Non-Dual—Inherently indivisible, and, therefore, never composed of "two" (or "self" and "not-self").

"object" / "objective"—Adi Da consistently places the words "object", "objective", "objectify", and so forth, in quotation marks. He does this in order to indicate that, in Reality Itself, there is no such thing as an "object" that is separate from the "subject".

"Perfect Knowledge"—The direct, tacit Realization of the Indivisible Unity of Reality Itself—prior to any presumption of separation between "knower" and "known". "Perfect Knowledge" contrasts with all forms of ordinary "knowledge"—which are based on the presumption of an irreducible separation between "knower" and "known", or "subject" and "object".

Perfectly Subjective—In the phrase "Perfectly Subjective", the word "Subjective" does not refer to "the inward experience of an individual". Rather, it points to Reality Itself—the True Source (or "Subject") of all apparent experience, which exists prior to any apparent individual "self".

"point of view"—By placing this phrase in quotation marks, Adi Da is communicating that, in Reality, every ordinary "point of view" is an illusion—

because all ordinary viewpoints are founded in the presumption of the separate existence of "I".

prior unity—Adi Da's term "prior unity" points to the unity that exists prior to all the apparent differences and conflicts in the world. That unity, in other words, is senior to all apparent signs of disunity. Adi Da also calls this the "unifying life-principle" and the "cosmically extended pattern of Oneness". In the phrase "prior unity", Adi Da uses the word "prior" in the sense of "a priori", or "inherent" (not in the sense of "previous"). Please see p. 35 for a full discussion.

psycho-physical—A phrase which Adi Da uses to indicate that the human being (and the world altogether) is not a purely physical phenomenon, but a phenomenon with both physical and mental/psychic dimensions.

Reality Itself—See **conditionally manifested reality / Reality Itself**.

Real God—Adi Da uses the term "Real God" to refer to Reality or Truth Itself, rather than any conventional anthropomorphic idea of God as "Creator".

save face—To "save face" is to try to "look good", or to maintain whatever presumed-to-be-positive self-image one tends to present to the world. See **lose face**.

scientific materialism—The predominant philosophy and worldview of modern humanity, the basic presumption of which is that the material world is all that exists. In scientific materialism, the method of science, or the observation of "objective" phenomena, is made into a philosophy and way of life that suppresses awareness of the inherent unity of existence and the native human impulse to Realize Reality Itself.

"self" / not-"self"—The two categories of egoic illusion: that which one identifies with ("self"), and everything else (not-"self"). Adi Da places "self" in quotation marks to indicate that the presumption of a truly separate entity is an illusion—generated in response to the fact of bodily existence.

"self"-contraction—The fundamental presumption (and activity) of separation. Also called "ego", or "ego-'I'".

"self"-fulfillment—Ultimate and permanent happiness and satisfaction for the separate "self", which Adi Da defines as an inherently unattainable goal.

Self-Nature, Self-Condition, and Self-State—While pointing out that there is no such thing as a separate egoic "self", Adi Da uses this phrase to indicate that Reality Itself is the true "Self" (capital "S") of all existence.

stave in the wheels—To describe the ego's obstructing effect on systems, Adi Da uses the analogy of sticking a large pole, or "stave", into the wheel of a cart. If you do so, you interrupt the wheel's ability to do what it is built to do—and the cart wheel becomes incapable of rotating. The removal of the "stave" allows the cart to function as it should.

sublated—The verb "sublate" means "to remove" or "to negate"—in the sense of "rendering no longer effective".

Transcendental Spiritual—Adi Da uses this phrase as a description of the two fundamental aspects of Reality Itself, and also of the process of Reality-Realization (or Enlightenment). "Transcendental" refers to Existence (or Being, or Consciousness) Itself, and "Spiritual" refers to Energy (or Light) Itself. Adi Da has revealed that these two aspects inherently coincide in Reality Itself, Which is Indivisible.

"tribalism"—Adi Da uses the terms "tribal" and "tribalism" to refer to the ego in its collective form. Please see p. 37 for a full discussion.

Unifying Life-Principle—See **prior unity**.

Witness—The natural "Position" of Consciousness Itself is to Stand as the Mere Witness of all that arises, Prior to egoic "self"-identification with the body-mind-complex.

World-Friend—See p. 333.

"zero-point"—With the term "zero-point", Adi Da is describing the "place" (or reality) that is prior to the root-gesture of separation. Thus, "zero-point" is synonymous with "egolessness". The quotation marks indicate that its meaning is limited to the specific definition described here.

INDEX

totality, human *(continued)*
presumed powerlessness of, 201–2
recognizing the single, 97
self-management by, 52–54
subordination and attack of, 202–3
as targets of war, 272
"zero-point" pattern-process of, 216–18
See also everybody-all-at-once
toxicity, 65
tradition, cultural, 219, 220–21
transcending ego
as consumption-unit, 266–67
as desire, by love, 137
ego cannot accomplish, 208
as ideas, in Reality Itself, 278
via identifying with "not-self", 299–300
via law of love, 311–12
as "objectification", 155, 158, 163
as reactivity, 281
as religious conflict, 117, 120–22
right life as based on, 205
as "self", by Reality Itself, 298
as separativeness, 139–40
universal embrace of, 108–10, 111
Transcendental Spiritual Reality, 340
"tribal" culture/"tribalism"
as archaic and irrelevant, 87–88, 93
defined, 37, 340
destructiveness of, 41–42, 45
as dysfunctional, 54, 230–34
and hierarchy, 68
is finished, 54
must stop, 91
political leaders in, 43
prior unity as context of, 122
and "self"-preservation, 241
as "stave in the wheels", 228–29
stepping beyond, 38, 43
three egoic myths of, 213–15
"zero-point" education relinquishes, 81–82
Truth, the
egoic subordination of, 149–50
life proof of, 115
"Perfect Knowledge" of, 287
pure warriors for, 53
religion as subordinate to, 121
restoration to life in, 163
as self-evident, 71–72
Three Great Principles of, 285–86
transcends religion, 117–19
TV, 151–52

twoness
is not-peace, 258
superimposed on zero and infinity, 304–5

U
understanding
action based in moral, 148
call to intrinsic, 248
as cooperative community basis, 129–30
of ego "self", 111, 128, 130
of human knowledge patterns, 223–24
of "not-two", 248–49
and relinquishing conflict, 108–10
transcends "objectification" of "self", 155
"zero-point", 209–10
United Nations, 250
unity
prior (*See* prior unity)
separation cannot achieve, 239, 243–44
speaking virtuously about, 232
"working toward", 150, 160
Unity-Principle. *See* Prior-Unity-Principle of Reality Itself
"us" vs. "them"
irresponsibility of, 49–50
as root of fear and conflict, 37
warlike mindset of, 43
See also "self" and "not-self"/"other"
utopia
double-mindedness and, 124
as an illusion, 326
impossibility of, 168

V
violence
of presuming opposites, 248–49
subduing physical, 141–42

W
war
abandoning the politics of, 107–9
civilians as targets of modern, 271–72
as ego-made, 105–6
global cooperative to deal with, 166
global destruction via, 106–7
as no longer applicable, 89, 90
serves no one, 238–39
total, 44–45
as "tribal" confrontations, 41–42

Prior Unity
The Basis For A New Human Civilization
by the World-Friend Adi Da

The presumption of prior unity—rather than the conflict between opposing identities—needs to be the basis for life in human society.

—Adi Da

A compact book of Adi Da's invaluable wisdom on going beyond the separate worldview to peaceful, cooperative coexistence. This is not a book about politics as we know it. It is about uncovering the true basis for a new politics, a new social contract that is founded in, and expressive of, how things really are.

It is impossible to endorse this book adequately enough. It is a rare event in human history when a truly enlightened master speaks directly to the world situation, what must be done about it, and the consciousness from which all action, individual and collective, must proceed. The message in this book is urgent. We do not have a lot of time on this planet to get it right. In order for a globally just, sustainable, and thriving future to emerge, we must co-create that future on the most truthful of principles.

Adi Da, in this book, provides the core truth upon which that future must be built. Adi Da does not give us a blueprint, nor a plan of action. Instead, he asks us to meditate on and into the truth of our inherent and prior unity. He asks us to be transformed into hero-servants who take responsibility for the welfare of the whole world—everybody-all-at-once. He asks us to become the change we want to see in the world. He asks us to source all action in love. He asks us to walk through the boundary of our apparently separate selves to the place where I leave off and you begin. He asks us to be so deeply "in love" and "as unity" that we can only act in service of our mutual and highest interest. He asks that unity become the foundation of the new world civilization.

This is a profound book. We must take it seriously.

BOB ANDERSON
Founder and Chairman, The Leadership Circle

128 pp., **$12.95**
www.priorunity.org

For more information
about the social wisdom of
the World-Friend Adi Da, visit:

www.nottwoispeace.org

www.priorunity.org

www.da-peace.org

I S   P E A C E   7 2 3